DAVID TANIS MARKET COOKING

DAVID TANIS MARKET COOKING

Recipes and Revelations
Ingredient by Ingredient

Photographs by Evan Sung

ARTISAN | NEW YORK

Library of Congress Cataloging-in-Publication Data is on file.

ISBN 978-1-57965-628-7

Cover and book design by James Casey
Cover photographs by Evan Sung

Artisan books are available at special discounts when purchased in bulk for premiums and sales promotions as well as for fund-raising or educational use. Special editions or book excerpts also can be created to specification. For details, contact the Special Sales Director at the address below, or send an e-mail to specialmarket@workman.com.

Published by Artisan
A division of Workman Publishing Company Co., Inc.
225 Varick Street
New York, NY 10014-4381
artisanbooks.com

Published simultaneously in Canada by
Thomas Allen & Son, Limited

Printed in China
First printing, October 2017

10 9 8 7 6 5 4 3 2 1

Also by David Tanis

A Platter of Figs
Heart of the Artichoke
One Good Dish

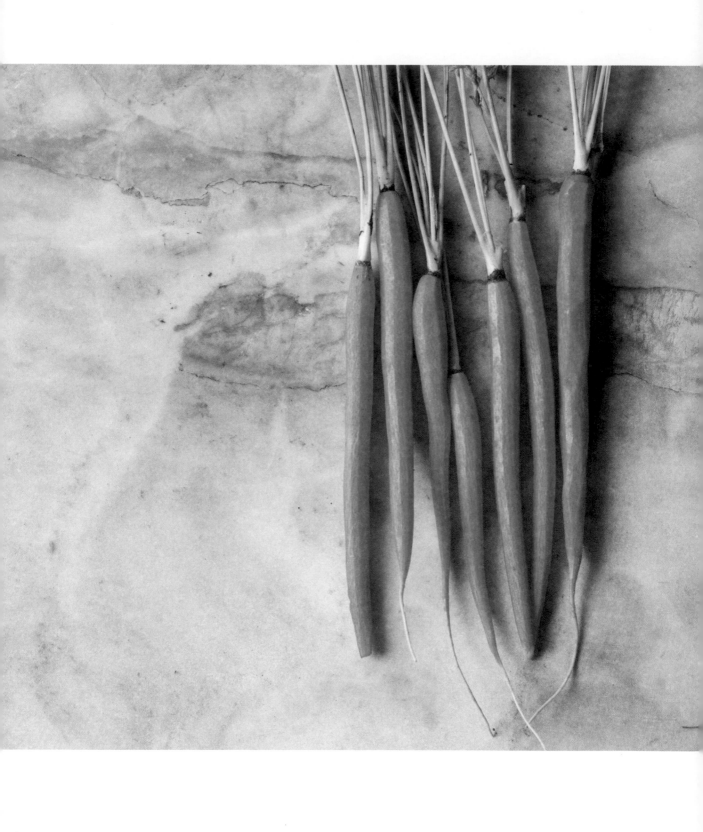

CONTENTS

WHERE COOKING BEGINS

When I say "market cooking," I'm referring to a common French term. If a French chef (or an acclaimed home cook) is asked which cuisine is his or her specialty, the response may well be "*la cuisine du marché.*" It would be my response too. It implies a philosophy as much as a style of cooking. Loosely translated, it means: I go to the market, see what looks best, *and then* decide what will go on the menu.

The fresh ingredients provide inspiration for the meal. I don't go with a fixed idea of what I want; I look for the most sparkly fish, the most tantalizing vegetables. I want them to be fresh, local, and seasonal—hardly a new concept, but a most admirable one. The best cooking I know depends upon it. It's the age-old, traditional, normal way, even if today's chefs and foodies lay claim to the farm-to-table moniker. A new generation is discovering the value of foraging, seeking out organic produce, and cooking over live fire. These are ancient practices. And for much of human history, sourcing local and seasonal produce was not a lifestyle choice—it was the only way to cook.

A key aspect of market cooking is simplicity—letting the natural flavors of the ingredients shine. Delicious food doesn't have to be complicated. When tomatoes are truly vine-ripened, a little salt and olive oil are all you need. A roasted head of garlic gives immediate satisfaction; freshly picked asparagus needs just a few minutes of steaming and a good vinaigrette.

How did we stray so far from this place-based, seasonal approach? One-stop shopping at big-box stores may be convenient, but several stops at a couple of smaller shops may make a great difference. It means not settling for generic industrial eggs when a side trip from life's busy thoroughfare will give you a better egg and a better meal. And perhaps a small adventure to boot. There really can be joy in marketing.

What follows is a collection of recipes for some of the dishes and ingredients I like best—my own, admittedly sometimes quirky, favorite foods. Hence garlic, onions, and potatoes are given pride of place, and I wholeheartedly celebrate hot chiles and the power of *picante*. What's more, the majority of the recipes are vegetable-based. Vegetables are central to a meal. I try to make them the focus, even if meat or fish is on the menu.

Some of the recipes here are quite precise, others are presented in a more suggestive fashion. But a recipe can only go so far. More important is understanding the process, the how and why, the technique, the feel; ultimately, recipes offer guidelines and quantities, but only experience can make you a better cook. Mastering kitchen fundamentals will increase your comfort and your enjoyment in the kitchen.

Cooking can be both a personal expression and a cultural one, connecting us to past, present, and future. It is at once creative and introspective. I also cook because I really want a good meal, and often the most satisfying way to get it is to make it myself—at home. Cooking (and, it follows, dining) is what makes a house a home, whether alone or with a companion, a few friends, or a large group.

There are a thousand good reasons to stay home and cook. When you get in the habit of cooking, it's easy to weave it into your daily routine. If you cook once in a blue moon, there's no continuity; you may feel rusty or reticent or less than rhythmic.

But a trip to the market will help get you in the mood. In every season, there are colorful fruits and vegetables to seduce you. Your "market" may be a supermarket or a farm stand or a corner store that has fresh figs from the owner's tree. If you're lucky, there's a regular farmers' market in the vicinity. In any case, your goal is to procure the freshest ingredients and to cook them simply.

Previous pages: A head of radicchio Tardivo.
Right: Daikon radish.

ALLIUMS UNITED

One could nourish oneself quite happily only on humble alliums before ever venturing into the larger vegetable kingdom. These workhorses of the kitchen, so often taken for granted, can and should be appreciated in their own right. Any one of these allium family members—garlic, onion, leek, shallot, or scallion—can make a meal. Soups come to mind immediately, made from just one or another, or a combination. A rustic onion soup, a creamy leek potage, and a simple garlic broth can all be magnificent.

But perhaps alliums are best known in their supporting roles. Every cook is familiar with the ritual of slowly softening onions in butter, olive oil, lard, or poultry fat—is there any lovelier aroma?—as the necessary first step to building flavor before other ingredients are added. It's fitting that we call this "sweating," since alliums do a lot of the heavy lifting when it comes to making a good meal. They boost tomatoes toward an eventual sauce, they give depth to a simple paella, and they add character to a braised chicken.

Nearly every allium can be roasted, grilled, stewed, caramelized, pickled, or fried. All these techniques serve to emphasize their innate sweetness, taming their sharp bite. But often they don't require cooking at all. Toasted bread rubbed with raw garlic is divine. Thinly sliced crisp raw onions are welcome in a salad. A little minced raw shallot or a bit of raw garlic are de rigueur for a good vinaigrette. A sprinkle of slivered raw scallions or of chives, another allium family member, is often just the right finish.

GARLIC, ALWAYS

Why does garlic come at the beginning of the book? Because it's one of the most indispensable items in the kitchen. At least I think so. It's on my short list of "can't cook without" ingredients. Garlic quickens the appetite—it gets the juices flowing. Many a good meal begins with garlic gently sizzling in a pan in a little olive oil, sending its singular aroma wafting throughout the kitchen. It signifies to anyone within smelling distance that good things are soon to come.

If you want to understand how garlic grows, plant a few cloves in a flowerpot and observe what happens. First you'll see a pale green shoot, like a skinny scallion. (When you go to the farmers' market in early spring, you can often find foot-long young garlic shoots, also called green garlic. Green garlic is tender top to bottom, so aside from a little trimming, you can use it all. The flavor is fresh, mild, and sweet, in a garlicky way.) After spending another month in the ground, a bulbous head begins to form at the root. A few weeks later, when the cloves within have fully formed, they have a pungent, bright flavor, undeniably garlicky. New-crop garlic, ready by early summer, is divine; this is garlic at its best. At the market, you'll know it by its colorful large heads, still fresh pink and purple, for sale before the majority of the crop goes to the drying barns to cure for use throughout the year.

Even if you store it in a cool, dark place, your garlic will begin to stir, as each clove develops a green sprouting center. That's because it's still alive, with the innate instinct to reproduce. (Some people remove the green sprout before chopping—I don't unless it's enormous.) The sprouted cloves are the living future, so long as they escape the kitchen knife. Plant a few of these sprouted cloves, and the cycle begins again.

Garlic gloriously improves the flavor of nearly any dish.

Clockwise from bottom left: Pounding garlic in a mortar, pink-tinged Rocambole garlic, popping the skin, slicing peeled garlic, and trimming whole heads for roasting.

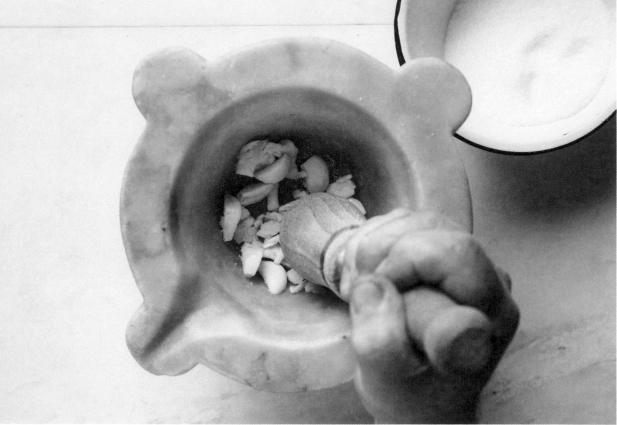

Spanish Garlic Toast for Breakfast

In Spain, breakfast is toast. Whether you are in Seville or Barcelona, strolling along early morning streets, the smell of toasting bread is everywhere. There are two choices: with butter and marmalade or with garlic and oil. I say go for the garlic. The ideal bread is a crusty, rustic hearth-style loaf. You toast thick slices and rub the top surface with a garlic clove, not too vigorously (you are essentially grating garlic right into the bread, so meter the amount). Drizzle the toast generously with a tasty, fruity olive oil and, if you wish, sprinkle it with a little flaky salt and pepper. Aficionados wash it down with strong coffee or, if they've just seen the sunrise on their way home from a night of revelry, with something stronger—or with both.

Pan con Tomate

If you have a ripe tomato, Spanish garlic toast can become *pan con tomate* (in Catalunya, it's *pa amb tomàquet*). Rub the toast first lightly with garlic, then forcefully with a halved ripe tomato to make the bread red and juicy. Finish with a drizzle of oil and salt and pepper. And perhaps an anchovy fillet or a slice of *jamón*. Eat it for breakfast or at any time of day. Perfect as a tapa to serve with drinks; it is very red wine friendly.

Garlic and Parsley, a Dynamic Duo

Employing the classic combination of chopped garlic and parsley is a simple but sure way of adding flavor and brightness. Just a small amount can catapult your cooking to delicious heights.

Persillade

Persillade is the French term for a mixture of chopped garlic and parsley (the proportions can vary to taste, but it's generally a couple of garlic cloves and a handful of parsley). Add a sprinkling of raw persillade to a dish for a pungent garlicky effect, or let it cook a bit for a tamer garlic taste. For example, sprinkle persillade over hot Golden Panfried Potatoes (page 285) at the last minute and serve immediately. Or, to enhance any vegetable—say, sautéed zucchini or green beans—add persillade to the pan in the last few minutes of cooking.

To make persillade, mix together ½ cup chopped flat-leaf parsley and 3 or more finely minced garlic cloves.

Gremolata

Gremolata, an Italian version of persillade, includes grated lemon zest in the garlic-parsley mixture. It's brilliant. Traditionally gremolata is sprinkled over osso buco, braised veal shanks, but it's just as good on steamed vegetables or grilled fish or pasta. Like persillade, use it raw when you want a sharp garlic hit or cook it briefly to mellow the flavor. I occasionally add some chopped capers and grated orange zest to gremolata, or a small amount of rosemary and crushed red pepper.

To make gremolata, mix ½ cup chopped flat-leaf parsley with 2 finely minced garlic cloves and the grated zest of 1 lemon.

ROASTING WHOLE GARLIC HEADS

Raw or briefly cooked garlic is pungent, strong, and wild, whereas long-cooked garlic has a mellow sweetness. That's why the French can invent a dish called "chicken with 40 cloves of garlic" and get away with it, and why even the most garlic-phobic can love a garlic head that has been roasted for a long time, oozing with tender caramelized cloves. Use a fork to press the soft roasted garlic cloves from the skin, then spread on bread or whatever else is on the dinner plate.

To roast whole garlic heads, clean them up a bit, trimming the root ends and rubbing off any extraneous papery skin. (Some cooks cut off the tops of the heads, but I find that unnecessary.) Nestle the heads into a bed of coarse salt, if you wish, to keep them upright—the salt also conducts heat for even cooking. Or lay them in one layer in a baking dish on a bed of thyme sprigs. Drizzle with olive oil and bake for about 1 hour at 375 degrees, until completely softened and beginning to caramelize. It's wise to count at least one head of garlic per person. Summer is a fine time to do it, with new-crop garlic, but it's good all year round, as long as the garlic is meaty and firm, not sprouty.

Garlic Cloves en Chemise

You can roast individual cloves, either on a baking sheet or in a cast-iron pan. Just break the cloves apart, without peeling them, then cook them dry or toss lightly with olive oil and roast in a 375-degree oven for about 30 minutes, until softened. (Faster than cooking a whole head.) The French call this cooked unpeeled garlic *en chemise*, meaning still with its shirt on.

Garlic Confit

To make a luscious confit with that slow-cooked garlic sweetness, simmer a good dozen peeled garlic cloves very slowly in an inch of olive oil until completely softened and just barely tinged with color. They should be done in about 30 minutes. Lift them out of the oil and salt them lightly. Spoon the whole warm cloves over fish fillets, braised meat, or scrambled eggs, or mash to spread on toast. (Use any leftover oil in marinades, for cooking vegetables, or for toasting croutons.)

A whole soft, oozing caramelized garlic head for each lucky diner.

Roast Chicken with Whole Garlic Heads

As with all roast chicken recipes, it is crucial to start with a wholesome, strapping free-range bird. Salt generously, and let a few sprigs of thyme and rosemary lend their herby perfume, along with a dozen garlic heads. The garlic is coaxed to sweetness with the long cooking. Serve each person one or two heads.

*1 organic free-range chicken
(about 4 pounds), at room temperature
Salt and pepper
1 small bunch thyme*

*1 small bunch rosemary
A dozen heads of garlic, trimmed for
roasting whole (see photo on page 17)
1 cup dry white wine or water*

Heat the oven to 425 degrees. Season the chicken generously inside and out with salt and pepper, then massage the skin to distribute the seasoning evenly. Put the thyme and rosemary into the cavity, then put the bird in a shallow earthenware baking dish or roasting pan. Tie the legs together if you wish. Surround with the garlic heads and add the wine to the dish.

Roast the chicken, uncovered, for 20 minutes. Reduce the oven temperature to 350 degrees and continue roasting for 45 to 60 minutes more, until the juices run clear when a thigh is probed with a paring knife. The bird should be well browned and the garlic soft and caramelized. Remove from the oven, tent loosely with foil, and let rest for 15 minutes. Carve and transfer to a warm platter. Surround with the garlic heads and serve the garlicky pan juices separately.
MAKES 6 SERVINGS

Roasted Chicken Legs with 40 Cloves of Garlic

Scatter some rosemary and thyme sprigs over the bottom of a shallow earthenware baking dish or roasting pan and then scatter over 40 peeled garlic cloves. Season 6 large chicken legs (drumstick and thigh) generously with salt and pepper and lay them on top. Add 1 cup dry white wine and roast uncovered at 400 degrees for 45 minutes or so, until the skin is browned and crisp and the juices run clear when a thigh is probed with a paring knife. To serve, spoon some pan juices and 6 or 7 soft garlic cloves over each leg. MAKES 6 SERVINGS

NOTE: Egg noodles tossed with the precious pan juices and a few soft garlic cloves are delightful too, with or without the chicken.

Garlic heads surround and perfume a fat chicken.

Garlic Chips

Garlic chips make a festive and tasty garnish for not much effort. Count on at least 1 large garlic clove per person. Slice them paper-thin using a sharp knife or mandoline. Heat an inch of olive oil to 350 degrees in a small skillet. Add the garlic slices and gently fry just until light golden but not browned (golden tastes sweet, browned tastes bitter), about 1 minute. Remove from the oil, blot on paper towels, and season with a little salt. Sprinkle these tiny crisp garlic chips over mashed potatoes, onto pasta, into salads, or over pan-seared fish.

Sweet golden garlic chips with sea salt.

Three Garlic Sauces

There are a variety of garlicky condiments enjoyed throughout the Mediterranean, most of which are made of garlic and olive oil pounded to a thick, creamy sauce. The most famous are French aïoli, Greek *skordalia*, and Spanish *all-i-oli*. Which came first is a matter still up for debate. And there are more: Lebanese *toum* and Turkish *tarator*, among many others, which are equally fine. All have a spreadable, dollopy, mayonnaise-like consistency and are used with abandon to accompany lamb, grilled fish, fish soups, and vegetables of every kind, cooked or raw. For garlic lovers only—no apologies. (Think height of summer, with a glass of chilled rosé in hand.)

To make any of these, you need an ingredient to bind the emulsion: bread, potato, nuts, or egg. For *skordalia*, cooked and mashed potatoes are used to that effect (though my Greek friend Aglaia makes hers with pounded blanched almonds). Aïoli is generally thickened with egg yolk, like mayonnaise. Lebanese *toum* sometimes uses egg white; *tarator* relies on pounded walnuts. Old-fashioned *all-i-oli* uses only garlic for thickening.

These garlic sauces are traditionally served on the thickish side, but I prefer them with a soft-whipped consistency, so I usually dilute them with a little cold water, whisking in a tablespoon or so at the end. It should go without saying that if you're making a sauce of mostly garlic, the garlic should be of the highest quality, preferably fresh summer garlic. Oh, and lemon juice or vinegar? There's no right or wrong way. Some use it and some shun it altogether.

Skordalia (Greek Garlic Sauce)

Try *skordalia* as a dip for potato chips or crudités. It's also perfect in a pita sandwich of lightly salted tomato slices or as a sauce for grilled fish or shrimp. For a delightful alternative, substitute 1 cup cooked chickpeas for the potatoes.

½ pound medium potatoes,
   such as Yukon Gold or russet
   (not waxy red or white ones)
6 to 8 garlic cloves

Salt and pepper
1 cup extra virgin olive oil
1 to 2 tablespoons lemon juice
1 tablespoon sherry vinegar

Boil or steam the potatoes until tender; let cool and peel. Sprinkle the garlic with a bit of salt and, using a mortar and pestle or the side of a heavy knife, smash to a paste. Transfer the garlic paste to a medium bowl, add the potatoes, and mash together. Using a wire whisk or heavy wooden spoon, incorporate the olive oil 2 tablespoons at a time, beating well with each addition. Once the mixture thickens, thin it with a tablespoon or two of lemon juice (if the mixture becomes too thick, beat in a little water). Finish with the vinegar, mixing well. Season with salt and pepper and thin with more water if needed to achieve a milkshake-like consistency.   MAKES ABOUT 1½ CUPS

Aïoli (French Garlic Sauce)

In olden days, the French garlic sauce called aïoli was made by moistening and squeezing out day-old bread, then whisking garlic and olive oil into it to achieve the desired emulsified texture. Nowadays people use egg yolks instead of bread. So prevalent was it at the table in the south of France that aïoli became known as *le beurre Provençal*, used as liberally as butter in the north. (Aïoli, by the way, is not the name for any other sauce, so when you encounter impostors such as Yuzu-Wasabi Aïoli, Bacon-Chipotle Aïoli, or the like, be polite but not overfriendly. Somehow the name has been co-opted to describe creative mayonnaise variations; to be true aïoli, there must be only garlic as flavoring.)

2 large egg yolks
4 to 6 garlic cloves, mashed to a paste
with a pinch of salt

2 cups olive oil, or 1 cup fruity olive oil
plus 1 cup vegetable oil
About 2 tablespoons cold water
Salt

Put the egg yolks and garlic in a heavy bowl and beat with a wire whisk for a minute or so, until slightly thickened. Slowly drizzle in the oil, starting with a teaspoon of oil at a time, whisking in a circular motion and making sure the oil is thoroughly incorporated each time before adding the next teaspoon. Once the sauce begins to thicken, graduate to a tablespoon at a time, remaining vigilant to fully incorporate each new addition of oil before continuing. Failing to do so, or adding too much oil at once, will cause the emulsion to break. (If this happens, start over with a new egg yolk and whisk in the curdled mixture as if it were oil.) When you've added 1 cup of the oil and the sauce is quite thick, thin it by whisking in a tablespoon or two of cold water. Then gradually whisk in the remaining cup of oil. Thin again as necessary. I usually add a big pinch of salt at this point and then let the sauce sit for a few minutes before tasting, allowing the salt to dissolve. The garlic flavor will intensify as the aïoli sits, so make it at least 30 minutes before serving—but be sure to use it the day it's made.

MAKES ABOUT 2½ CUPS

NOTE: You can also make aïoli with a handheld electric mixer or a stand mixer fitted with the whisk attachment. Alternatively, make it with a food processor or immersion blender (see All-i-oli, following page). See also the photos of making mayonnaise on page 432.

All-i-oli (Spanish Garlic Sauce)

Spanish purists insist that the ultimate *all-i-oli* (also called *ajoaceite*) is made only from garlic cloves, pounded to a paste in a mortar, and olive oil, added drop by drop to make a thick sauce. This old-fashioned method requires not a little skill and a saint's patience. Most modern cooks use a machine and an egg, so today *all-i-oli* is basically a very garlicky mayonnaise, quite similar to aïoli. A stick-type immersion blender, which accomplishes the job in seconds, is the tool of choice. I even know a chef who makes a delicious *all-i-oli* this way using a half cup of milk instead of an egg—the powerful blender can create a thick emulsion with no egg at all. Though I'm not usually much for such tools, I had to try it. Here is my version. This *all-i-oli* is pure white.

½ cup whole milk
3 small garlic cloves, roughly chopped
Generous pinch of salt

½ cup olive oil
1 cup vegetable oil
Lemon juice (optional)

Put the milk, garlic, and salt in the jug of an immersion blender or another tall narrow container. Whiz the milk to make it frothy and then, with the blender running, trickle in the olive oil and blend for 30 seconds or so, until somewhat thickened. Now drizzle in the vegetable oil with the blender at high speed, raising and lowering it until the whole mixture has emulsified, a minute or two. Transfer the sauce to a serving bowl and thin it by beating in a tablespoon or two of water or lemon juice, as desired. Taste and adjust the seasoning if necessary.   MAKES ABOUT 2 CUPS

NOTE: If you like, replace the milk with 1 large egg.

A garlic lover's favorite condiments (*clockwise from top*): *all-i-oli, skordalia,* and aïoli.

Three Garlic Soups for the Soul

Soups are comforting, nourishing, and fortifying—and none more so than garlic soup. Countless renditions exist. In addition to tasting wonderful, a simple garlic broth is a tonic.

Oaxaca-Style Garlic Soup

Every summer afternoon in Oaxaca, in the highlands of Mexico, the sky clouds over and for an hour or two, a hard and refreshing rain pours down. Then in the cool air of the evening, you go out for a bowl of *sopa de ajo*, made with the rich wholesome chicken broth Mexican cooks are famous for. The garlic cloves are first toasted in their skins on a hot *comal*, or griddle, then simmered to impart a mild garlic flavor. Now *this* is soup, nurturing and substantial but not heavy. With some chopped jalapeño, a squeeze of lime, and a basket of steaming tortillas, it makes an exemplary restorative meal.

8 garlic cloves, unpeeled
3 cups Blond Chicken Broth (page 460)
Salt
2 large eggs, at room temperature

1 jalapeño or serrano chile,
  minced or sliced
½ cup roughly chopped cilantro
Lime wedges

Toast the garlic cloves, in their skins, on a hot steel *comal* or in a cast-iron skillet over high heat until lightly charred, about 5 minutes.

Bring the chicken broth to a simmer in a medium saucepan. Add the toasted garlic cloves to the chicken broth and simmer for about 15 minutes, until completely softened. Taste the broth for salt and adjust.

Meanwhile, place two soup bowls in a 350-degree oven. Once the bowls are hot, take them out of the oven and crack a raw egg into each one. Immediately ladle the piping-hot broth over the eggs, and give each bowl some of the garlic cloves. At the table, each diner uses a spoon to break and stir the egg into the soup. Pass the chopped chile, cilantro, and lime wedges.   MAKES 2 SERVINGS

Consider a garnish of lightly fried tortilla strips.

Provençal Garlic Soup

This bare-cupboard Provençal soup is insanely good. The ingredients are nothing more than a lot of garlic, some sage leaves, water, a little olive oil, and salt and pepper. It takes only 10 to 15 minutes to cook, but when you taste it, you'll swear it is a long-simmered garlicky chicken broth.

Like chicken broth, garlic soup is said to have all sorts of medicinal properties. It's believed to both prevent and cure hangovers, strengthen the immune system, and aid digestion. It makes a perfect light lunch or supper on a hot summer day when you don't feel much like cooking. When serving it as a first course, some cooks whisk a beaten egg, or a couple of beaten yolks, into the broth at the end to give it a rich, creamy consistency. Many brothy rustic versions—including this one—add a poached egg and toasted bread to make the dish more substantial.

2 tablespoons extra virgin olive oil

2 heads garlic, preferably new-crop, cloves peeled and sliced or roughly chopped

12 sage leaves

Salt and pepper

6 cups water

4 large eggs

4 thick slices day-old French bread, toasted

Chopped parsley, scallions, or chives

Warm the oil in a heavy pot over medium heat. Add the garlic and sage and let sizzle a bit without browning, about 2 minutes. Season with about 1 teaspoon salt and a few grinds of pepper. Add the water and bring to a boil, lower to a brisk simmer, and cook for 10 to 15 minutes, until the garlic has mellowed slightly and the broth is flavorful. Adjust the seasoning if necessary. Keep warm over low heat.

Ladle about an inch of the soup into a large skillet and bring to a brisk simmer over medium heat. Carefully crack the eggs into the pan, leaving ample space between them, and poach for about 3 minutes, until the whites are set but the yolks are still runny.

To serve, place a slice of toast in the bottom of each of four shallow soup bowls and top each with a poached egg. Ladle the hot soup over the eggs and sprinkle with a little parsley. MAKES 4 SERVINGS

Garlic-Tomato Soup

This is a great summertime soup. Made with vine-ripened tomatoes, sweet onions, and new garlic, lightly cooked and pureed, it can be served hot or cold. Adjust the cayenne and vinegar to suit your taste, but it does need a little of both. A drizzle of fruity olive oil makes a fine garnish, as do snipped chives and basil.

4 large tomatoes (about 2 pounds), cored and halved

2 tablespoons extra virgin olive oil, plus more for drizzling

1 large onion, thinly sliced

2 heads garlic, preferably new-crop, separated into cloves (about 12 large cloves total) and peeled

Pinch of cayenne

A thyme sprig

A bay leaf

Salt and pepper

2 cups water

1 tablespoon sherry vinegar, or to taste

1 tablespoon snipped chives

A handful of basil leaves

Heat the broiler. Place the tomatoes skin side up on a baking sheet and broil until aromatic and softened, about 8 minutes; set aside.

Meanwhile, put a heavy-bottomed soup pot over medium-high heat and add the olive oil. When it is hot, add the onion, garlic, cayenne, thyme, and bay leaf and season generously with salt and pepper. Stir the mixture and sauté until the onion is softened and the garlic is lightly colored, about 10 minutes.

Add the tomatoes, water, and vinegar and bring to a boil, then reduce to a simmer and cook for 15 minutes.

Remove the thyme and bay leaf. Transfer the mixture to a blender and puree, then strain through a medium-fine sieve. Thin with a little water if necessary. Taste and adjust the seasoning. Serve topped with the herbs and a drizzle of olive oil. MAKES 4 TO 6 SERVINGS

Mussels with Green Garlic and Fregola

Mussels with garlic is an age-old, deeply satisfying combination. In the springtime, use fresh green garlic shoots. Green garlic is somewhat mild, so you can add it with abandon. Mussels need some starchy accompaniment. Bread for sopping the savory juices is usually the approach. But some kind of toothy pasta, like the fregola (sometimes called Sardinian couscous) used here, also works well.

Salt

1 cup fregola

2 tablespoons extra virgin olive oil

½ cup chopped green garlic, both white and tender green parts (or substitute 4 garlic cloves, grated or minced)

½ teaspoon crushed red pepper

½ teaspoon pimentón, preferably dulce

4 pounds mussels, well rinsed and beards trimmed

½ cup dry white wine

2 tablespoons roughly chopped parsley

Bring a medium pot of generously salted water to a boil. Add the fregola and cook until al dente, 12 to 15 minutes. Drain the fregola and divide among four large soup bowls. Put on a baking sheet and keep warm in a low oven.

Meanwhile, put the olive oil in a large heavy-bottomed soup pot or Dutch oven and heat over medium heat until hot. Add the garlic, crushed red pepper, and pimentón and let sizzle for 30 seconds, without browning. Add the mussels, stir to coat, and increase the heat to high. Add the wine and put on the lid. After 2 minutes, give the mussels a stir, then cover and continue cooking until all the mussels have opened, 6 to 8 minutes.

Pile the mussels into the bowls of fregola, ladle the broth over, and garnish with chopped parsley. MAKES 4 SERVINGS

Clockwise from bottom:
Freshly picked
green garlic, brothy
mussels with fregola,
and rustic toasted
Sardinian fregola.

ONIONS

The humble onion—life in the kitchen without it is unimaginable. It's comforting to remember that, in any season, an onion is standing by, like a steadfast friend; practically every dish benefits by association. Peeling and dicing onions is a meditative ritual, tears and all, and one that most cooks perform on a daily basis.

Onions come in every shape, color, and size, from tiny pearl onions to hefty, flat Bermudas. There are petite "boiling onions" and fat-bulbed fresh spring onions, perfect for grilling or roasting. Red, yellow, or white, they are at their best and juiciest when freshly harvested. They look pretty, pristine, and dewy at the farmers' market bunched with their tender green tops. Walla Walla sweets are ideal for slicing and eating raw. Likewise, some Southern folk say Vidalia onions are as crisp and sweet as apples. Elongated red torpedo onions, originally from the Calabrian town of Tropea, are a great multipurpose variety favored all over Italy. They make cute diminutive onion rings too.

You'll want to make onion tarts and pickled onions, or sweet-and-sour spiced onions for an antipasto. Any type of onion, thickly sliced and grilled or broiled until slightly charred, can accompany whatever you happen to be serving—meat, fish, or lentil salad. A whole long-cooked onion, baked in an oven or in glowing embers until utterly soft, can make a meal on its own, lavished with olive oil and sea salt, perhaps with a drop of sweet vinegar.

Keep a bag of onions in the pantry at all times and hunger will be kept at bay—one way or another.

Onions are quite possibly a cook's most important ingredient. Where would we be without them?

Onion and Bacon Tart

An onion tart is a beautiful way to show off the bulb's many virtues. A classic example is this pizza-like *tarte flambée* or *Flammeküche*. An Alsatian specialty, it has only a few ingredients: onions, crème fraîche, fromage blanc, and bacon. Originally it was a frugal treat on bread-baking day, made from a scrap of bread dough and baked on the stone floor of the village's communal wood-fired oven.

FOR THE DOUGH
$\frac{1}{2}$ cup lukewarm water
1 teaspoon active dry yeast
$1\frac{1}{2}$ cups all-purpose flour
$\frac{1}{2}$ teaspoon salt
$1\frac{1}{2}$ tablespoons butter, melted, or olive oil

FOR THE TOPPING
2 tablespoons butter or olive oil
3 large onions (about $1\frac{1}{2}$ pounds), sliced
   $\frac{1}{8}$ inch thick

Salt and pepper
$\frac{1}{2}$ teaspoon caraway seeds
2 garlic cloves, grated or minced
$\frac{1}{4}$ pound thick-sliced smoked bacon,
   cut into $\frac{1}{4}$-inch-wide lardons
4 ounces fresh ricotta
$\frac{1}{2}$ cup crème fraîche
A splash of milk if needed

To make the dough, pour the water into a medium bowl and stir in the yeast. Stir in $\frac{1}{4}$ cup of the flour and let the mixture get bubbly, 10 to 15 minutes. (You can made the dough with a stand mixer if you like.)

Add the salt, melted butter, and the remaining $1\frac{1}{4}$ cups flour and stir until the dough forms a rough ball. Then turn the dough out onto a lightly floured surface and knead for about 5 minutes, until smooth. Cover the dough with a damp towel or plastic wrap and let rise until doubled in size, about 1 hour. (Or transfer the dough to a zippered plastic bag and let rise in the refrigerator for several hours, or overnight.)

To make the topping, melt the butter in a large skillet over medium-high heat. Add the onions and cook, stirring occasionally, until wilted and lightly browned,

Building an
irresistible
onion tart.

about 5 minutes. Season generously with salt and pepper. Stir in the caraway seeds and garlic and cook for 2 minutes more. Let cool to room temperature.

Put the bacon in a small pan and cover with 1 inch of water. Simmer for 2 minutes, then drain and cool.

Heat the oven to 375 degrees. Punch down the dough, transfer to a lightly floured surface, and knead into a smooth ball. Let relax for a few minutes.

Using a floured rolling pin, roll out the dough to a circle about 12 inches in diameter. Transfer to a 12-by-17-inch baking sheet lined with parchment. Stretch the dough to an elongated oval about 11 inches by 15 inches.

Mix the ricotta with half the crème fraîche and dab spoonfuls of the mixture evenly over the dough. Spread the cooked onions over the dough, leaving a ½-inch border all around. Top with the bacon, scattering it evenly. Drizzle the tart with the remaining crème fraîche. (Beating the crème fraîche with a fork should loosen it enough for drizzling; otherwise, thin with a little milk.)

Bake the tart for 30 to 35 minutes, turning the baking sheet around if necessary for even cooking, until the crust is well browned. Cool on a rack for a few minutes and serve warm, or let cool and serve at room temperature.

MAKES 4 TO 6 SERVINGS

Onion and Olive Tart

For a tart with a Provençal inflection, replace the ricotta with soft goat cheese, the caraway with chopped thyme, and the bacon with olives. Garnish with strips of anchovy fillet if you wish.

Venetian Onions

This is a classic sweet-and-sour dish of small onions braised in wine with spices, raisins, and pine nuts. Every one of these ingredients but the onion was once considered extravagant.

Peel a pound of cipollini or boiling onions. Put them in a pan with 3 tablespoons olive oil over medium heat and season generously with salt and pepper. Crumble a pinch of saffron and mix it into 1 cup dry white wine to harness its flavor and color, then add this to the onions and bring to a gentle simmer. Stir in a half teaspoon each of cinnamon, coriander, dried ginger, and cloves. Add ½ cup golden raisins, ½ cup currants, ½ cup packed brown sugar, and 3 tablespoons white wine vinegar, then add water to barely cover and put on the lid. Simmer very gently for 30 to 40 minutes, until the onions are soft.

Remove the lid and turn up the heat. Reduce the cooking liquid until it is syrupy and coats the onions like a glaze. Serve at room temperature, with a few lightly toasted pine nuts sprinkled over the top.   MAKES 4 SERVINGS

Lebanese Kibbeh with Caramelized Onions

Kibbeh, made with spiced ground lamb or beef and bulgur, are little fried football-shaped savory treats eaten throughout the Middle East. This extraordinarily fragrant family-style version is baked and can be eaten hot, warm, or cold.

1 cup fine bulgur

1 pound finely ground lamb shoulder

4 cups sliced onions (¼ inch thick), plus ¼ cup grated onion

1 teaspoon cumin seeds, toasted and ground

Pinch of cayenne

Salt and pepper

½ cup ice water, or as needed

3 tablespoons olive oil, plus more for oiling the baking pan

½ cup pine nuts, lightly toasted

Thick plain yogurt for serving

Rinse the bulgur well, put in a bowl, cover with cold water, and soak for 20 minutes. Drain well.

Put the drained bulgur, lamb, grated onion, cumin, and cayenne in a large bowl. Add 2 teaspoons salt and ½ teaspoon pepper and mix well with your hands to distribute the seasoning. With a wooden spoon, beat in the ice water. The mixture should be smooth and soft.

Heat the olive oil in a large cast-iron skillet over medium heat. Add the sliced onions and fry gently, stirring occasionally, until they soften, about 5 minutes. Season generously with salt and pepper. Raise the heat, add ¼ cup of the lamb mixture, and fry until the meat is crumbly and the onions are nicely browned, another 10 minutes or so. Stir in the pine nuts and taste for seasoning. Let cool to room temperature.

Heat the oven to 350 degrees. Lightly oil a 9-by-13-inch baking pan, then press half the remaining lamb mixture evenly over the bottom. Spread half the onion mixture over the meat. Add the rest of the meat to the pan, pressing with wet hands to make a smooth top. Score with a sharp paring knife to make a diamond pattern, cutting at least ½ inch deep.

Bake for 35 to 45 minutes, until the top is golden. Spread the top with the remaining onion–pine nut mixture. Serve in squares, with a dollop of yogurt alongside. MAKES 4 TO 6 SERVINGS

The best part is the sweet, darkly caramelized onion topping.

Buttermilk is
a miraculous
ingredient that
renders fried food
crisp and flaky.

Spicy Buttermilk Onion Rings

Deep-frying at home may seem like a messy task, but you'll be surprised by how easy, and how delectable, homemade onion rings are. A quick dip in a buttermilk bath and a light dusting of flour gives you just enough coating to yield a crisp, flaky crust. Banish any fast-food memories; these onion rings are really superior. This flour-and-buttermilk technique works well for just about anything else you might want to fry—and why not, while the oil's hot? A cast-iron pan works fine, but an old Italian cook I know swears by an electric skillet, and her fried food is spectacular.

Use small onions—red, white, or yellow—so the rings aren't unwieldy. Peel 2 onions and cut them into ¼-inch slices. Separate each slice into rings, put the rings in a bowl, and cover them with buttermilk. Put 1 cup all-purpose flour in a bowl. Season the flour with salt, pepper, and a bit of cayenne. Pour about an inch of vegetable oil into a frying pan and heat the oil to 350 degrees; adjust the heat as necessary to keep the temperature steady.

Take one ring from the buttermilk, dip it quickly into the flour mixture, and carefully slip it into the oil. Add more coated onion rings, without crowding the pan, and fry for a minute or so on each side, just until golden. Remove the rings from the oil with a spider or slotted spoon and drain on paper towels. Sprinkle the warm onion rings lightly with salt. Repeat with the remaining onion rings. Pass them to nibble with drinks or serve to accompany a meal.

If you want to make a larger quantity, you can stockpile the fried rings in a low oven, on a rack on a baking sheet, while you fry more. But the truth is, it's best to serve them as soon as they are ready so the rings don't get soggy.

MAKES 4 SERVINGS

Red Onion Soup with Cheese Toasts

Onion soup is an excellent antidote to blustery, cold weather. Though often made with beef broth, Jacques Pépin showed me this frugal version, made with onions and plain tap water (his mother made it that way, he said). His wise counsel: Don't overcrowd the pan, or the onions won't brown. Keep the heat high but not too high, so the onions don't cook too fast and burn. Be generous with the salt and pepper. Bay leaf and thyme are essential, everything else is negotiable. A little red wine is welcome, a splash of Cognac couldn't hurt.

Olive oil

3 pounds red onions, sliced ⅛ inch thick

Salt and pepper

About 10 cups water

1 cup dry red wine

2 bay leaves

1 small bunch thyme, tied with string

8 garlic cloves, roughly chopped

2 tablespoons Cognac or other brandy (optional)

6 slices day-old bread, lightly toasted

6 ounces Gruyère cheese, grated

1 tablespoon chopped sage

1 teaspoon chopped thyme

Set two wide skillets over medium-high heat (if you have only one pan, work in smaller batches). When the pans are hot, put 1 tablespoon oil and a large handful of the sliced onions in each pan. Season the onions generously with salt and pepper and sauté, stirring occasionally, until they are a ruddy dark brown, about 10 minutes.

Transfer the onions to a soup pot and return the pans to the heat. Pour ½ cup of the water into each pan to deglaze it, scraping with a wooden spoon to dissolve any brown bits, then pour the deglazing liquid into the soup pot. Wipe the pans clean and begin again with more oil and sliced onions. Continue until all the onions are browned.

Put the soup pot over high heat, add the wine, bay leaves, thyme, and garlic, and cook for 5 minutes. Add 8 cups water and bring to a boil, then turn the heat down to maintain a gentle simmer and cook for 45 minutes.

Remove and discard the thyme. Skim off any surface fat, taste the soup, and adjust the seasoning. (The soup can be prepared to this point up to 2 days in advance and refrigerated; bring back to a simmer before proceeding.)

This homemade version is far better than the kind served in tourist traps, bubbling with molten cheese.

Just before serving, add the brandy, if using, and simmer for 5 minutes.

Meanwhile, make the cheese toasts: Heat the broiler. Place the toasted bread on a baking sheet. Mix the grated cheese with the chopped sage and thyme, along with a generous amount of pepper. Heap the cheese mixture on the toasts and broil until the cheese bubbles and browns slightly.

Ladle the soup into wide bowls and top each with a toast.   MAKES 6 SERVINGS

LEEKS

In France, there's a leek in every shopper's market basket—not a bad habit to get into. What a wonder simply cooked leeks are, simmered in salted water, butter-stewed, or slowly charred over coals. They are a sweet, tender, elemental pleasure. Leeks are the mildest allium. Unlike scallions, they are almost always eaten cooked, and they are quite versatile—adding depth to vegetable soups and stews or served on their own, grilled or simmered.

But leeks require careful, mindful cooking. Undercooked and still crunchy, they are unpleasant—but they mustn't be cooked to smithereens either. Note that small leeks are more tender and require less cooking time.

When prepping leeks for cooking, you'll need to peel off and discard at least one tough outer layer, but don't cut off the green top entirely; the tender pale green center is too good to waste. Large leeks should be halved lengthwise before chopping.

To wash chopped leeks, swish them in a large bowl of warm water, then let them float to the surface so any sand and dirt can sink to the bottom. Lift the leeks out of the water, leaving the sand and dirt behind. If they are still gritty, soak them again.

For a delicious, simple way to cook chopped leeks, stew them gently in a saucepan with a good knob of butter and a small amount of water, until tender but still bright green, seasoned with salt, pepper, and perhaps a little thyme. Spoon these stewed leeks over poached fish or chicken, add to an omelette, or stir into mashed potatoes.

Medium or large leeks are halved lengthwise before chopping.

Velvety Green Leek Soup

A creamy soup doesn't always mean lots of cream—or any, as in this case. The pureed leeks in the soup provide body as well as flavor, and a handful of rice gives it a smooth consistency. For a striking green taste and color, let the soup cool completely before blending in the spinach. And take the time to strain the soup through a fine-mesh sieve for the silkiest texture.

6 medium leeks (about 3 pounds)
4 tablespoons butter
Salt and pepper
4 garlic cloves, grated or minced
Pinch of cayenne
1/2 cup white rice

8 cups Blond Chicken Broth (page 460), heated, or hot water, or as needed
10 ounces baby spinach, washed
Grated nutmeg
1/2 cup crème fraîche
2 tablespoons thinly sliced chives
2 tablespoons thinly sliced tarragon

Trim the leeks of the tough outer layers and the root ends. Halve lengthwise and chop the white and tender green parts (discard the tough gray-green parts) into 1/2-inch pieces. Swish the chopped leeks in a large bowl of warm water, then let them float to the surface so sand and dirt can sink to the bottom of the bowl. Lift the leeks from the water, leaving any sediment behind. To make sure no grit remains, soak them again in fresh water, then lift out and drain.

Melt the butter in a heavy-bottomed soup pot over medium heat. Add the leeks, season well with salt and pepper, and cook, stirring, until wilted, 8 to 10 minutes.

Add the garlic, cayenne, and rice and cook for 1 minute. Add the hot broth and bring to a boil, then reduce to a gentle simmer and cook until the rice is very soft, about 25 minutes. Remove from the heat and let cool completely.

Using a blender, puree the spinach with the cooled soup mixture, working in batches if necessary. Strain the soup through a fine-mesh sieve into a saucepan; discard any fibrous solids. Adjust the seasoning and add a little nutmeg. Thin the soup with broth or water if necessary.

To preserve the bright green color, don't reheat the soup until just before serving. Then garnish each serving with a tablespoon of crème fraîche and a sprinkling of chives and tarragon. MAKES 8 SERVINGS

Leeks Vinaigrette with Chopped Egg

In traditional French bistros, cooked whole leeks are dressed with a tart vinaigrette and served as a classic first course, sometimes called "poor man's asparagus" (leeks are cheaper there than in North America). Leeks vinaigrette can be wonderful or dull, depending on several variables: the size of the leeks, the quality of the olive oil, the care taken to cook them perfectly. Don't use giant ones; choose medium to small leeks for tender results. Another caveat: Cooked leeks should have no crunch. Err on the well-cooked side.

Salt and pepper
8 medium leeks (about 4 pounds)
3 tablespoons red wine vinegar
1 tablespoon Dijon mustard

1 small garlic clove, minced
6 tablespoons extra virgin olive oil
3 hard-cooked eggs (see How to Boil an Egg, page 431), roughly chopped

Bring a large pot of salted water to a simmer. Meanwhile, trim the roots from the leeks and peel away any tough outer layers. Trim the tops but leave the tender green parts. With a paring knife, make a lengthwise slit halfway down each leek. Soak the leeks in a large bowl of lukewarm water, swishing to dislodge sand. Let stand briefly, then lift from the water and drain. Repeat once more with fresh water, then lift out and drain.

Add the leeks to the pot and simmer for 6 to 8 minutes. The thickest part should be tender when probed with a paring knife. Transfer the leeks to a bowl of cold water. Drain and blot dry on a kitchen towel, and leave at room temperature.

To make the vinaigrette, whisk together the vinegar, mustard, and garlic in a small bowl. Season with salt and pepper, then whisk in the olive oil.

Arrange the leeks on a serving platter or individual plates. Season lightly with salt and pepper, then spoon the vinaigrette evenly over the leeks. Top with the chopped egg.   MAKES 4 SERVINGS

SHALLOTS

Attention shoppers: Don't bypass the shallot bin in your quest for edible alliums. The onion's oft-forgotten cousins, shallots seem to be more popular in Europe, but they're readily available here these days. The copper hue of their outer skin is beautiful; ditto for their sweet pink-purple flesh. There are gray-skinned white-fleshed shallots, too, popular in France despite being somewhat difficult to peel. The marvelously mild pink shallots grown in Vietnam are found in countless Vietnamese dishes, employed with more frequency than onions. (They are available at most Asian groceries.) Crispy Fried Shallots (page 63) are often added as a crunchy topping for good measure.

Shallots come into play when subtlety is needed, adding more elegance than onions can. One small finely diced shallot can elevate a vinaigrette or salsa verde, give steak tartare the subtle punch it requires, or be used to make a simple pan sauce for steaks or fish fillets.

But pretty much anything you can do with an onion can be done with a shallot; be prepared to fry, pickle, braise, or roast.

Shallot Vinaigrette

All you really need for a great vinaigrette is flavorful oil and good vinegar. But if you add a finely chopped shallot to your vinegar, in ten transformational minutes you will have turned your dressing from pedestrian to superb. Use this vinaigrette for mixed green salads or spoon it over grilled fish.

1 small shallot, finely diced　　　　*Salt and pepper*
2 tablespoons red wine vinegar　　　*6 tablespoons olive oil*

Put the shallot in a small bowl and add the vinegar, a good pinch of salt, and a little black pepper. Leave the mixture to macerate for 10 minutes.

Beat in the olive oil with a fork, or shake the mixture in a jar if you like. Use within a day or two.　MAKES ABOUT ½ CUP

Quick Pickled Shallots

This is a dead-easy method for a super-quick pickle, similar to macerating shallots for vinaigrette. These go well with prosciutto and any kind of salumi, and with pâtés or other charcuterie.

4 large shallots, sliced ¹/8 inch thick
¹/2 cup red wine vinegar
¹/2 teaspoon salt
¹/2 teaspoon sugar
A thyme sprig

Put the shallot slices in a small bowl, using your fingers to separate them into rings. Stir together the vinegar with the salt and sugar until they are dissolved and pour over the shallot rings. Add the thyme sprig and make sure the vinegar is covering everything. The pickles will be ready in 15 minutes, and they can be refrigerated for up to a week.   MAKES ABOUT 1 CUP

Braised Shallots with Pancetta

The shallot's size lends itself to cooking whole, like cipollini or pearl onions. Serve these warm to accompany any kind of roast.

2 ounces sliced pancetta or bacon, cut into ¼-inch-wide lardons

2 tablespoons butter

12 medium shallots

Salt and pepper

2 tablespoons sherry vinegar

½ cup Blond Chicken Broth (page 460) or water

Put a large skillet over medium heat, add the pancetta, and cook until barely browned, about 3 minutes. Add the butter and shallots and season generously with salt and pepper, stirring to coat the shallots. Let the shallots brown for a few minutes, stirring occasionally. Then add the vinegar and broth, cover the pan, turn the heat down, and simmer gently for about 20 minutes, until the shallots are tender when pierced.

Remove the lid, turn up the heat, and cook off most of the remaining liquid, basting the shallots with the reduced pan juices to finish.   MAKES 4 SERVINGS

Crispy Fried Shallots

These crispy shallots are brilliant in both Western and Asian recipes, where they add a little sweet crunch. Make a large batch to store in a jar in the pantry. The trick is to start the shallots in room-temperature oil and cook them very slowly. The leftover cooking oil can be saved and used for stir-fries.

1 cup vegetable oil
3 large shallots, sliced lengthwise about 1/8 inch thick
Salt

Put the oil in a small saucepan, add the shallots, and set over medium heat. Cook the shallots gently, stirring occasionally, for about 15 minutes (turn down the heat if they seem to be coloring too quickly), until they turn golden brown.

Place a fine-mesh sieve over a bowl. Transfer the shallots to the sieve and let drain well. Then blot with paper towels. They will crisp as they cool. Sprinkle lightly with salt.   MAKES ABOUT 1 CUP

Butcher Steak with Shallot Pan Sauce

The preferred French cut for steak-frites is *onglet*—what we call hanger steak in the States. Butchers know it to be more flavorful, if less tender, than some expensive cuts. It's best cooked in a hot pan, rather than grilled, with a pan sauce thrown together once the meat is done and resting. If your butcher doesn't have hanger steak, ask her to recommend another similar unusual cut. Most butchers have something inexpensive and delicious they keep for their regular clientele, such as bavette, sirloin flap, and regional, well-marbled cuts like Newport or Bohemian steaks (another reason to get to know your butcher).

Set a cast-iron pan over high heat while you season 2 butcher steaks (5 ounces is a good portion) with salt and pepper. Put a film of olive oil in the pan, and when it is almost smoking, put in the steaks. Reduce the heat to medium-high and let the steaks brown well on the first side, about 3 minutes, then turn them over. After 2 or 3 minutes, when you see red juices begin to appear on the surface, transfer the steaks to a warm plate. The meat should be rare to medium-rare, or it will be tough.

Add a tablespoon of butter to the pan, throw in some finely diced shallot, and let it begin to color. Stir with a wooden spoon to loosen any brown bits on the bottom of the pan, then add 1 cup beef or chicken broth and ¼ cup dry red wine and deglaze the pan, scraping the bottom with the spoon. Boil to reduce the liquid by half. You should have a dark, concentrated sauce. Turn off the heat and swirl in another tablespoon of butter. Taste for salt, then spoon the sauce over the steaks. Serve with a big bunch of watercress and Golden Panfried Potatoes (page 285). SERVES 2

Luscious pan-cooked hanger steak. Skirt or flank steaks are also good options.

SCALLIONS

Scallions go by many names. They're also called green onions, and some call them spring onions, though true spring onions are larger, and the bottoms are bulbous. Gardeners call them bunching onions, since they can be planted close together. They grow straight and tall, never form a bulb, and can be harvested relatively soon after planting, in eight to ten weeks. Confusingly, scallions are called shallots in Louisiana, owing to the region's French culinary roots, so when you see "shallots" on menus in New Orleans or in Creole cookbooks, it's green onions they're talking about.

Scallions are mild enough to use generously. A handful of chopped scallions can improve the flavor of nearly any savory dish. Even something as mundane as scallion cream cheese shows how scallions can add dimension to the simplest preparations.

I tend to use both the green top and white bottom, mixed together, especially if they are finely sliced. They are beautiful cut Asian-style, at a sharp angle, but they can also be sliced crosswise. I dice them small to include in mixtures of freshly chopped herbs for a brighter, livelier green garnish.

For the most part, I use scallions raw, sprinkled into broth or over all kinds of noodles, for instance, or folded into soft-scrambled eggs. And there's an old James Beard recipe for thin-sliced raw onion sandwiches built on good white bread, slathered with mayonnaise. I make a version with scallions instead. They are not as dainty as cucumber-and-watercress tea sandwiches—better with beer.

Scallions can be cooked whole, charred in a hot skillet or over coals; simmered in a buttery bath to serve as a side vegetable; or steamed and sauced with a vinaigrette, like miniature leeks.

Golden Scallion Crepes

There are lots of versions of scallion pancakes, and it's hard not to love them all. These are modeled after the Vietnamese crepes called *banh xeo*, made with a savory rice flour batter. This is a vegetarian version, bright with the flavor of basil and mint and the crunch of mung bean sprouts. The way to eat them is to wrap a bit of pancake in a lettuce leaf, then dunk it in a spicy dipping sauce. Serve these for lunch. (Actually, I'd have them for breakfast too.)

FOR THE BATTER
1 cup rice flour
½ teaspoon ground turmeric
½ teaspoon salt
1½ cups cold water

Vegetable oil for cooking the crepes
6 scallions, thinly sliced
1 cup mung bean sprouts, rinsed
A handful of mint leaves
A handful of basil leaves
6 large crisp lettuce leaves
Dipping Sauce (recipe follows)

To make the batter, whisk together the rice flour, turmeric, and salt in a medium bowl. Add the cold water and whisk until smooth. Cover and leave at room temperature for 1 hour.

To make the crepes, heat 1 tablespoon oil in a crepe pan or small shallow skillet over medium-high heat until hot. Ladle ½ cup of the batter into the pan, tipping and swirling the pan to spread the batter to the edges. Sprinkle a small handful of sliced scallions over and cook until the bottom of the crepe is brown and crisp, 2 to 3 minutes (these crepes are cooked on one side only). Remove the crepe and blot gently on a paper towel. Make 5 more crepes in the same manner (don't stack them).

Top each crepe with a few bean sprouts and some mint and basil leaves and fold in half. Serve with the lettuce leaves and dipping sauce.   MAKES 6 SERVINGS

Dipping Sauce

1 Thai or serrano chile (or more if
  desired), thinly sliced
2 garlic cloves, finely chopped
2 teaspoons finely minced or grated
  fresh ginger

2½ teaspoons sugar, or to taste
⅓ cup lime juice
¼ cup fish sauce (such as Red Boat,
  a high-quality Vietnamese brand)

Combine the chile, garlic, ginger, sugar, lime juice, and fish sauce in a small bowl.
Add more sugar if desired, or add water by the tablespoon if needed to soften
the flavors.   MAKES ABOUT ⅔ CUP

No eggs in this batter.
The golden color
comes from turmeric.

Scallions cut
crosswise (*in bowl*)
and diagonally
(*on board*).

Japanese Scallion Custard

This Japanese savory egg custard, *chawanmushi*, is light and silky, perfect for a first course. It's traditionally steamed in decorative little porcelain vessels, but you can certainly make it in small ramekins or tiny coffee or teacups. Served warm, it's a nice alternative to soup.

4 large eggs
1½ cups Blond Chicken Broth (page 460)
   or Dashi (page 461)
3 scallions, thinly sliced crosswise
1 teaspoon toasted sesame oil

1 teaspoon soy sauce
1 tablespoon sake
1 teaspoon mirin
½ teaspoon salt

Beat the eggs in a medium bowl, then whisk in the broth. Add the scallions, sesame oil, soy sauce, sake, mirin, and salt and mix thoroughly. Ladle into six small ramekins, using ⅓ cup of the mixture for each.

Place the ramekins in a steamer set over rapidly simmering water, lay a kitchen towel over the top (to avoid drops from condensation), and put on the lid. Steam for 7 to 8 minutes, or until the custards are just set. Carefully remove from the steamer and serve.　MAKES 6 SERVINGS

A fine custard is not
always rich and sweet.

Scallion Schmear

A m I really arguing that you should make your own scallion cream cheese? Yes. This way, you can use first-rate cream cheese, which will make a better schmear. There is plenty of nostalgia for gummy Philadelphia-style cream cheese, but I prefer the fresher, natural, less-processed type available at any decent cheese shop. Better cheese and freshly chopped scallions make all the difference, and it takes no time. Just mix ½ cup slivered scallions into 8 ounces (1 cup) room-temperature cream cheese.

Charred Scallions

The most luscious scallions are flash-cooked over high heat, in a hot wok or cast-iron skillet or over a bed of glowing coals, and quickly, for only a few minutes. The exterior of the scallions gets charred, but the center stays tender, sweet, and green. This is a relatively primal way of cooking, with immediate, visceral appeal. You can leave the scallions whole, just trimming off the roots—best for grilling—or chop them into bite-sized 1-inch pieces so they can go straight from the scorching-hot wok to the diner's rice bowl. It's good messy fun to eat the whole scallions straight from the grill, when they are almost too hot to handle. In either case, coat the scallions lightly with oil and give them a pinch of salt before you char them.

MAD FOR VEGETABLES

I have always had a great fondness for vegetables. Even as a child, I always requested creamed spinach at birthdays. Though I grew up mostly on vegetables from the freezer, to me they were the best part of any meal.

My feelings haven't changed. If anything, they have deepened. When I go to the market in the early morning at the height of the season, the sight of all those vegetables, freshly picked and piled high at stand after stand, is compelling and inspirational. So many colors, shapes, textures, tastes, and aromas, and so many ways to cook them all. Be still my heart.

If you want more than lackluster generic vegetables, it can take a little bit of sleuthing. Relish it. Take a quick pass through the farmers' market, checking out each stand to see who has the best of what is on offer. No farmers' market nearby? Take a detour to that place in Chinatown that always has the best flowering mustard greens or to the little produce store that gets fresh lettuces on Tuesday.

Looking forward to a vegetable's true season provides yearly excitement, not to mention superior flavor. Say no to winter asparagus shipped from Peru and wait for the crop grown locally.

As for how the following vegetables are organized, my loose approach was to list them from lighter to heavier, not alphabetically and not seasonally. And if your favorite vegetable didn't make the list, it was for lack of space, not lack of love. Sadly, okra and fava beans didn't get in. Mea culpa.

LETTUCES & LEAVES

Alas, I grew up on only one kind of salad: a sad naked wedge of iceberg lettuce, with bottled dressing on the side. It's not that other lettuces didn't exist—just not in our household. The only variation was that, occasionally, the iceberg was chopped or sliced. And salad was always something in a shallow bowl to the left of the dinner plate, served with the meal rather than as a course of its own. My horizons expanded when we visited my aunt, who served the most delicious salad of mixed lettuces with sliced cucumbers and radishes. She made her own simple dressing with oil and vinegar, right in the bowl. It was easy for even my young taste buds to discern the difference; watching her prepare a salad was an early lesson in cooking.

If I was salad conscious as a boy, it's fair to say I'm now salad obsessed. I'm absolutely enamored of salad, from the most tender Bibb lettuce leaves with a delicate dressing to forceful, bitter leaves like dandelion and radicchio, which pair so beautifully with anchovy and garlic in a highly seasoned dressing.

I'm jealous of anybody with even the smallest vegetable garden. To me, one of the most heavenly cooking experiences is going out and cutting a head of lettuce (or gathering a bowlful of snipped salad leaves) just before a meal, for the most alive-tasting, freshest salad imaginable. Lacking a garden, you have to be vigilant in selecting your salad greens wherever you find them, the goal being to find lettuces that feel and taste freshly picked.

Obviously the freshest offerings will be at the farmers' market or farm stand, but even there quality can vary from stall to stall and time of day (get there early!). In the supermarket setting, don't settle for grab and go. Prewashed salad mixes in a plastic bag or clamshell are generally less than ideal (to put it politely), and they may not contain the mix that is actually wanted. And washing your own salad greens can be relaxing, a pleasure, not a chore—or am

Choose sturdy smallish to midsized lettuces for the best mixed salads. Tiny baby lettuce leaves quickly wilt when dressed.

I living in an alternate universe? My preference is to buy a variety of medium-sized heads of lettuce and make my own mix, which may include small red or green oak leaf, curly endive, Little Gem, and small Bibb lettuces. I also may use arugula, herbs, watercress . . . anything that's fresh, leafy, and vibrant.

When you're choosing large lettuces like romaine, in addition to general appearance and the perkiness of the leaves themselves, check out the root ends to gauge freshness—they should look freshly cut, juicy, and pale green, not brown.

Most lettuce heads need a little cleaning up. This means you may need to jettison the tough outer leaves to the compost bin or save them to use as cooking greens. It is the tender unblemished leaves that you want for a good salad.

Ultimately, my obsession (and hopefully yours too) is about not only the freshness of the salad leaves, but also the care taken in seasoning and dressing them. Always use a light hand. You'll be much happier.

Tender Lettuce Salad
with Crème Fraîche Dressing

An old French custom is to dress tender lettuces lightly with cream and lemon, rather than with oil and vinegar. (Unfortunately, in France and many parts of Europe, this has devolved into commercial "salad cream," a sad, thin, mayonnaise-based dressing in a squeeze bottle.) Butter lettuces like Buttercrunch, Boston, and Bibb or similar soft, broad-leaved heads are the ones to choose for this salad, though the slightly crisper Little Gem lettuces would also be good.

Put ½ cup crème fraîche in a small bowl, add 1 teaspoon strong Dijon mustard, a pinch each of cayenne, salt, and pepper, ½ teaspoon grated lemon zest, and about 1 tablespoon lemon juice, and beat with a fork to combine. The consistency should be like heavy cream; thin with a little cream or milk if necessary.

Be ruthless in removing the lettuces' tough outer leaves. Wash and gently dry the lettuce leaves (you'll need 4 large handfuls) and put them in a wide salad bowl. Sprinkle very lightly with sea salt and drizzle with about 3 tablespoons of the dressing. Dress the salad quickly with your hands, using your fingers to help coat the leaves lightly, then add a little more dressing if needed. Sprinkle with chopped dill, chervil, or chives if desired.   MAKES 4 SERVINGS

Mixed-Leaves Salad

It's an absolute pleasure to eat a green salad that is well made, dressed perfectly, and in balance, but it takes a good cook to do it. You must develop a feeling for the taste and texture of the greens. For certain salads, you may want the delicious flavor of the oil to predominate, so you use only a few drops of lemon juice. Other salads, especially those with soft or fragile leaves that should be dressed very lightly, need a dressing with more acid so the salad tastes bright. Also consider that some vinegars are sharper than others and sometimes the garlic is more pungent.

Though so-called baby lettuces are trendy (and not to dismiss them), I usually prefer a midsized lettuce, one that has been allowed to grow long enough to acquire some vigor, that won't wilt immediately upon contact with the dressing, with leaves about 4 inches in length. At the market, look for Lollo Rosso, red romaine, red or green oak leaf, frisée (curly endive), watercress, mâche, or arugula, or for Merveille des Quatre Saisons, deer tongue, salvius, Tango, or other regional varieties. A beautiful mix is the ideal, but a vibrant green salad made with only one type of lettuce can also be perfect.

Make a basic vinaigrette with 2 tablespoons red wine vinegar, 1 tablespoon sherry vinegar or Banyuls vinegar, 1 smashed garlic clove, salt and pepper, and 6 tablespoons olive oil: Whisk these together in a bowl or shake the mixture in a jar. For an emulsified vinaigrette with more body, add ½ teaspoon Dijon mustard.

Put 4 large handfuls (about ½ pound) of washed salad leaves (make sure they are dry, or the dressing will be diluted) in a wide shallow bowl. Sprinkle very lightly with salt and toss the leaves with your hands. The challenge now is to dress the salad perfectly. Be miserly with the dressing—it's better to dress twice than to risk the sad sight of a salad's death-by-drowning. MAKES 4 SERVINGS

Washing and drying lettuce: Lift the salad leaves from the water, allowing the grit to sink to the bottom of the basin. Drain well in a colander, giving the colander a good shake. (You might prefer to use a salad spinner, but I find this method most effective.) Since water is the enemy of a good vinaigrette, blot the washed lettuce leaves and carefully roll them up in a kitchen towel. Refrigerate for up to 2 days in the towel, in a loose-fitting plastic bag.

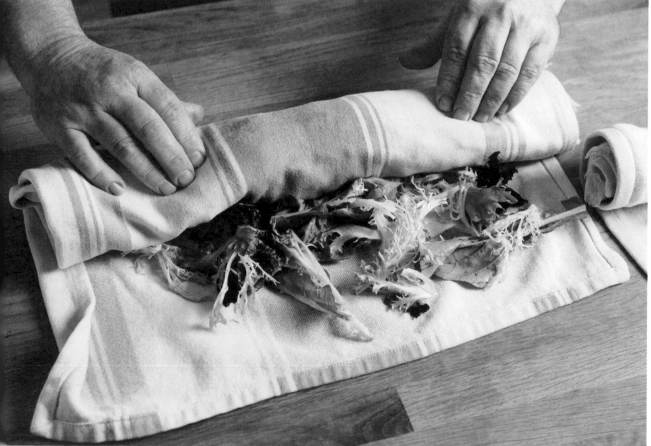

Romaine Leaves with Lemon and Parmesan

This is a bright, crisp, and satisfying salad. You can use supermarket organic hearts of romaine to make this salad year-round, but seasonal locally grown romaine will make the salad that much better. A whole romaine head has lots of outer leaves that are not salad worthy, though, so I save them for cooking (they're delicious chopped and cooked in butter or olive oil).

2 large heads romaine lettuce, hearts only, or organic hearts of romaine

3 tablespoons lemon juice

1 teaspoon Dijon mustard (optional)

1 garlic clove, smashed to a paste with a little salt

¼ cup fruity extra virgin olive oil

Salt and pepper

A chunk of Parmesan, for shaving

Wash the romaine leaves in cool water, then drain well. To dry the leaves, place them in one layer on kitchen towels, then stack the towels, roll them into a cylinder, and refrigerate. (Or use a salad spinner if you prefer.)

To make the vinaigrette, put the lemon juice in a small bowl and whisk in the mustard and garlic. Whisk in the olive oil and and season with salt and pepper. The dressing will be quite tart, but the flavor of the oil should be evident too.

Put the romaine leaves in a wide salad bowl. Sprinkle very lightly with salt, then drizzle on half the vinaigrette. Toss quickly with your hands to coat the leaves. Taste a leaf and adjust the seasoning, also adding more vinaigrette as necessary. With a sharp vegetable peeler, shave Parmesan curls or shards over the salad. Add a little freshly ground pepper and serve immediately.   MAKES 4 SERVINGS

Grilled Romaine Hearts

To make a warm version of this salad, first halve the romaine hearts lengthwise. Paint the cut sides lightly with olive oil and grill briefly over coals (or under the broiler), just until the cut sides are charred and slightly softened. Arrange one heart on each plate and spoon the vinaigrette over them. Add shaved or grated Parmesan, some garlic toast, and an anchovy fillet or two to each salad.

Above: A platter of tender fragrant salad herbs, ready to be nibbled raw or dressed. *Left:* A garlicky salad of Italian flat-leaf parsley.

Herb Salads

Although you might think of an herb salad as something froufrou served in a restaurant where the cooks use tweezers, it absolutely can be a nice thing at home.

There are many approaches. One is to offer a gorgeous pile of delicate herbs and lettuces simply presented on a platter with no dressing at all, as is common in Vietnamese and Persian cuisines. The fragrant herbs are meant to be nibbled on as a refreshing accompaniment to the meal. The herb mixture may include tiny tender lettuce leaves, parsley sprigs, pale celery leaves, basil leaves, dill fronds, cilantro sprigs, baby mizuna greens or baby spinach, young arugula, chervil sprigs, tarragon leaves, hyssop leaves, borage flowers, and more.

Another way is to dress a small bowlful of tender leafy herbs in the lightest possible way—with a teaspoon of buttery olive oil, or perhaps a nut oil, massaged ever so gently with your fingertips, followed by a little salt and a few drops of lemon or lime juice. In any case, the salad should be barely dressed, nearly naked.

Sometimes even an herb salad can have a forceful personality. For instance, I like to dress a handful of flat-leaf parsley leaves lightly with a garlicky citrus dressing and a light dusting of grated pecorino cheese or Parmesan. This sort of zippy parsley salad tastes good scattered on a pizza or over a steak.

Mixed Chicories
with Anchovy, Garlic, and Lemon

Chicories are sturdy cool-weather salad greens, though to call them greens is a little misleading. The most common in the produce section of the supermarket are the round-headed radicchio di Chioggia, mostly crimson with white veins, and ivory-hued pointy-leaved Belgian endive. At the farmers' market, you may encounter other colorful radicchios, like the oxblood red elongated Treviso and the curlicue Tardivo, or other chicory family members, such as pale speckled Castelfranco, escarole, and frisée. With all chicories, whether raw or cooked, a slight pleasant bitterness is expected.

For a beautiful mixed chicory salad, tear radicchio or Castelfranco leaves into rough 2-inch pieces or slice them into wide ribbons and put them in a salad bowl. Add some frisée (just the pale tender center leaves) and the leaves of 2 or 3 Belgian endives. You'll need 4 large handfuls (about 6 cups). Make an assertive dressing with 2 garlic cloves and 4 anchovy fillets pounded together, 1 teaspoon Dijon mustard, 2 tablespoons red wine vinegar, 1 tablespoon lemon juice, and a little salt. Whisk in 6 tablespoons extra virgin olive oil and some freshly ground pepper.

Season the leaves lightly with salt and drizzle with 3 or 4 tablespoons of the dressing. Toss well and leave the salad alone for about 5 minutes. Then toss again, taste, adding a little more dressing if necessary, and serve.   MAKES 4 SERVINGS

NOTE: This dressing is also good with dandelion greens (another type of chicory) or any crisp lettuce leaves.

Chicories with Balsamic Vinegar

For a simpler chicory salad, sprinkle the leaves with coarse sea salt and dress lightly with a flavorful extra virgin olive oil. Distribute among individual salad plates. Drizzle a small spoonful of aged balsamico over each portion.

Dandelion Greens with Mustard Dressing

For the best dandelion salad you want the leaves to be relatively small and tender—the large dandelion bunches you see in the supermarket are often better cooked (though you could use just the top 6 inches of them for this salad and save the tougher bottoms for cooking). Of course, you can forage for young wild dandelion under the right conditions. If you can't get dandelion, use sturdy spinach leaves, mizuna, or frisée.

FOR THE VINAIGRETTE
1 garlic clove, grated or minced
3 tablespoons red wine vinegar
1 tablespoon Dijon mustard
6 tablespoons extra virgin olive oil
Salt and pepper

2 ounces thick-cut bacon, cut crosswise into ¼-inch-wide lardons
2 bunches young dandelion greens (about ¾ pound), stems trimmed
Salt and pepper
4 soft-center hard-cooked eggs (see How to Boil an Egg, page 431)
Shavings of Gruyère cheese (optional)

To make the vinaigrette, put the garlic, vinegar, and mustard in a small bowl. Whisk in the olive oil and season to taste with salt and pepper.

Fry the lardons gently in a large cast-iron skillet over medium heat for about 5 minutes, until golden—they should be crisp but with some give. Blot on paper towels.

Put the greens in a large salad bowl and season lightly with salt and pepper. Dress with half the vinaigrette, tossing to coat, then add more as needed. Arrange the greens on individual plates and distribute the bacon among the salads. Cut the eggs in halves or quarters and season with salt and pepper, then garnish each salad with a halved egg. Add shavings of Gruyère, if using.

MAKES 4 SERVINGS

Belgian Endives with Tangerine

Belgian endives are juicier and milder when raw than their chicory brethren, so they make a tamer, crisper, more user-friendly salad for your scaredy-cat dining friends. Either a sweet citrus vinaigrette or a more aggressive anchovy-and-garlic one suits them well. You may also want to experiment with how you present them: Simply cut the petal-like leaves free and dress them, or slice them lengthwise into ribbons.

1 small shallot, finely diced
1 teaspoon sherry vinegar
Salt and pepper
½ teaspoon grated tangerine zest
¼ cup tangerine juice, with the pulp

¼ cup fruity extra virgin olive oil
6 Belgian endives
½ cup pecan halves, lightly toasted
  (optional)

Put the shallot in a small bowl, add the vinegar and a little salt, and let macerate for 10 minutes. Whisk in the tangerine zest, juice, and olive oil. Taste for seasoning.

Trim the bottoms of the endives and discard any withered outer leaves. Arrange the endive leaves on a platter or individual plates, season with salt and pepper, and spoon the vinaigrette over. Crumble the pecans over the top, if using, and serve.

Alternatively, cut the endives lengthwise into ¼-inch strips and put in a shallow salad bowl. Season with salt and pepper and toss with half the vinaigrette, coating well. Taste and add more dressing if needed. Garnish with the crumbled pecans. MAKES 4 SERVINGS

Endives with Blood Orange

Instead of tangerine juice, use blood orange juice. Substitute toasted walnuts for the pecans and add a little crushed red pepper and a bit of walnut oil.

GLORIOUS HERBS

Why have herbs become so mysterious? To me, they're as essential as salt and pepper—an everyday affair.

Some herbs are tender and green, like parsley, and some are more resinous and hardy, like rosemary. Among the first kind, which tend to be sweeter and leafier, there's also chervil, basil, cilantro, mint, hyssop, lovage, chives, tarragon, and dill; among the woodier variety, there's thyme, marjoram, savory, oregano, and sage.

Most herbs don't require washing. They simply need their leaves removed from their stems to be used, chopped or not. Bunches of parsley and cilantro, however, need to be swished in a large basin of water as they tend to be sandy and gritty. Lift them from the bowl, give them a good shake, and wrap them in a kitchen towel placed in a loose-fitting plastic bag.

You can go to any supermarket and buy a pricey little package of sage or thyme or rosemary. But often you just want a wee sprig of thyme. You don't need all three dollars and ninety-nine cents' worth. There's something wonderful about having those herbs available, but there's also something horrible about their being packaged in plastic and expensive and often not terribly fresh. Oh, for an herb garden!

The next best thing to having your own herb garden is having a half dozen pots of herbs on the windowsill—or a friend with an herb garden. You can buy potted herbs at the farmers' market, and even in supermarkets. Pluck the few leaves you need and then plant the whole thing in a larger pot so it can flourish. (I had basil all summer long from a plant I got at the supermarket.)

If you do end up with a bunch of extra rosemary that will surely rot if left in the fridge, tie a string around it and hang it out to dry. You'll have the freshest dried rosemary around.

Top to bottom: Parsley, cilantro, thyme and chervil, tarragon and chives, and rosemary and basil.

Paris Omelette with Fines Herbes

This may not be strictly true, but for the sake of argument, let's just say that any run-of-the-mill neighborhood bistro in Paris will give you a pretty decent omelette for a fine lunch with a nice glass of wine. I'd rarely risk this in a U.S. restaurant. French cooks seem to know intuitively how omelettes should be—soft, custardy, and nearly but not quite runny inside. They can be quite plain, just seasoned with salt and pepper, or there may be cheese or ham inside. For sheer simplicity and elegance, though, the classic mixture of snipped sweet herbs called *fines herbes*—parsley, chervil, tarragon, and chives—is the ideal flavoring for a well-made omelette.

2 large eggs	*2 tablespoons butter*
2 tablespoons water	*1 tablespoon chopped fines herbes*
Salt and pepper	*(chives, chervil, parsley, and tarragon)*

Beat the eggs in a bowl, then whisk in the water and season with salt and pepper. Heat a carbon steel omelette pan or small nonstick skillet over medium heat. Add the butter and swirl it around the pan to evenly coat—you do not want it to brown. When the butter is foamy, add the eggs and, using a spatula, stir constantly to create soft curds. As the eggs begin to set up, lift up the sides to let any runny uncooked egg make contact with the skillet (leave a little bit of runny egg on the top). Cook for an additional minute or so, shaking the skillet (this will make it easier to slide the omelette out of the pan), then sprinkle the herbs over the omelette, fold it onto itself, and slide onto a warm plate. The whole process should take only 3 or 4 minutes.   MAKES 1 SERVING

A good omelette has a soft, nearly runny, custardy center.

Lebanese Tabbouleh

You may not know that a proper tabbouleh, as served in the Middle East, is really a parsley salad with a little bulgur wheat, not the other way around, as many people here know it. Light and herby, tabbouleh is a refreshing way to begin a meal, either on its own or with an assortment of other salads. Of course you need tasty olive oil, ripe tomatoes, and tender, flavorful parsley. The pomegranate seeds add lovely texture and sweetness but are not required.

3/4 cup fine bulgur

Salt and pepper

3 tablespoons lemon juice

4 scallions, minced

1/2 cup finely chopped mint

About 4 tablespoons extra virgin olive oil

2 cups roughly chopped flat-leaf parsley
  (about 3 bunches)

4 small tomatoes, cut into 1/2-inch dice

1/2 cup pomegranate seeds (optional)

Soak the bulgur in cold water for 30 minutes.

Drain the bulgur, pat dry with a tea towel, and transfer to a bowl. Season generously with salt and pepper, then stir in the lemon juice and toss well. Add the scallions and mint and toss. Drizzle in 3 tablespoons of the olive oil, stirring, then taste and adjust the seasoning. Add half the parsley and mix well.

Spoon the tabbouleh onto a platter and sprinkle with the rest of the parsley. Put the tomatoes in a bowl, season with salt and pepper, and drizzle with the remaining olive oil. Garnish the tabbouleh with the seasoned tomatoes and the pomegranate seeds, if using.   MAKES 4 TO 6 SERVINGS

A proper tabbouleh is heavier on parsley than bulgur.

Double-Coriander Sea Bass Ceviche

Ceviche is essentially a spicy raw fish salad, typically given a quick cure with salt and lime juice. There is no cooking involved, just a little shopping and chopping. Bright and refreshing, ceviche is excellent for hot weather—good any time of day with an ice-cold beer—but there's no reason not to eat it year-round. The process is simple: Bathe hand-chopped raw fish or shellfish in a lime juice mixture until it becomes firm and opaque, giving it a gently cooked feel while adding flavor. Chopped onions and hot chiles are a given. And so is cilantro. Cilantro is known as green coriander in much of the English-speaking world. I like to add pounded coriander seeds as well, either from the spice jar or plucked green from the plant when it's in flower (coriander flowers taste delicious here too).

One ½-pound sea bass or other firm white-fleshed fish fillet

Salt

1 teaspoon coriander seeds, toasted and ground

¼ teaspoon crushed red pepper

⅓ cup finely diced red onion

1½ tablespoons lemon juice

1½ tablespoons lime juice

1 serrano chile, minced

1 tablespoon olive oil

½ cup roughly chopped cilantro leaves and tender stems

24 small crisp lettuce leaves, such as Little Gem

Cut the fish into ¼-inch cubes, place in a small bowl, and set the bowl over ice. Sprinkle with ½ teaspoon salt, the ground coriander, and red pepper, then mix in the onion, lemon juice, lime juice, chile, and olive oil. Let stand for 15 to 20 minutes.

Stir the cilantro into the ceviche. Fill each lettuce leaf with a tablespoon of the ceviche and arrange on a platter. Sprinkle lightly with salt and serve.

MAKES 4 SERVINGS

This superior ceviche features both leafy green coriander and toasted coriander seeds.

Roasted Red Snapper
with Lemon and Fennel

When you buy a fennel bulb or two at the market, don't discard the beautiful tops. They're flavorful too. The tender green feathery bits can be chopped and used in herb mixtures and the tougher stalks can also be put to good use. Here they are used as an aromatic bed, in place of a roasting rack, for a whole fish. Fish cooked on the bone is always more succulent. You could also roast a chicken, or a pork loin, for that matter, in the same way.

Coat a gutted and scaled 2-pound fish lightly with olive oil, then season the inside and outside generously with salt, pepper, 1 teaspoon crushed toasted fennel seeds, and 1 tablespoon chopped fennel fronds. Arrange a bed of washed fennel stalks on a baking sheet. Lay the fish on top and tuck thin lemon slices underneath, in the cavity, and on top of the fish. Leave at room temperature for 30 minutes.

Heat the oven to 450 degrees. Place the fish on the top shelf of the oven and roast, uncovered, for 15 to 20 minutes, depending on the thickness of your fish, until it is firm when probed with a paring knife and flakes at the thickest part. Remove from the oven and let rest for 5 minutes.

To serve, use a small knife and a spatula (or two large soupspoons) to remove the top fillet; transfer to a platter. Gently pull the spine away and transfer the bottom fillet to the platter. Serve with a little dish of sea salt, some lemon wedges, and a cruet of fruity extra virgin olive oil.   MAKES 2 SERVINGS

A fine fresh snapper,
before and after.

Herb-Roasted Chicken Legs

If you don't feel like grilling, here's another way to cook chicken legs with decidedly aromatic results. Roast them on masses of herb branches—thyme, rosemary, sage. The herbs don't actually burn, but they do char a bit in the hot oven, adding an almost smoky taste. Their flavor and perfume permeate the meat.

6 large chicken legs (about 4 pounds)
Salt and pepper
6 garlic cloves, grated or minced

Extra virgin olive oil for drizzling
1 large bunch each thyme, rosemary, and sage

Season the chicken legs on both sides with salt and pepper, then rub with the garlic and drizzle with olive oil. Let stand for 30 minutes to 1 hour at room temperature.

Heat the oven to 425 degrees. Spread the herb branches evenly in the bottom of a baking dish or roasting pan big enough to hold the chicken legs in one layer. Place the chicken legs on top of the herbs. Roast, uncovered, for 15 minutes, or until the skin is beginning to crisp. Add 1 cup water to the pan and lower the heat to 375 degrees. Continue cooking for 45 minutes to an hour, basting the chicken with the herby liquid in the pan every 10 minutes or so, until the juices run clear when a leg is probed at the thickest part with a paring knife and the legs are nicely browned.   MAKES 6 SERVINGS

Easier than roasting a whole chicken, and roasted legs are guaranteed to be juicy.

French Chicken Tarragon

Tarragon doesn't get enough love. Most people know it only in its dried form, and administered with a heavy hand. But a few sprigs of fresh tarragon can be lovely. It's a traditional component of the mixture called *fines herbes*, contributing sweetness and an almost anise-like flavor. It happily finds its way into salads, vinaigrettes, and homemade mayonnaise, and it is often the herb of choice for chicken or fish. Tarragon is especially well suited for these braised chicken thighs, complementing the white wine and crème fraîche.

6 large chicken thighs (about 3 pounds)
Salt and pepper
2 tablespoons unsalted butter
2 shallots, finely diced
2 garlic cloves, grated or minced
2 teaspoons chopped tarragon, plus whole leaves for garnish
1 cup Blond Chicken Broth (page 460)
½ cup dry white wine
½ cup crème fraîche
½ teaspoon grated lemon zest

Season the chicken generously with salt and pepper. Let stand for 30 minutes to 1 hour at room temperature.

Heat the oven to 400 degrees. Put an enameled cast-iron Dutch oven over medium heat. Add the butter and shallots and cook, stirring, until softened and lightly browned, about 5 minutes. Add the garlic and chopped tarragon and cook for 1 minute (be careful not to let the garlic brown). Arrange the chicken thighs in the pot in one layer, add the broth and wine, and bring to a simmer.

Put the lid on and place the pot on the middle shelf of the oven. Bake for 15 minutes, then lower the heat to 350 degrees and continue baking for 45 minutes, or until the thighs are tender. Put the thighs on a platter, cover loosely, and keep warm.

Strain the pan juices through a fine sieve into a saucepan and spoon off any rising fat. Place the pan over medium-high heat, add the crème fraîche and lemon zest, and simmer until the sauce is slightly thickened, about 5 minutes. Taste and adjust the seasoning.

Spoon the sauce over the chicken, garnish with tarragon leaves, and serve. MAKES 6 SERVINGS

NOTE: A sprinkling of very thinly sliced scallions and chives could also be nice.

Tuscan Pork Roast

Porchetta, that beyond-divine traditional Italian roast pork specialty, is usually made with a whole small pig, generously seasoned with wild fennel, rosemary, sage, and black pepper. This version uses a pork loin or shoulder roast. The loin is leaner, and a bit more expensive; ask the butcher for a front loin piece that has both a fat and a lean end to satisfy all tastes. But boneless pork shoulder makes a succulent roast too, and it has the perfect ratio of fat to lean throughout. (Lamb shoulder makes a fine substitute for those who don't care for pork. Or use the seasoning for a roast capon or chicken.)

*1 boneless pork loin or shoulder roast
    (about 4 pounds)*
Salt
8 garlic cloves, grated or minced
*½ cup roughly chopped fennel fronds,
    preferably from wild fennel*
*2 teaspoons fennel seeds, crushed in a
    mortar or spice mill*
1 teaspoon fennel pollen (optional)
1 teaspoon grated lemon zest

*2 tablespoons roughly chopped rosemary,
    plus a few extra sprigs*
*2 tablespoons roughly chopped sage,
    plus a few extra sprigs*
*2 tablespoons roughly chopped marjoram,
    plus a few extra sprigs*
½ teaspoon crushed red pepper
1 teaspoon coarsely ground black pepper
2 tablespoons olive oil

Season the pork generously on all sides with salt. In a small bowl, combine the garlic, fennel fronds, fennel seeds, fennel pollen (if using), lemon zest, the chopped rosemary, sage, and marjoram, the crushed red pepper, black pepper, and olive oil. Rub and pat the mixture all over the meat. Press the rosemary, sage, and marjoram sprigs against the roast, and use a few lengths of butcher's twine to secure them. Cover the roast with plastic wrap and refrigerate for several hours, or preferably overnight. Bring to room temperature before roasting.

Heat the oven to 400 degrees. Place the roast in a shallow baking dish and cook, uncovered, for about 1 hour, until the meat is nicely browned and a thermometer inserted into the thickest part of the roast registers 130 degrees. Let rest for at least 15 to 20 minutes before slicing.

Serve the porchetta, thinly sliced, warm or at room temperature.   MAKES 6 SERVINGS

A pork loin bundled
in herbs and ready
for the oven.

Flank Steak Tagliata with Salsa Verde

*T*agliata is Italian for sliced steak. You'll find it on nearly every Italian restaurant menu. But it's easy to make at home, and a great choice for an unfussy meal. (Sometimes it's also a good way to make one steak feed two.) Often tagliata is served simply with arugula leaves, shaved Parmesan, lemon, and olive oil, but a bright, acidic salsa verde, the Italian green herb sauce, adds bolder flavor. Make the salsa verde with as many herbs as you like, starting with parsley and adding mint, basil, marjoram, and perhaps a touch of rosemary.

Flank steak makes a great tagliata. It's relatively inexpensive and easy to cook. Skirt steak and sirloin are also good options, but if you're feeling flush, go with a thick rib-eye. While purists season tagliata only with salt, I'm inclined to make it highly seasoned, using lots of coarsely crushed black pepper as well as garlic and rosemary. Here is the method for cooking the steak in a cast-iron skillet, but grilling over coals is also a good option.

1 flank steak (about 2 pounds)
Salt
Black peppercorns
A few sprigs of rosemary
6 garlic cloves, sliced

2 tablespoons extra virgin olive oil
5 ounces arugula
A chunk of Parmesan, for shaving
Salsa Verde (recipe follows)
1 lemon, cut into wedges

Put the flank steak on a baking sheet and season on both sides with salt. Put a generous handful of peppercorns on a cutting board and crush them by pressing firmly with the bottom of a saucepan (or use a mortar and pestle or a spice mill to achieve a very coarse grind). Measure 1 tablespoon of the crushed pepper and sprinkle it on both sides of the steak.

Strip the leaves from the rosemary sprigs and sprinkle the meat evenly on both sides with the rosemary and garlic slices. Drizzle the olive oil over both sides of the steak, then massage it with your hands to distribute the seasonings, pressing the pepper, rosemary, and garlic onto the surface. Let the steak stand at

Arugula and shaved Parmesan invariably accompany a fine tagliata.

room temperature for an hour (or refrigerate for several hours; bring to room temperature before proceeding).

Meanwhile, place a cast-iron skillet large enough to hold the steak (or a heavy roasting pan) on the upper rack of the oven and heat the oven to 450 degrees. Let the pan heat for at least 30 minutes.

Carefully put the flank steak in the pan and close the oven door. After 5 minutes, flip the steak (it should be well browned on the bottom) and cook for 2 to 3 minutes, just until juices appear on the surface and a thermometer registers 120 degrees for rare, or for a few minutes more for medium-rare meat. Transfer the steak to a carving board and let rest for 10 minutes.

Cut the meat on a diagonal, against the grain, into ¼-inch-thick slices. Arrange the meat on a large platter and surround with the arugula. With a vegetable peeler, shave about 2 ounces of cheese over the arugula. Serve with the salsa verde and lemon wedges. MAKES 4 SERVINGS

Salsa Verde (Green Herb Salsa)

Garlic clove
Salt
2 anchovy fillets, roughly chopped
1 teaspoon roughly chopped capers
¾ cup fruity extra virgin olive oil

½ cup finely chopped flat-leaf parsley
2 tablespoons finely chopped mint
1 small shallot, minced
1 teaspoon grated lemon zest
1 tablespoon lemon juice

Put the garlic in a mortar with a pinch of salt and pound to a paste. Add the anchovies and capers and roughly mash them. Stir in the olive oil, parsley, mint, shallot, and lemon zest. (You can make the sauce to this point up to several hours in advance.)

Just before serving, stir in the lemon juice. (Don't add it earlier or your bright green sauce will fade.) Taste and adjust the seasoning. MAKES 1 CUP

Green Basil Oil

Basil oil is a simple little sauce. Hardly anything at all—basil leaves, salt, and olive oil, with a few parsley leaves to enhance the green color. Make it just before you use it, as the flavor of fresh basil is fleeting. Compared with the more complex pesto, it's delicate, and it can enhance a beautiful piece of fish, for instance, without masking its flavor. The oil is also wonderful drizzled over a spring vegetable soup or freshly sliced garden cucumbers or tomatoes. Use a mortar and pestle, a mini food processor, or a blender.

Pick the leaves from a fine bunch of basil, about 2 small handfuls. You also want a handful of tender Italian parsley leaves and 1 grated or minced garlic clove. Puree these well with ¾ cup fruity extra virgin olive oil and ½ teaspoon salt. You will have a bright green not-very-thick sauce. It doesn't really hold an emulsion, so stir before using.   MAKES ABOUT 1 CUP

ASPARAGUS

Holding out for regional produce may seem absurdly romantic, or even a little stubborn, but there's no denying the thrill when, after months of potatoes, apples, and sturdy greens, suddenly asparagus appears in full force at the market. Finally, spring has arrived.

Anticipation is half the fun. Celebrating the return of a favorite food is a pleasure. In France, there's a charming custom of drinking a toast to first-of-the-season produce, especially asparagus, after a long, cold winter.

I prefer to prepare the early crop as simply as possible: briefly boiled, quickly stir-fried, or even raw. Cooking time is crucial. Generally speaking, it's better to err on the bright side of slightly undercooked than risk veering into the sad army-drab territory of several minutes too long. Grilling or roasting asparagus has become popular, but it's not the method I use for early asparagus. Later, though, toward the end of the season, when the flavor of asparagus becomes a bit grassy, the slight char of the grill or roasting pan is welcome, as is more aggressive seasoning.

Perfectly Steamed Asparagus

Simmering asparagus briefly in well-salted water is the way for first-of-the-season asparagus. A stellar first course or a light lunch.

1½ pounds large or medium asparagus

1 small shallot, finely diced

2 tablespoons red wine vinegar

Salt and pepper

2 tablespoons Dijon mustard

¼ cup extra virgin olive oil

4 soft-center hard-cooked eggs

  (see How to Boil an Egg, page 431),

  halved or quartered

1 tablespoon finely snipped chives

Snap off and discard the tough bottom ends of the asparagus spears. If using large asparagus, peel the lower ends with a vegetable peeler; medium asparagus does not need peeling.

To make the vinaigrette, put the shallot, vinegar, and a pinch of salt in a small bowl and let the shallot soften for 5 minutes. Stir in the mustard to dissolve, then whisk in the olive oil to make a thick dressing. Season to taste with salt and pepper.

Bring 4 quarts well-salted water to a rolling boil in a large nonreactive pot. Add the asparagus and cook for 3 to 5 minutes, until just done. (Alternatively, cook the asparagus in a steamer.) Remove the asparagus with a large spider or tongs and spread out on a baking sheet lined with a clean kitchen towel. The asparagus can be served warm or at room temperature.

To serve, place the asparagus on a platter or individual plates. Spoon the vinaigrette over it, garnish with the halved or quartered eggs, and sprinkle with the chives.

MAKES 4 SERVINGS

When peeling asparagus, lay them flat and use a light touch.

Shaved Asparagus Salad

You can get asparagus from South America all winter long, and early spring asparagus from Mexico and Southern California. This is not a dish to make with those. You need sweet, just-picked asparagus, preferably from your local farmers' market, for this simple salad of raw asparagus ribbons. Accompany with a platter of sliced prosciutto if desired.

½ pound large or medium asparagus
2 tablespoons lemon juice
3 tablespoons fruity extra virgin olive oil

Salt and pepper
6 ounces arugula, washed and dried
A chunk of Parmesan, for shaving

Snap off and discard the tough bottom ends of the asparagus. Slice the asparagus lengthwise into paper-thin ribbons.

To make the dressing, whisk together the lemon juice and olive oil in a small bowl. Season to taste with salt and pepper.

Place the asparagus ribbons in a shallow salad bowl. Season lightly with salt and pepper, add half the dressing, and toss to coat. Add the arugula, tossing gently to distribute the asparagus. Drizzle with the remaining dressing. With a vegetable peeler, shave thin curls of Parmesan over the salad.   MAKES 4 SERVINGS

Shave asparagus
with a mandoline,
if you have one,
or cut slices with
a thin-bladed knife
on a long diagonal.

Spicy Asparagus Stir-Fry

Asparagus doesn't have to be treated as a delicate, fragile thing, napped only with butter or a creamy sauce, or served plain with olive oil and salt. That's fine for the first few weeks of the season, but then it's time to dial up the interest factor and add some spice. Asparagus actually stands up quite well to assertive flavors. A quick toss in a hot wok with garlic, ginger, and chiles doesn't overwhelm it at all, at least if you don't overcook the spears. Instead, the vegetable's sweetness becomes accentuated by contrast.

1½ pounds medium or pencil asparagus
2 tablespoons vegetable oil
2 or 3 small dried red chile peppers
Salt and pepper
½ teaspoon fermented bean paste
1 teaspoon grated or minced garlic
1 teaspoon grated fresh ginger

½ teaspoon grated orange zest
1 jalapeño or serrano chile, finely chopped
  (seeds removed if desired)
2 teaspoons toasted sesame oil
½ cup roughly chopped cilantro
3 scallions, slivered
1 tablespoon toasted sesame seeds

Snap off and discard the bottom ends of the asparagus, then cut into 2-inch pieces (halve any thicker pieces lengthwise).

Set a wok or wide skillet over high heat and add the vegetable oil. Add the dried chiles and let sizzle for a moment or so, then add the asparagus, tossing well to coat. Season with salt and pepper and stir-fry for a minute or so, then add the bean paste, garlic, ginger, orange zest, and jalapeño and continue stir-frying for a minute, maybe less, until the asparagus is cooked but still firm and bright green. (It will continue cooking briefly off the heat.)

Mound the asparagus on a serving platter and drizzle with the sesame oil. Sprinkle the cilantro, scallions, and sesame seeds over the top.   MAKES 4 SERVINGS

White Asparagus
with Savory Whipped Cream

White asparagus can be sublime. In Europe, they are highly prized as a springtime delicacy. Usually cigar-sized, they have a sweet flavor, tinged with a pleasant faint bitterness, and are most often served at room temperature with a rich, creamy sauce (termed *sauce onctueuse* on Parisian menus). On this side of the pond, white asparagus tends to be skinnier, and scarcer, but it is no less delicious. White asparagus spears always need peeling and take a little longer to become tender. So they really are rather different from the green. I serve mine with a garnish of light savory whipped cream. It's like *crème Chantilly*, but for vegetables.

1 cup heavy cream
Salt and pepper
Pinch of cayenne
1 teaspoon Dijon mustard
    (or ½ teaspoon dry mustard)
2 teaspoons finely sliced chives,
    plus more for garnish

2 teaspoons chopped chervil,
    plus more for garnish
2 teaspoons chopped tarragon,
    plus more for garnish
1 pound white asparagus
4 slices prosciutto (optional)

To make the savory whipped cream, beat the cream in a bowl with a whisk or electric mixer only until it begins to thicken—keep it quite loose. Season with salt and pepper and the cayenne. Dilute the mustard with some of the cream in a small bowl, then fold the mustard mixture into the rest of the cream with a rubber spatula. Fold in the chives, chervil, and chopped tarragon. (Notice that the cream will thicken with each addition, so be careful not to agitate it too much. You want it not quite pourable, but nearly.)

Cut off the tough bottoms of the asparagus and discard. With a vegetable peeler, lightly peel each spear, beginning just under the tip.

Bring a deep wide nonreactive skillet of well-salted water to a boil. Add the asparagus and simmer until tender when pierced with a paring knife, 8 to 10 minutes. Lift the asparagus from the water with a spider or tongs and spread out on a towel-lined baking sheet to cool.

To serve, divide the asparagus among four plates. Spoon the savory whipped cream generously across the spears, leaving the tips exposed. Sprinkle with chives, chervil, and tarragon. Drape with the prosciutto if desired.   MAKES 4 SERVINGS

Savory Whipped Cream, Other Ways

When flavoring whipped cream, consider saffron and lemon zest, or a bright mixture of curry spices. Try savory whipped cream with other vegetables, or spoon on a dollop to garnish a bowl of pureed vegetable soup. It's also very good with salmon (smoked, poached, or grilled).

CUCUMBERS

I'm fond of the expression "cool as a cucumber"—and cucumbers are indeed cool. Unfortunately, many of us know only the common supermarket variety, with its thick, waxy skin and big seeds, or the hothouse-grown English cuke, always shrink-wrapped in plastic. There are better choices, at least during the summer growing season. At the market, look for ridged Armenian cucumbers, which, when picked young and pale green, are delectable, skin and all. Or the smooth-skinned Japanese varieties, or Persian cukes. Or try Kirby pickling cucumbers, designed for a life in brine but also quite good raw.

Generally speaking, the younger the cucumber, the smaller the seeds, so no need to remove them. Larger cucumbers must be split lengthwise so their seeds can be easily scraped out with a spoon.

Because there are so many good ways to eat cucumbers raw, I'm not very inclined to cook them. But of course it can be done, with lovely results, in Asian stir-fries, or with butter and tarragon as in some older French recipes. While we don't instantly think of cucumbers as having a particular aroma, they certainly do. Sliced cucumbers lend a subtle perfume when added to a healthy pitcher of "spa water," and they're now finding their way into all sorts of trendy cocktails.

Fresh, smooth-skinned, and firm—not fat, not waxed, not smothered in plastic.

Japanese Cucumber Salad

Cucumber and miso is a stunning combination. You don't have to use Japanese cucumbers to make this, but if you can find this slender, smooth-skinned variety, use them. Inspired by a recipe from Nancy Hachisu, this gorgeous salad of cucumbers in miso dressing is flecked with the fragrant herb shiso, sometimes called perilla. It has a bright lemony, peppery, hyssop-like flavor. Green shiso leaves are sold in little packages at Japanese and other Asian groceries, and the plant can be easily cultivated in a home garden (it grows like a weed). Use basil leaves if you can't find shiso.

1½ pounds small cucumbers, sliced ⅛ inch thick
1 teaspoon salt
3 tablespoons toasted sesame seeds

3 tablespoons red miso (see Note)
2 tablespoons rice vinegar
1 tablespoon grated fresh ginger
12 shiso leaves, cut into thin strips

Put the cucumbers in a bowl, sprinkle with the salt, and toss. Let sit for 10 minutes.

Grind the sesame seeds to a paste in a suribachi mortar, if you have one, or use another type of mortar, a spice mill, or a mini food processor. Transfer the paste to a small bowl. Add the miso and vinegar and mash to a creamy mixture.

Squeeze the cucumbers to rid them of excess liquid and transfer to a serving bowl. Stir in the sesame-miso sauce. Stir in the ginger and shiso and serve.
MAKES 4 SERVINGS

NOTE: Miso, the salty, nutty Japanese seasoning paste, is made from fermented soybeans, or grains such as brown rice or barley. The two most common types are the delicate white shiro miso and the more robust red aka miso. Miso is so flavorful, it takes only a little dashi (page 461) or chicken broth to produce a simple soup. It's often used to glaze broiled vegetables (see page 265) or fish.

Cucumbers with Miso Dip

For a simpler version, my Japanese neighbor serves cucumber sticks with a bowl of red miso for dipping and a stack of shiso leaves for wrapping—an easy hands-on snack with cocktails.

Cucumbers in Yogurt

Throughout the eastern Mediterranean, you'll find cucumber salads with yogurt, mint, and garlic. The names change—*cacik, tzatziki*—but the concept is of a piece. The combination is great as a salad or a saucy side dish. I sometimes increase the balance of yogurt to cucumber for a quick chilled soup. I don't recommend the thick Greek-style yogurt commercially available these days, which has none of the desired acidity of real Greek yogurt. Too creamy and bland—you want some sourness.

2 cups diced or thinly sliced peeled
    cucumber
Salt
2 cups plain whole-milk yogurt
    (not Greek-style)
2 garlic cloves, grated or minced
2 tablespoons roughly chopped mint

2 teaspoons chopped dill
Pinch of Maras pepper or other crushed
    red pepper
½ teaspoon cumin seeds, toasted and
    ground
2 tablespoons extra virgin olive oil

Put the cucumbers in a colander and season lightly with salt. Leave for 10 minutes to drain, then rinse briefly with cold water and blot with a kitchen towel.

Put the yogurt in a bowl. Whisk in ½ teaspoon salt, the garlic, mint, dill, red pepper, and cumin, then whisk in the olive oil. Fold in the cucumbers. Cover and chill for at least 30 minutes, or up to a few hours (if held longer, it loses its fresh taste).

Just before serving, taste and adjust the seasoning.　MAKES ABOUT 3 CUPS

Other Cucumber Thoughts

For a simple variation, finish with a drizzle of olive oil and and a sprinkle of za'atar. A Persian version of this dish, *mast-o-khiar*, might include golden raisins and walnuts, along with crushed dried rose petals. Some have garlic, some have shallot. Some use a combination of dried and fresh mint.

Mexican Cucumber Spears

In Mexico, wedges of cucumber are sprinkled with salt, hot chile powder, and lime juice and sold from carts on the street. It's a brilliant trio, good on nearly any fruit or vegetable you can think of. Try it on melon, mango, avocado, or jicama. Or pineapple, apples, or oranges. It's refreshing any time of day (and may change your notions of what fast food can be).

Choose smallish cucumbers—Kirbys, Japanese, Persian, or Armenian, peeled if necessary—and cut them lengthwise into long wedges. Put them on a plate. Make a mixture of salt and hot red chile powder; the proportions will depend upon the strength of the chile (start with 2 tablespoons salt to 1 teaspoon chile powder). Cut a small lime in half, dip it in the spiced salt mixture, and use it to smear the salt on the cucumber spears, then squeeze it to give them a bit of lime juice.

Sublime in its
simplicity: salt,
red chile powder,
and lime.

ZUCCHINI & SUMMER SQUASH

My long-ago first encounter with garden-fresh summer squash was in a starkly simple preparation that left an impression. They were crookneck squash, a variety that you don't see so much at the market these days, simply simmered with butter and water and topped with fresh snipped dill. Astonishingly good. The method is fine for pattypan or other summer squash.

The word *zucchini* is a diminutive of the Italian *zucca*, a large squash. So zucchini should be on the small side. Not tiny baby squash, picked too young, which tend to have tough, slightly bitter flesh, but younger and smaller than what you find in most supermarkets. (Commodity zucchini are usually grown to a particular length so they fit in a crate of a certain size, and they must grow straight for packing. Flavor is secondary.) Look for smaller zucchini and summer squash at the market or ask a neighbor with a vegetable garden, who will be only too happy to oblige. I have a thing about unblemished squashes. They look so beautiful still on the vine, firm and shiny-skinned—though if you look closely, you'll notice a very fine coating of fuzz. That's the squash ideal I aim for. Small, tender zucchini cook quickly, but fatter zucchini and yellow Gold Bar squash are best cut into biggish chunks for long, slow cooking.

Stewed Zucchini Pasta with Ricotta and Basil

Crisp stir-fried zucchini is great, but this is not that. Sometimes longer cooking really brings out the best, and it surely does here. The softened onions, garlic, olive oil, and zucchini coat the pasta in a lovely way, along with creamy ricotta, lemon zest, and basil pesto.

1 medium onion, finely diced

6 tablespoons extra virgin olive oil

2 pounds zucchini, cut into 1/2-inch-thick slices (for larger zucchini, cut in half lengthwise before slicing)

Salt and pepper

2 garlic cloves, grated or minced

About 2 cups basil leaves

1 pound ziti or penne

12 ounces (1 1/2 cups) fresh ricotta

Pinch of crushed red pepper

Grated zest of 1 lemon

2 ounces Parmesan or pecorino cheese, or a mixture, grated (about 1 cup), plus more for serving

Put a large pot of water on to boil. Meanwhile, in a large skillet, cook the onion in 3 tablespoons of the olive oil over medium-high heat until softened, 5 to 8 minutes; reduce the heat as necessary to keep the onion from browning. Add the zucchini, season generously with salt and pepper, and cook, stirring occasionally, until rather soft, about 10 minutes. Turn off the heat.

While the zucchini cooks, use a mortar and pestle to pound the garlic, basil, and a little salt into a rough paste (or use a mini food processor). Stir in the remaining 3 tablespoons olive oil.

Salt the pasta water well and add the pasta, stirring. Cook per the package instructions, but make sure to keep the pasta quite al dente. Drain the pasta, reserving 1 cup of the cooking water.

Add the pasta to the skillet with the zucchini and turn the heat to medium-high. Add 1/2 cup of the cooking water, then add the ricotta, crushed red pepper, and lemon zest, stirring to distribute. Check the seasoning and adjust as necessary, then cook for 1 minute more. The mixture should look creamy; add a little more pasta water if necessary. Add the basil paste and half the grated cheese and quickly stir to incorporate.

Spoon the pasta into warm soup plates and sprinkle with the remaining cheese. Serve immediately. MAKES 4 TO 6 SERVINGS

Raw Zucchini Salad

Slicing zucchini into long ribbons with a mandoline (or a sharp knife) gives plenty of surface area for this bright dressing of lemon, olive oil, and crumbled wild oregano. The salad can share the plate with meaty slices of tomato for a perfect summer antipasto.

Ricotta salata, available from most cheese shops, is made from sheep's-milk ricotta that is salted and aged only briefly. It is similar to a mild feta but has a firmer texture, which allows it to be sliced, shaved, or crumbled. But this salad is just as good with shavings of Parmesan or pecorino.

*2 pounds small yellow zucchini or
  other summer squash
Salt and pepper
Extra virgin olive oil
2 tablespoons lemon juice*

*12 squash blossoms (optional)
8 ounces ricotta salata
  (or substitute mild feta)
Dried oregano (wild if possible),
  for garnish*

Trim both ends of each zucchini. Using a mandoline (or a sharp thin-bladed knife), cut the squash lengthwise into very thin slices. Put the squash in a large bowl and cover with a damp towel until you are ready to serve—it takes only a minute or two to finish the salad. (You can do this an hour or two ahead of time.)

Just before serving, season the squash lightly with salt and pepper and toss gently. Drizzle with olive oil just to coat, then add the lemon juice. Toss again, taste, and adjust the seasoning.

Mound the dressed squash on a platter. If using squash blossoms, tear them (petals only) into strips and scatter them over the salad. With a sharp vegetable peeler, shave the cheese over the top of the salad, and sprinkle with a pinch of crumbled oregano. Serve immediately.   MAKES 4 TO 6 SERVINGS

Steamed Squash Blossoms with Ricotta and Herbs

Beautiful squash blossoms are always a temptation at the market. If you have access to a vegetable patch, pick only the male blossoms, the ones standing tall with long stems; the female flowers are attached to the bottoms of as-yet unborn squash. Deep-frying the blossoms doesn't always do them justice. Gently steaming them with a bit of butter brings out their vegetal goodness. Use the best fresh ricotta you can get. The squash blossoms may look fragile, but they're actually fairly sturdy, so there's no need to worry as you spoon the herbed ricotta inside them. The effect here is ravioli-like, so I serve this as a first course.

1 cup fresh ricotta
¼ cup grated Parmesan
½ teaspoon grated lemon zest
2 tablespoons finely chopped chives
½ teaspoon finely chopped thyme
Salt and pepper
Tiny pinch of cayenne

12 squash blossoms
3 tablespoons butter
1 cup Blond Chicken Broth (page 460)
*   or water*
Chopped flat-leaf parsley or basil
*   (optional)*

Put the ricotta in a small bowl, add the Parmesan, lemon zest, chives, thyme, ½ teaspoon salt, a little freshly ground pepper, and the cayenne and stir everything together.

Carefully pull the squash petals open and put a heaping tablespoon of the filling mixture inside each blossom. Bring the petals back to surround the filling and reshape the blossom with your hands, flattening it a bit.

Melt the butter in a wide skillet over medium heat. Arrange the blossoms in the pan in one layer and sprinkle lightly with salt. Add the broth, put on the lid, and simmer gently for about 5 minutes, until the blossoms are heated through.

Lift the blossoms from the pan with a small spatula and arrange in shallow soup bowls. Spoon some of the buttery juices over and sprinkle with parsley, if using.
MAKES 4 TO 6 SERVINGS

Fresh squash
blossoms are filled
with herbed ricotta,
then simmered
and served in a
buttery broth.

PEAS

Fresh green peas in the pod are luxurious, well worth the effort required to shuck them. Keeping up with peas in the garden is hard work—you must catch them when the pod still has some give and the peas within are small, not overstuffed with large starchy peas. The same holds true for sugar snap and snow peas, which should be smooth, slender, and bright green. (Of course, use these guidelines at the market too; in a pinch or out of season, frozen peas may be your best choice.) Snow peas must be picked young to be sweet.

Canned peas, with their drab color, may seem drastically overcooked to us, but people used to cook them that way, and some still do. "Cooked-down" peas are favored by many, with bacon or pancetta (in the American South and Italy) or highly spiced (India). It's simply a different approach, and it's a good way to deal with starchy larger peas.

Sugar Snap Peas with Chinese Flavors

The whole point of a quick stir-fry like this is to keep the snap peas crisp, green, and juicy. Ginger, sesame, and hot chiles accentuate the sweetness of peas. For a less spicy rendition, use only one or two chiles.

2 tablespoons vegetable oil

6 to 8 small dried hot red chiles

1 pound sugar snap peas (or snow peas), trimmed at both ends

Salt

1 teaspoon grated fresh ginger

1 teaspoon grated or minced garlic

½ teaspoon toasted sesame oil

½ teaspoon toasted sesame seeds

3 or 4 scallions, slivered

Put the oil in a wok or large cast-iron skillet over high heat. When the oil is hot, add the chile peppers and let them sizzle for a few seconds, then follow with the snap peas. Season well with salt, add the ginger and garlic, and toss with two large spoons to coat the peas. Stir-fry for 2 minutes, then add ¼ cup water and continue stirring until the water completely evaporates, about 1 minute. Add the sesame oil, sesame seeds, and scallions, toss to coat, and transfer to a serving platter.   MAKES 4 TO 6 SERVINGS

The whole dried chiles add hot, bright flavor to the oil and beauty to the dish, but don't make the mistake of eating them.

Young Peas and Lettuce with Ham

Peas in the pod are often called English peas or garden peas. Shucking them is fairly easy work, and if picked small, they cook quickly. Serve this herby dish in wide shallow soup bowls, all the better for spooning up the buttery juices.

2 tablespoons butter
2½ cups small English peas
 (about 2 pounds in the pod)
Salt and pepper
¼ cup sliced scallions
2 heads Little Gem lettuce, cut into
 long thin wedges
1 ounce good ham, cut into small cubes

2 tablespoons roughly chopped flat-leaf
 parsley
1 tablespoon finely sliced chives
2 teaspoons chopped tarragon
Grated zest and juice of ½ lemon
A few pea tendrils (optional)

Melt the butter in a large saucepan over medium-high heat. Add the peas and season with salt and pepper. Add the scallions, lettuce, and ham and stir to coat. Add an inch of water to the pan, cover, and bring to a boil, then reduce the heat and simmer for about 5 minutes, until the peas are tender. Add the chopped parsley, chives, and tarragon and stir in the lemon zest and juice.

With a slotted spoon, divide the peas among four shallow bowls. Spoon the juices over them and serve, garnished with pea tendrils, if you like.   MAKES 4 SERVINGS

An old-fashioned way to cook peas and lettuce, teased with scallions, herbs, and a bit of salty-sweet ham.

Curried Peas with Potato

This is my version of a traditional Indian dish—peas and potatoes cooked with aromatic spices. A little hot chile, or a lot, is essential to complement the peas' sweetness. Of course, while it's best with fresh garden peas, frozen peas cooked this way can brighten a meal year-round.

2 tablespoons ghee (see page 440), butter, or vegetable oil
½ teaspoon black mustard seeds
½ teaspoon cumin seeds
1 small red onion, finely diced
Salt and pepper
1 russet potato, peeled and cut into small cubes
½ teaspoon grated fresh ginger
½ teaspoon grated or minced garlic
½ teaspoon ground turmeric
⅛ teaspoon cayenne
1 tablespoon tomato paste
1 cup water
2½ cups small English peas (about 2 pounds in the pod)
2 teaspoons minced Fresno or other medium-hot fresh red chile

Heat the ghee in a large saucepan over medium-high heat. Add the mustard and cumin seeds. When the mustard seeds begin to pop and the cumin seeds have colored a bit, add the onion and season with salt and pepper. Cook, stirring, until the onion is softened, about 5 minutes.

Add the potato, ginger, garlic, turmeric, cayenne, and tomato paste and stir well. Add the water and bring to a boil. Turn the heat down to medium and cook until the potatoes are tender, 5 to 8 minutes. Add the peas and simmer, covered, until tender, about 5 minutes more (starchy peas may take 10 to 15 minutes). Stir in the chile, taste, and adjust the seasoning, then transfer the mixture to a serving dish.   MAKES 4 SERVINGS

Let's be practical—sometimes frozen peas are the best and only option.

FENNEL

The mildly licorice-scented fennel bulb is delicious raw or cooked, and it has many uses, from salad to soup to antipasto. In Italy, no one is surprised to see fennel at the market, but in the States, it still has a bit of an exotic aura.

Unfortunately, much of the fennel on offer in American supermarkets is well past its prime, even if the frilly fronds are still attached. The root end has turned brown, and the exterior, instead of being a beautiful pale celadon green, has gone dull, white, and stringy. Not at all what you want, and quite disappointing.

Sometimes you can salvage an over-the-hill bulb by peeling away a good deal of the outer layer to reveal a fresher-looking center, but it's a pity to have to do so. In the best of all worlds, fennel is freshly picked—crisp, sweet, and redolent of anise. Still, the bulb should be good-sized—those tiny, immature picked-too-early embryonic ones tend to be stringy.

Trimming a fennel bulb yields a lot of usable debris. Save frilly fronds to make fritters or for seasoning a pork roast. Use tough stalks to make broth, or place them under a roast in lieu of a metal rack. Slice the bulb crosswise as thinly as possible for salads or cut into wedges for roasting or making gratins.

Fennel al Forno

This is an excellent vegetarian main dish if paired with a pile of sautéed dark leafy greens. But you can also send it to the table alongside a roast chicken or pork loin or some Italian sausages. The fennel is briefly blanched, then baked with mozzarella, Parmesan, and bread crumbs. The flavor is amplified with fennel seed, garlic, crushed red pepper, rosemary, and a little olive oil. Expect raves.

4 medium fennel bulbs (about 2½ pounds), trimmed, a few fronds reserved for garnish
Salt and pepper
3 tablespoons extra virgin olive oil, plus more for the baking pan
½ teaspoon fennel seeds, crushed or roughly powdered in a mortar or spice mill
3 garlic cloves, smashed to a paste with a little salt
½ teaspoon chopped rosemary, plus 2 teaspoons whole leaves
⅛ teaspoon crushed red pepper
8 ounces fresh mozzarella, sliced or shredded
¼ cup coarse dry bread crumbs, homemade from an Italian or French loaf
½ cup grated Parmesan
2 tablespoons chopped flat-leaf parsley, or a mixture of parsley and fennel fronds

Heat the oven to 375 degrees. Remove a thin layer of the fennel bulbs' tough exterior. Cut the fennel crosswise into ½-inch slices.

Bring a large pot of salted water to a boil. Add the fennel and boil for 1 minute, then drain and put it in a bowl of cold water to stop the cooking; drain and pat dry. Season the fennel with salt and pepper.

Lightly oil a large baking dish. Layer in the fennel to a depth of 1½ inches (pushing it down if necessary).

In a small bowl, stir together the olive oil, fennel seeds, garlic, chopped rosemary, and crushed red pepper. Drizzle 2 tablespoons of this mixture over the fennel. Sprinkle with the rosemary leaves. Cover with the mozzarella, then sprinkle with the bread crumbs. Drizzle the remaining oil mixture over the top, then sprinkle with the Parmesan. (The dish can be prepared to this point several hours ahead.)

Bake the fennel, uncovered, for 20 to 25 minutes, until nicely browned. Garnish with the chopped parsley.   MAKES 6 SERVINGS

Fennel, Radish, and Mushroom Salad

For the most divine fennel salad, simply dress very thinly sliced very fresh fennel with salt, lemon juice, and olive oil—*basta*. This one goes a tiny bit further, adding sliced raw button mushrooms and radishes. If you have somehow acquired a few firm, fresh porcini mushrooms, use them, sliced paper-thin, instead of the cultivated mushrooms for a far more flavorful version.

1 garlic clove, smashed to a paste with a little salt

½ teaspoon grated lemon zest

2 tablespoons lemon juice

Salt and pepper

¼ cup olive oil

3 fennel bulbs, trimmed and thinly sliced

¼ pound firm white mushrooms, wiped clean and thinly sliced

6 radishes, trimmed and thinly sliced

A chunk of Parmesan, for shaving

Flat-leaf parsley leaves (optional)

Arugula (optional)

Put the garlic in a small bowl and add the lemon zest and juice and a little pepper. Whisk in the olive oil.

Put the fennel, mushrooms, and radishes in a salad bowl and season lightly with salt and pepper. Add about three-quarters of the dressing and toss gently. With a vegetable peeler, shave curls of Parmesan over the salad. Garnish with a few arugula and parsley leaves, if you like. Drizzle with the remaining dressing. MAKES 4 SERVINGS

NOTE: This salad must be dressed at the very last minute, just before serving, or it will be hopelessly wilted and soggy.

Deluxe Fennel Salad

If you get hold of a deeply perfumed white truffle from Italy, shave it over the salad just before serving. That would cost a small fortune, though, so ask a rich aunt or uncle to buy it for you. (Do not, however, substitute truffle oil, which is synthetically produced in a laboratory and not even made from truffles.)

Fennel Frond and Spinach Fritters

Fragrant wild fennel is particularly well loved in Sicily, Turkey, and Greece. It also grows abundantly in temperate climates of North America, notably California, and in Australia, where some consider it an invasive weed. (I wish some wild fennel would invade my neighborhood!) Wild fennel has a much stronger scent (and flavor) than cultivated, and it doesn't form a bulb.

The best time to gather wild fennel is early spring, when the bright green, tender new fronds begin to appear. Usually the feathery fronds are simmered in water, then chopped for various uses. (The dried seeds and even the pollen are also valued for seasoning all sorts of pastas, soups, fish, and meat.) For these fritters, I use the fronds of cultivated fennel instead. The fritters are silver-dollar size and just right with drinks.

½ pound spinach leaves
½ pound bushy green fennel fronds
3 large eggs, beaten
1 cup grated Parmesan or pecorino cheese
1 cup coarse bread crumbs (made from day-old bread), or as needed

½ cup chopped flat-leaf parsley
1 teaspoon crushed red pepper
1 teaspoon fennel seeds, lightly toasted, then ground to a powder
Salt and pepper
Extra virgin olive oil for frying

Bring a large pot of lightly salted water to a boil. Drop in the spinach leaves, just to wilt them, then transfer to a colander using a slotted spoon. Rinse the spinach with cool water, drain, and squeeze dry. Add the fennel fronds to the boiling water, reduce the heat, and simmer for 15 to 20 minutes, until tender. Drain, cool, and lay the fronds on a kitchen towel to dry.

Put the spinach and fennel fronds on a cutting board and finely chop together. With your hands, squeeze out any excess water from the mixture. You should have about 1 cup. Transfer to a medium bowl and add the eggs, cheese, bread crumbs, parsley, crushed red pepper, and ground fennel. Season generously with salt and pepper and mix well. Add some more bread crumbs if the mixture doesn't hold together. Form into 24 small (2-inch-diameter) patties.

Pour olive oil to a 1-inch depth into a large cast-iron skillet and heat to 350 degrees. Working in batches, fry the fennel patties, turning once, until golden, about 3 minutes per side. Remove and blot briefly on paper towels. Serve warm, sprinkled with a little salt.   MAKES 24 FRITTERS

An adaptation of my Sicilian friend Angelo's famous recipe.

CORN

Corn (maize) was sustenance in the Americas for thousands of years (thousands!) before the Spanish conquerors arrived, and not only in the alimentary sense. Corn was money, corn had religious significance, corn was culture. So it is interesting to know that the white man has known corn for a mere five hundred years or so, and that it remains essentially a New World crop, even if cornmeal has been adopted by some European cuisines—think Italian polenta, for instance. (Oddly, in Switzerland, cold canned corn [Green Giant brand!] is often part of a mixed green salad, along with canned beets, shredded carrots, and a sort of Swiss ranch dressing they call *Französiche*—"French.") But for the most part, in Europe corn is grown for cow fodder.

In the States, in the early twentieth century, fresh summer corn— what we call corn on the cob—was known as green corn, to differentiate it from mature dried corn.

It wouldn't seem like summer without truckloads of fresh corn at every farm stand. In the not-so-distant past, before modern varieties were developed, corn fanatics would insist on getting the pot of water boiling before running out to the field to pick just enough corn for dinner. Given that the sugars would begin turning to starch immediately upon picking, this was the way to ensure tender, sweet corn. Newer cultivars stay sweet for several days, but it's still a good idea to get your corn as fresh from the farm as possible. Corn is cooked either on the cob or cut off the cob; off-the-cob is sometimes considered more civilized eating.

Corn on the Cob

Corn on the cob slathered with good butter and sprinkled with salt is so very American, and you can't argue with its wonderful simplicity. But corn on the cob is a popular street food worldwide, most often grilled over glowing coals and topped with delicious regional flavors.

How to boil an ear of corn? Quickly, in briskly simmering, well-salted water. Don't leave it longer than 5 minutes. For grilling over coals, allow at least 45 minutes if you are leaving the husks on (remove the silk first; the corn essentially steams inside the husk) or about 15 minutes for grilling shucked corn, turning frequently to allow some kernels to char a bit.

Red Chile and Lime

Mix ½ cup sea salt with 1 teaspoon, more or less, hot red chile powder (the proportions will depend upon the strength of the chile and your personal taste). Cut a few small limes in half. Dip the cut sides into the spiced salt mixture. Use the lime halves to rub the salt mixture on each ear, then squeeze it to give the corn a bit of juice.   ENOUGH FOR 8 EARS

Green Chile Butter

Mix together ½ cup softened butter, 1 minced jalapeño or serrano chile, the grated zest and juice of 1 lime, ½ teaspoon ground toasted cumin seeds, ½ teaspoon salt, and 3 tablespoons chopped cilantro. Spread on boiled or grilled corn.   ENOUGH FOR 8 EARS

Indian Spices

Mix together ½ cup softened butter, 1 tablespoon coconut oil, 1 teaspoon toasted coconut flakes, ½ teaspoon ground turmeric, ⅛ teaspoon cayenne, ¼ teaspoon ground cloves, ¼ teaspoon ground cardamom, ½ teaspoon salt, and the juice of 1 lime. Spread on boiled or grilled corn.   ENOUGH FOR 8 EARS

Chinese Street Food–Style

Mix together 1 tablespoon sesame paste, 1 teaspoon toasted sesame oil, 1 tablespoon brown sugar, 1 teaspoon grated or minced garlic, 2 teaspoons grated ginger, ½ teaspoon ground Sichuan pepper, ½ teaspoon salt, and ⅛ teaspoon cayenne. Paint the corn with this mixture before grilling. Keep it moving on the grill so the coating caramelizes but doesn't burn.   ENOUGH FOR 8 EARS

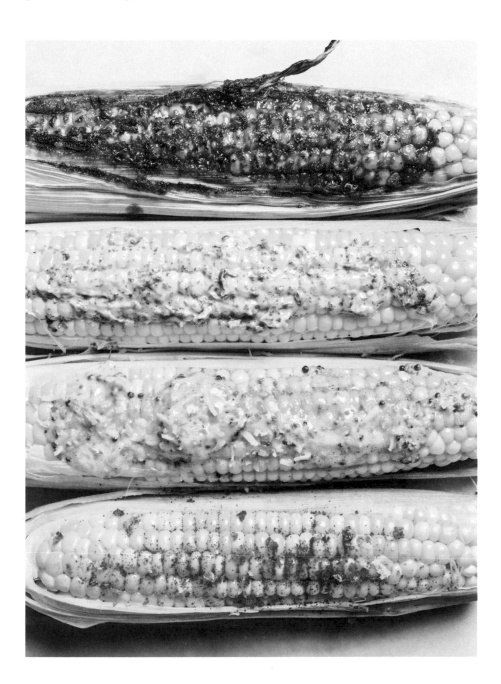

For the most tender
kernels, don't cut too
close to the cob. Save
the cobs to make a
light vegetarian broth.

Improved Creamed Corn

In the right hands, creamed corn can be delicious, but most people know it as something bland from a can that doesn't contain a drop of cream. It doesn't have to be that way. You can improve your creamed corn exponentially with cumin, jalapeño, and crème fraîche.

2 tablespoons butter
1 onion, very finely diced
Salt and pepper
Kernels from 4 ears corn (about 2 cups)
1 teaspoon cumin seeds, toasted and
 ground

1 jalapeño chile (green or red), seeds and
 veins removed and very finely chopped
1 cup crème fraîche or heavy cream
Juice of 1 large lime
1 tablespoon very thinly sliced chives
A few cilantro sprigs

Melt the butter in a 10-inch sauté pan over low heat. Add the onion, salt lightly, increase the heat to medium, and cook, stirring gently, for 5 to 8 minutes, until the onion is completely soft and translucent. Add the corn kernels, season with salt and pepper, and cook for 1 minute. Add the cumin, jalapeño, and crème fraîche, stir well, and simmer for 2 minutes, until slightly thickened. Taste for seasoning, add the lime juice, and stir once more.

Transfer the corn to a serving dish. Garnish with the chives and cilantro sprigs and serve.   MAKES 4 TO 6 SERVINGS

Corn Soup with Indian Spices

Corn defines summer eating for me. But at a certain point, one tires of corn on the cob and its perfect simplicity, and it's time to do more than boil or grill. Once you have shucked the corn and cut off the kernels, use the cobs to make a light broth. The kernels get simmered with butter and a few offerings from the spice cupboard. Puree the soup to a velvety creaminess.

4 tablespoons butter
1 medium onion, diced
2 garlic cloves, grated or minced
1 tablespoon grated fresh ginger
½ teaspoon ground turmeric
½ teaspoon cumin seeds
½ teaspoon black mustard seeds
Large pinch of cayenne
3 cups corn kernels
   (from 4 or 5 large ears)

Salt and pepper
4 cups water or corn broth (see Note)
Milk (optional)

FOR THE GARNISH
¾ cup plain whole milk-yogurt
1 tablespoon chopped chives
Cilantro sprigs
Lime wedges (optional)

Melt the butter in a heavy-bottomed soup pot over medium heat. Add the onion and cook until softened, about 10 minutes. Add the garlic, ginger, turmeric, cumin, mustard seeds, and cayenne and sizzle for a minute or so.

Add the corn kernels and season generously with salt and pepper. Cook, stirring, for 2 minutes. Add the water or corn broth and bring to a boil, then reduce the heat and cook gently for 10 to 15 minutes, until the corn is tender. Remove from the heat.

Puree the soup in a blender, then strain through a fine-mesh sieve into a saucepan. Check the seasoning and adjust if necessary. Thin the soup with water or milk if it seems too thick.

To serve, reheat the soup and ladle into small bowls. Garnish each bowl with 2 tablespoons yogurt and sprinkle with the chives and cilantro. Add a squeeze of lime to each one if you like.   MAKES 6 SERVINGS

NOTE: To make corn broth, put 4 shucked and halved cobs in a large saucepan with 1 onion, thickly sliced; a sprig of parsley; and a sprig of thyme. Add 6 cups of water and simmer for 30 minutes. Strain and refrigerate for up to 2 days.

For the loveliest texture, you really must strain the soup.

Fresh Corn Griddle Cakes

Stirring fresh corn kernels, chopped jalapeño, and chives into the cornmeal batter is a fine idea. And a zippy salsa of chopped summer peppers and tomatoes makes a delicious topping, too. Serve them hot off the griddle as an appetizer, or as an accompaniment to fried eggs or grilled pork chops. You can prep the wet and dry ingredients for the batter in advance if you like, but for the fluffiest texture wait to combine them until just before cooking.

FOR THE BATTER

1¹/₂ cups cornmeal
¹/₂ cup all-purpose flour
2 teaspoons baking powder
1 teaspoon baking soda
1 teaspoon salt
2 teaspoons sugar (optional)
1¹/₂ cups buttermilk
2 large eggs, lightly beaten
6 tablespoons butter, melted, or
    vegetable oil
2 cups corn kernels (from about 4 ears)
1 small jalapeño chile, finely chopped, or
    to taste
3 tablespoons thinly sliced chives or
    scallions

FOR THE SALSA

1¹/₂ cups finely diced red or white onions
1¹/₂ cups finely diced bell peppers,
    preferably a mix of colors
1¹/₂ cups finely diced firm but ripe
    tomatoes, preferably a mix of colors
1 small jalapeño chile, finely chopped, or
    to taste
1 teaspoon salt
Juice of 2 limes, or more to taste

Butter or vegetable oil for greasing
    the griddle
1 cup crumbled queso fresco
    (or substitute mild feta)
1 cup roughly chopped cilantro

To make the batter, stir together the cornmeal, flour, baking powder, baking soda, salt, and sugar, if using, in a large bowl. In a medium bowl, whisk together the buttermilk, eggs, and melted butter. Add to the cornmeal mixture and whisk briefly to make a thick batter. Add the corn kernels, jalapeño, and chives and stir to combine.

To make the salsa, put the onions, peppers, tomatoes, jalapeño, and salt in a medium bowl and toss to combine. Add the lime juice and toss again. (The salsa can be prepared up to 2 hours ahead and refrigerated.)

Set a griddle or large cast-iron skillet over medium heat. When it is hot, grease lightly with butter or oil, using a folded paper towel or pastry brush. Spoon slightly less than ¼ cup batter onto the griddle for each cake. Cook for about 1½ minutes, until golden on the bottom, adjusting the heat as necessary to keep the cakes from browning too quickly. Carefully flip with a spatula and cook for another 1½ minutes. Serve the griddle cakes as soon as they are ready, or keep the first batches hot in a low oven until all the batter is used.

To serve, garnish each cake with a generous spoonful of salsa, a little queso fresco, and a sprinkling of cilantro.   MAKES 18 TO 20 CAKES (4-INCH DIAMETER)

Polenta

Properly cooked polenta is a delight. Polenta is basically cornmeal porridge, once a staple of Italian peasant fare and still popular throughout the northern part of the country. It doesn't need to say polenta on the box; you can use any kind of cornmeal—ground coarse, medium, or fine. The better the cornmeal you start with, though, the better your result in the kitchen. The real key to perfect polenta is cooking it for a sufficient amount of time, which, in most cases, is at least an hour. You need to allow the cornmeal to swell slowly and become fully cooked. That way, you bring out the sweet corn flavor (undercooked cornmeal has an unpleasant texture and bitterness). Polenta must be cooked over very low heat and stirred frequently. It needs monitoring, and an occasional splash more liquid when it begins to look dry. Don't worry if it sticks to the bottom of the pot—that's normal. You want to get the salt right too, but be sure to cool the polenta on your spoon before tasting, or you risk a scalded tongue.

The recipe below gives instructions for making both soft and firm polenta. Serve firm polenta as a side to nearly anything. Soft polenta can be served in a bowl as a simple meal on its own, or as an accompaniment to the main course.

5 cups water
Salt and pepper
1 cup medium-grind polenta
(see Note, following page)
6 tablespoons butter
(if making soft polenta)

Grated Parmesan
(for soft polenta; optional)
Extra virgin olive oil, as necessary
(if making firm polenta)

Bring the water to a boil in a medium heavy saucepan over high heat. Add 1 teaspoon salt, then slowly pour the polenta into the water, stirring with a wire whisk or wooden spoon. Continue stirring as the mixture thickens, 2 to 3 minutes. Turn the heat to low and cook for at least 45 minutes, stirring every 10 minutes or so. If the polenta becomes quite thick, thin it with ½ cup water, stir well, and continue cooking; then add up to 1 cup more water as necessary to keep the polenta soft enough to stir. The grains should be swollen and taste cooked, not raw. Taste a spoonful (let it cool first) and add salt as needed and pepper if desired. The consistency should be like soft mashed potatoes.

For soft polenta, add the butter to the pan and stir well. This gives the polenta a creamier texture. Serve immediately, or transfer to a double boiler set over low heat, cover, and keep warm for up to an hour or so. (Or set the saucepan in a skillet of barely simmering water.) Serve with grated Parmesan, if desired.

For firm polenta, do not add butter. Brush a small baking sheet or a shallow baking dish (approximately 8½ by 11 inches) with olive oil. Carefully pour the polenta into the pan and, using a spatula, spread it to a thickness of ¾ inch. Let cool to room temperature. Cover and refrigerate for at least 2 hours and up to 3 days ahead. To serve, cut into 3-inch squares or wedges, brush lightly with olive oil, and reheat until crisp by grilling, broiling, or panfrying.   MAKES 4 TO 6 SERVINGS

NOTE: If you are using artisanal stone-ground cornmeal or corn grits, be sure to rinse them before cooking, and skim off any chaff that rises to the water's surface as it cooks. The chaff never softens. Some types of heirloom stone-ground corn can take quite a bit longer to cook, even as long as 3 hours. I generally use a medium-grind organic Italian polenta or organic yellow corn grits (don't confuse corn grits for hominy grits, which have a different flavor).

Warm polenta on a cutting board (*left*) and grilled firm polenta (*right*).

Cutting Polenta with a String

The good old-fashioned way to serve polenta to accompany a roast or stew is to cut it with a string. Pour the warm polenta onto a cutting board in a mound and let it cool slightly. It will begin to firm as it sits on the board. At the table, take a 2-foot length of butcher's twine and pull it taut, slide it underneath the polenta, along the surface of the cutting board, and lift at 2- or 3-inch intervals to make slices. If you try to cut warm, soft polenta with a knife, it is impossible, but with a string, you get perfect slices.

GREENS

Spinach, chard, collards, and kale are greens with which we are all familiar. Why not expand your horizon to include morning glory greens, sweet potato greens, mizuna, tatsoi, and the other beautiful greens on display at outdoor markets? They're abundant sources of wholesome goodness, delicious by any standard, whether quickly wilted, stir-fried, creamed, long-cooked, or chopped for a filling. And don't forget that wild greens have long sustained folks all over the world.

Throughout the Mediterranean, there are examples of savory pies made with wild greens for a meatless meal. In many cultures, foraging for greens has often been the task of elderly women, the keepers of traditional wisdom. When I lived in New Mexico, I was always delighted to come across local lady foragers selling *quelites*, also known as lamb's quarters or wild spinach. Now there always seem to be some wild-foraged offerings at the Union Square Greenmarket in New York—wild watercress or purslane or amaranth.

I am sorry when I see people discarding leafy tops, like beet greens, at the market. It's like throwing money and food away (you've already paid for them!). You know you can cook those, I tell them. Radish and turnip tops, too, are wonderful. In any guise, cooked greens are fantastic. I just can't get enough. (Though I do get more than my share of cast-off beet tops.)

I can't help but think that we are hardwired to enjoy the deep, earthy flavor of cooked greens. *Clockwise from top left:* Chard, broccoli rabe, collards, Tuscan kale, and curly kale.

Chard Frittata

The curious thing about this delectable frittata is that the chard is added raw. You wouldn't imagine the chard could cook completely in the short time the frittata takes, but it does. Chard is among the most deeply flavorful cooking greens. If pressed, I might even call it a favorite.

3 large Swiss chard leaves, stems removed
and reserved for another use
4 large eggs
Salt and pepper

2 tablespoons grated Parmesan
2 tablespoons grated pecorino
2 tablespoons extra virgin olive oil

Stack and roll the chard leaves into a tight cigar shape. Cut the roll crosswise as thinly as possible.

Beat the eggs in a medium bowl. Season with salt and pepper. Stir in the chard, Parmesan, and pecorino.

Heat 1 tablespoon of the olive oil in a 9-inch cast-iron skillet over medium-high heat. Add the egg mixture and cook, tilting the pan and lifting the cooked edges with a spatula, until the eggs are nearly set, about 2 minutes.

Carefully place a plate or small cutting board on top of the skillet, flip the frittata onto the plate, and return the skillet to the stove. Add another tablespoon of olive oil to the pan, then gently slip the frittata back into pan (cooked side up) and cook for another 2 minutes, or until firm. Cut into wedges and serve.

MAKES 2 SERVINGS

My friend Amy Dencler, a chef at Chez Panisse and one of the best cooks I know, introduced me to my new favorite frittata.

Southern Greens with Ham Hocks

The two most important things for a respectable pot of long-cooked greens are that the greens cook for at least an hour, preferably more, until they melt in the mouth, and that the copious broth be assertively seasoned. Other constants are smoked pork jowls or hocks or a meaty ham bone, lots of onion, and collards for at least some portion of the greens. Don't stint on hot pepper or vinegar—both are necessary. I always drink a cup or two of the pot liquor on its own, which is as tasty and nutritious as the greens themselves. A bowl of greens and some warm cornbread—that's one fine dinner.

2 tablespoons butter

2 large onions, diced

Salt and pepper

4 garlic cloves, chopped

1 tablespoon tomato paste

1 teaspoon mustard powder

1/2 teaspoon crushed red pepper

1/8 teaspoon cayenne

1/2 teaspoon pimentón

1 smoked ham hock or a piece of slab bacon

4 cups water

4 pounds mixed cooking greens, such as collards, kale, chard, and mustard greens, washed and roughly chopped into 2-inch-wide strips

1 tablespoon apple cider vinegar

Melt the butter in a large Dutch oven or heavy-bottomed soup pot over medium-high heat. Add the onions, season generously with salt and pepper, and cook until softened, about 5 minutes. Add the garlic, tomato paste, mustard powder, crushed red pepper, cayenne, and pimentón, stir to coat, and cook for another minute.

Add the ham hock and water and bring to a boil. Add the greens a handful at a time, pushing them down with a wooden spoon to help them wilt into the liquid. When all the greens are in the pot, reduce the heat to a simmer and cook, partially covered, for at least an hour, until the greens are quite tender.

Taste the broth for salt and adjust as needed, then add the vinegar. Serve, or keep the cooked greens, in their liquid, in the refrigerator for up to 3 days; reheat before serving.   MAKES 6 TO 8 SERVINGS

Melted Spinach

Baby spinach is wonderful when wilted quickly in a little olive oil or butter—
the tender greens cook in less than a minute. (You can also try cooking baby
spinach in a flavorful seasoned oil or butter, such as the garlic oil left over from
making Garlic Confit, page 22, or leftover curry butter from the soft-shell crabs
on page 377.) But when you find yourself with larger, sturdier spinach, leave them
in the pan a little longer, until they have started to break down but haven't lost
their appealing deep green color.

Wash 2 pounds large spinach leaves well and remove the tough stems (it's always
a good idea to wash spinach three times to be sure it is free of sand and grit).
Melt 2 tablespoons butter in a large heavy-bottomed soup pot over medium-high
heat. Add the spinach leaves a handful at a time and let them wilt, stirring with
a wooden spoon. When all the spinach has wilted, season with salt and pepper,
turn the heat down to medium, and continue cooking and stirring. After 5 or
6 minutes, the leaves should be at the tender stage I like to call melted: well-
cooked, but not disintegrated.   MAKES 4 SERVINGS

Wilted Kale Salad with Pecorino

I think kale is far too fibrous to be considered a raw salad green, trends be damned. Instead, I prefer to wilt it a bit, for something along the lines of a warm dandelion salad.

To make croutons, remove and discard the crust of a day-old French loaf. Tear the bread into rough pieces about an inch in diameter, place in a bowl, drizzle with olive oil to coat, and season with salt. Spread on a baking sheet and bake at 375 degrees until crisp and golden, about 15 minutes. Set aside.

Cut a pound of lacinato kale (also called Tuscan kale or cavolo nero) into 2-inch-wide ribbons. Cut 2 slices bacon or pancetta into ¼-inch-wide lardons. Put the lardons and 1 tablespoon olive oil in a wide skillet over medium-high heat and cook until the bacon is crisp but not brittle. Remove and blot on paper towels. Add the kale to the pan, season with salt and pepper, and sauté until wilted, about 5 minutes.

Dress the kale with a garlicky mustard vinaigrette (page 91), top with the lardons, pecorino shavings, and croutons, and add halved 8-minute hard-cooked eggs (see How to Boil an Egg, page 431) for richness. Serve the salad warm.
MAKES 2 SERVINGS

Broccoli Rabe Lasagna

Broccoli rabe makes a stellar vegetarian lasagna. The leaves, tender stems, and broccoli-like buds have a distinctive pleasant bitterness and deep flavor. I pilfer some of the cooked greens to make a garlicky pesto and then chop the rest and add it to the layers. It's worth making the pesto alone to sauce spaghetti.

FOR THE BÉCHAMEL SAUCE
4 tablespoons butter
¼ cup all-purpose flour
2 cups half-and-half, heated, plus
*   a little more if necessary*
Salt and pepper
Pinch of cayenne
Grated nutmeg

FOR THE LASAGNA
1 pound dried lasagna noodles

Salt and pepper
2 bunches broccoli rabe (about 2 pounds),
*   tough stems trimmed*
4 garlic cloves, grated or minced
½ cup extra virgin olive oil
1 pound ricotta cheese
½ teaspoon grated lemon zest
4 tablespoons butter, softened
4 ounces Parmesan or a combination
*   of Parmesan and pecorino, grated*
(about 1½ cups)

To make the béchamel, melt the butter in a small saucepan over medium heat. Whisk in the flour and cook for a minute, without browning. Gradually whisk in the half-and-half, about ½ cup at a time, to obtain a smooth, lightly thickened sauce. Turn the heat to low, add ½ teaspoon salt, black pepper to taste, the cayenne, and nutmeg to taste and cook, whisking, for 4 to 5 minutes. Thin it if necessary with a little more half-and-half—you want a pourable consistency. Place the saucepan in a hot water bath to keep the sauce warm.

Bring a large pot of well-salted water to a boil. Add the lasagna noodles and cook for 5 minutes. Lift the noodles from the water with a spider or tongs and rinse well in a bowl of cold water. Drain and lay flat on a kitchen towel.

Blanch the broccoli rabe in the same cooking water for 1 minute, or until just wilted. Drain in a colander, rinse with cool water, and squeeze dry. Roughly chop the broccoli rabe.

Put 1 cup of the chopped greens, the garlic, and olive oil in a food processor or blender and puree to make the pesto. Season with salt and pepper to taste and transfer to a small bowl.

Mix the ricotta and lemon zest in a small bowl and season with salt and pepper to taste.

Heat the oven to 375 degrees. Use 2 tablespoons butter to grease an 8-by-10-inch baking dish.

To assemble the lasagna, put a layer of cooked noodles on the bottom of the baking dish. Spoon a quarter of the béchamel over the noodles, then dot with a third of the ricotta. Complete the layer with one-third of the chopped greens, a good drizzle of pesto, and about one-quarter of the grated cheese. Continue the layering, finishing with a layer of pasta. Spread the last of the béchamel on top and sprinkle with the remaining Parmesan. (You will have 4 layers of pasta and 3 layers of filling.) Dot the top with the remaining 2 tablespoons butter. (The lasagna can be assembled ahead and left at room temperature for up to 3 hours.)

Cover the pan with foil and bake for 20 minutes. Uncover and bake for 20 minutes more, or until nicely browned on top and bubbling. Let lasagna rest for 10 minutes before serving. (Or set aside for up to several hours and reheat in the oven before serving.)   MAKES 6 TO 8 SERVINGS

ARTICHOKES & CARDOONS

Artichokes in a jar were all I knew until I moved to California, where everyone was artichoke conversant. Who would ever think to eat a thistle? To look past the thorns and the bitterness must have taken a visionary. I'm glad somebody persevered. What a plant to admire in the field, with its beautiful silvery gray foliage, and what a pleasure to eat.

The large globe artichoke is the most common variety in the United States these days. Most people are familiar with the ritual of plucking off the leaves one by one, dipping them in a sauce of choice, and sucking the bit of flesh that comes along with it, then getting to the prized heart once you've scraped away the hairy choke. But it's important to know about the diminutive "baby" artichokes that grow lower down on the same plant as side shoots. Their tender hearts are completely edible, having no developed choke.

Cardoons, the artichoke's feral-looking cousin from ancient Roman times, are a bit more work, as their large celery-like stalks need to be peeled and then parboiled, but are so worth the effort.

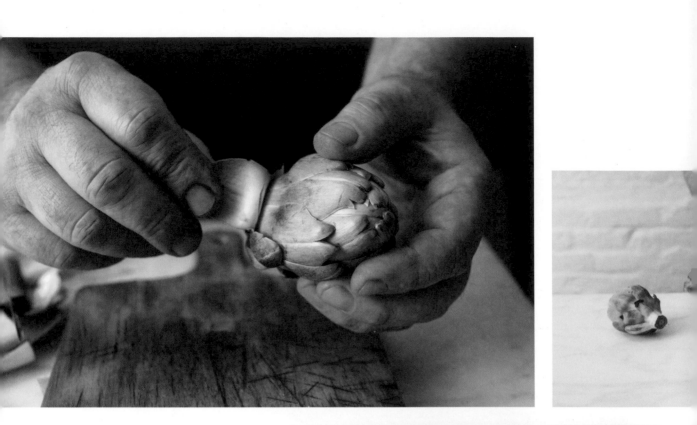

Trimming baby
artichokes: Remove
the outer leaves
to reveal the pale
tender center.

Trim tops and stems
with a paring knife.
Artichokes may
now be sliced or
quartered.

Baby Artichoke Sauté

Italy is a great place to eat artichokes. There artichokes of every size are as common as onions. It seems every neighborhood grocer has an overflowing crate of them sitting casually by the door, and small violet-tinged specimens with long edible stems are sold at outdoor markets. Baby artichokes can be found here too, albeit with much shorter stems. They are a bit fiddly: You peel off a layer of tough outer leaves from each artichoke and do a little trimming. Then cooking them is quick and easy.

24 baby artichokes (about 3 pounds)
Juice of 1 lemon
Olive oil for shallow-frying
Salt and pepper
½ teaspoon crushed red pepper
4 garlic cloves, finely chopped

3 tablespoons chopped flat-leaf parsley
Finishing salt, such as Maldon or fleur de sel
Lemon wedges or red wine vinegar for serving

Peel off and discard a few outer petals of each artichoke until you reach the paler tender leaves. Cut off the top and trim the stem end with a sharp paring knife, then quarter each artichoke. Put the artichokes in a bowl of cold water spiked with the lemon juice to prevent oxidation.

In a wide, heavy nonreactive skillet, heat ½ inch of olive oil over medium heat. Drain and blot the artichokes dry and, when the oil is nearly smoking, carefully add them to the skillet. Season well with salt and pepper, stirring to coat with oil. Let the artichokes cook and brown slightly, stirring occasionally, for 5 to 7 minutes, until they are tender when probed with a paring knife.

Add the red pepper, garlic, and parsley, stir well, and let sizzle for a minute or so. Transfer the artichokes to a platter, sprinkle with finishing salt, and serve with lemon wedges, or season sparingly with red wine vinegar. Eat hot or at room temperature.   MAKES 4 SERVINGS

Raw Artichoke Salad

In Italy and southern France, the smallest fresh artichokes are often eaten raw, thinly sliced and dressed with fruity olive oil and lemon juice. Peppery arugula leaves and shavings of Parmesan are often part of the story too. It may sound too plain to some, but it's very, very good.

4 baby artichokes
1 tablespoon lemon juice
1 small garlic clove, smashed to a paste
*   with a pinch of salt (optional)*

Salt and pepper
3 tablespoons extra virgin olive oil
2 handfuls of arugula
A chunk of Parmesan, for shaving

Peel off and discard a few outer petals of each artichoke until you reach the paler tender leaves. Cut off the top and trim the stem end with a sharp paring knife, then cut each artichoke in half vertically. Rinse in cold water, then blot dry.

Slice the artichokes as thin as possible with a sharp knife and place in a small bowl. Add the lemon juice and garlic, if using. Season well with salt and pepper, add the olive oil, and toss to coat.

Put the arugula in a shallow bowl or on a small platter. Spoon the artichokes over the greens and garnish with shavings of Parmesan.   MAKES 1 OR 2 SERVINGS

A raw artichoke salad is beautiful in its simplicity. Use a good full-flavored olive oil, and be generous with the Parmesan.

Plain Boiled Artichoke

Sometimes a plain boiled artichoke is just the thing. My Sicilian friend Fabrizia thinks so, at any rate, and she knows a thing or two about artichokes—she cooks them in the fireplace cinders, fries them, or turns them into caponata. After a day of hard work, she sometimes announces, "I'm tired and not very hungry . . . think I'll just boil an artichoke and go to bed." *Va bene*, I say, exhausting a large part of my limited Italian vocabulary.

Pick a nice medium-sized artichoke, fresh and firm. With scissors, snip off the thorny tips of each leaf (not necessary with thornless varieties). Cut an inch off the top of the artichoke and peel the stem, leaving it long if it looks good. Simmer the artichoke for about 30 minutes in well-salted water (use a stainless steel pot), until the heart is tender when pierced with a skewer. Remove and turn the artichoke upside down in a colander to drain. Eat hot or at room temperature with olive oil and salt. Other options for dipping are vinaigrette, homemade mayonnaise (see page 433), or melted butter.   MAKES 1 SERVING

Baked Cardoons

This is a project—there's no way around it. But if you're a cardoon lover like me, it's worth the effort.

First, peel the celery-like stalks (see page 194) with a sharp paring knife (some of the outer stalks may be too stringy and should be discarded). Cut them into ½-inch-thick batons about 2 inches long. As you work, put the cut pieces in a bowl of acidulated water so they don't oxidize. Simmer the pieces in well-salted water for 10 to 15 minutes, until tender. Drain and spread out on a towel-lined baking sheet to cool and dry.

Now you're ready to proceed: Butter a baking dish and arrange the pieces of cardoons in it in a single layer. Pour heavy cream over just to cover. Sprinkle with grated Parmesan and freshly ground black pepper. Bake in a 400-degree oven for about 30 minutes, until bubbling and nicely browned.

Fried Cardoons

Cardoons are also delicious fried. Dip the cooked pieces in flour, then in beaten egg, and roll them in bread crumbs. Shallow-fry in olive oil until golden, blot on paper towels, and sprinkle with salt. Serve with Aïoli (page 29) or a garlicky anchovy mayonnaise.

Left to right: A beautiful cardoon leaf, removing leaves from the stalk, trimming away stringy bits, cutting into batons, and prepped cardoons in lemon water.

FRESH BEANS

Beans, beans, beans! A highlight of summer abundance and one of the glories of the garden. Green beans are a joy to grow, because then you can pick them at just the right stage. They taste best on the smaller side, but you do have to keep after them—beans tend to go from tiny to jumbo when you have your back turned.

As a customer at the market, I'm usually the guy slowly picking through an overflowing bean pile for the best specimens. But my favorite farmer consistently harvests her beans at the perfect size, and I'm happy to pay a bit more per pound to make my life that much easier.

Green beans and yellow wax beans picked at their prime are a true delight. Romanos, also known as Italian flat beans, have a wonderful texture, and their shape helps catch tasty juices and dressings.

Italian cooks gravitate toward fresh summer shelling beans, as do American Southerners. You start seeing many of them at the market in mid- to late summer, sporting their colorful pods— cranberry beans, butter beans, cannellini, black-eyed peas, and many others. These cook more quickly than dried beans, usually in only 30 minutes or so, and have the loveliest creamy texture. But when the pod is left to dry, its contents become wintertime meals and next year's seeds (see Dried Beans & Legumes, page 210).

Glorious fresh shell beans: cranberries, pink runners, cannellini, limas, butter beans, and black-eyed peas.

Height-of-Summer Bean Salad

An easy summer salad that shows off the good stuff, with a gorgeous contrast of colors, sizes, shapes, and textures. Cooked separately by type, the beans are then reunited and tossed with a bright vinaigrette. (Not at all like those cafeteria three-bean salads of yore, drenched in cider vinegar.) This salad is best at room temperature, making it great for a picnic.

FOR THE VINAIGRETTE
3 tablespoons red wine vinegar
2 teaspoons Dijon mustard
2 garlic cloves, grated or minced
Salt and pepper
1/4 cup extra virgin olive oil

FOR THE SALAD
1 pound fresh shelling beans,
    such as cranberry beans or
    cannellini

1/2 pound small green beans or
    haricots verts
1/2 pound romano beans
1/2 pound small yellow wax beans
1 medium red onion, cut crosswise in
    1/4-inch slices (don't separate into rings)
A few sprigs of fresh marjoram or
    1/2 teaspoon dried oregano
2 tablespoons chopped flat-leaf parsley
A handful of oil-cured black olives
    (optional)

To make the vinaigrette, stir together the vinegar, mustard, and garlic in a small bowl. Add a good pinch each of salt and pepper, then whisk in the olive oil. Taste for seasoning and set aside.

Shuck the fresh shelling beans and simmer in lightly salted water to cover; they should be tender in about 30 minutes. Let the beans cool in their cooking water. (These can be cooked up to 1 day ahead.)

Cook the green beans, romano beans, and wax beans separately: Simmer each type in lightly salted water for 3 to 5 minutes, until just tender. Spread them out on a tray or plates to cool to room temperature.

Put a dry cast-iron skillet over medium-high heat. Lay the onion slices in the skillet and let them char and soften slightly on one side, about 5 minutes. Turn and char the other side. Set aside to cool.

continued

If using fresh marjoram sprigs, toast them in the hot skillet until they char slightly, about 1 minute; remove from the pan.

To assemble the salad, drain the shell beans (reserve the liquid for another purpose—bean broth is good in soups and pastas) and put them in a large serving bowl. Add the remaining cooked beans and the charred onions. Season with salt and pepper. Add the vinaigrette and toss well. Crumble the marjoram and sprinkle over the salad. Sprinkle with the parsley and serve, garnished with the olives if you like.   MAKES 4 TO 6 SERVINGS

Charred red onions for the bean salad (previous page).

Basic Fresh Shell Beans

This technique works well with any shell bean you like—choose whatever looks best at the market. Just barely cover the shelled beans with water, add a spoonful of olive oil, a peeled garlic clove, a rosemary sprig, and a little salt, and simmer gently. (If boiled hard, they'll burst.) After 20 minutes, begin tasting. If the beans are still crunchy, persevere and cook until delectably creamy. Fresh shell beans generally take about 30 minutes at most. Let them cool in their broth.

Reheat to serve, adding stewed onion or tomato if you wish. For me, a splash of good olive oil and a little sea salt will do just fine.

NOTE: Two pounds of shelling beans in the pod will yield about 3 cups, enough for 4 servings.

Wok-Cooked Romano Beans

Romano beans, also called flat beans, are terrific when cooked over high heat in a wok, Chinese-style. If you prefer to go Italianate, season them instead with olive oil, crushed red pepper, garlic, rosemary, and sage. You want a little color on the beans, but make sure they're still a vivid green.

1 tablespoon vegetable oil

3 small dried hot red chile peppers

1 pound romano beans,
*   cut into 3-inch lengths*

Salt

½ teaspoon grated or minced garlic

½ teaspoon grated fresh ginger

½ teaspoon toasted sesame oil

1 tablespoon soy sauce

3 scallions, thinly sliced on a diagonal

Roughly chopped cilantro

Heat the oil in a large wok over high heat. Add the chiles and let them sizzle for a minute, then add the beans and season with salt. Toss the beans rapidly for 2 minutes, allowing them to char and brown a bit. Add the garlic and ginger and let sizzle for 10 seconds. Add about ¼ cup water to help the beans steam a bit and cook for a minute or two more, until they are firm-tender. Add the sesame oil and soy sauce and toss to coat, then add the scallions. Adjust the seasoning, transfer to a serving platter, and sprinkle with cilantro.   MAKES 4 SERVINGS

Romano beans have been my lifelong obsession. They may become yours too.

Butter Bean Gratin

This shell bean marvel will remind you more of France than of New England—it's sort of an easy vegetarian cassoulet. It can be made in summer with succulent fresh shell beans, such as butter beans, or year-round with any large dried white beans, such as cannellini.

FOR THE BEANS
5 cups shucked fresh butter beans (about 4 pounds in the pod), or 3 cups dried white beans, soaked overnight in cold water to cover
1 medium onion, halved
1 medium carrot
A bay leaf
A small rosemary sprig
Salt

FOR THE BREAD CRUMBS
2 cups coarse homemade bread crumbs (from a day-old French loaf)
2 tablespoons extra virgin olive oil
1/2 teaspoon grated or minced garlic

1 tablespoon chopped flat-leaf parsley
1 teaspoon chopped sage
1 teaspoon chopped thyme
1 teaspoon chopped rosemary
Salt and pepper

FOR THE GRATIN
3 tablespoons extra virgin olive oil
1 large onion, finely chopped
Salt and pepper
2 teaspoons grated or minced garlic
1/2 teaspoon crushed red pepper, or to taste
1/2 teaspoon fennel seeds, coarsely crushed
1 tablespoon chopped thyme
1 tablespoon chopped sage

Put the shucked beans, onion, carrot, bay leaf, and rosemary in a large saucepan and add cold water just to cover. Bring to a boil, reduce the heat to maintain a simmer, and cook gently for 30 minutes or so, until tender. Add 1 tablespoon salt and remove from the heat. Let the beans cool in their liquid.

Alternatively, if using dried white beans, simmer slowly until tender, usually about 1½ hours. (The beans can be cooked up to 2 days in advance and refrigerated in their cooking liquid.)

Put the bread crumbs in a medium bowl. Stir together the olive oil and garlic and drizzle over the crumbs. Add the parsley, sage, thyme, and rosemary and mix well. Season with salt and black pepper to taste. Set aside.

Heat the oven to 350 degrees. Put the olive oil in a large skillet over medium-high heat, add the onion, and cook, stirring occasionally, until softened, about

10 minutes. Season generously with salt and black pepper, then add the garlic, crushed red pepper, and fennel seeds and cook for 1 minute. Remove from the heat.

Drain the beans, reserving the cooking liquid. Add the beans to the onion mixture and stir in the thyme and sage. Taste and adjust the seasoning. Transfer the beans to a shallow earthenware baking dish, at least 9 by 13 inches. Pour about 2 cups of the bean cooking liquid over the beans; there should be about an inch of liquid in the baking dish.

Sprinkle the bread crumbs evenly over the beans and cover the dish with foil. Bake for 45 minutes. Remove the foil and continue baking until the beans are bubbling in the center and the bread crumbs are golden brown, about 30 minutes more. Remove from the oven and let rest for at least 10 minutes before serving. (The gratin can be baked several hours ahead and reheated to serve.)   MAKES 6 TO 8 SERVINGS

Fresh cranberry beans (borlotti) in their brilliant crimson pods.

Shell Bean and Albacore Salad

In kitchens all around the Mediterranean, room-temperature salads of beans and tuna are common, often made with home-canned tuna and cooked dried white beans. For summer meals, I like to make this version with fresh shelling beans and a flavorful confit of albacore tuna cooked gently in olive oil. The Monterey Bay Aquarium Seafood Watch program recommends albacore as a sustainable choice.

FOR THE ALBACORE
1 pound fresh albacore steaks
Salt and pepper
½ teaspoon fennel seeds,
*   coarsely ground in a mortar*
A pinch of crushed red pepper
3 garlic cloves, roughly chopped
A small rosemary sprig
About ¾ cup extra virgin olive oil

FOR THE BEAN SALAD
1 cup finely diced mixed red and
*   yellow bell peppers*
½ cup finely diced sweet white or
*   red onion*
Pinch of crushed red pepper

2 tablespoons red wine vinegar
1 small garlic clove, smashed to
*   a paste with a little salt*
2 tablespoons extra virgin olive oil
Salt and pepper
3 cups cooked fresh shell beans (see Basic
*   Fresh Shell Beans, page 201)*
1 tablespoon chopped basil, plus a few
*   whole leaves for garnish*
A handful of halved cherry tomatoes
*   (optional)*
4 hard-cooked eggs (see How to Boil an
*   Egg, page 431), halved (optional)*

Aïoli (page 29) for serving (optional)

To make the albacore, heat the oven to 350 degrees. Cut the albacore into 1-inch-thick slices and put them in a small baking dish in one layer. Season generously with salt and black pepper. Sprinkle the fennel seeds and red pepper over the fish. Add the garlic and rosemary to the baking dish. Add olive oil to a depth of 1 inch, barely covering the fish.

Cover the dish and place in the oven for 10 minutes. Remove from the oven, turn the slices over, cover, and return to the oven for another 5 minutes. The albacore should be just cooked; take care not to overcook it. Let the fish cool in its dish, uncovered. (The fish can be stored in its cooking liquid in the refrigerator for up to 3 days. Bring to room temperature to serve.)

continued

To make the salad, toss the bell peppers, onion, crushed red pepper, vinegar, garlic, and olive oil with a little salt in a large serving bowl. Add the shell beans, draining them well first, and season lightly with salt and black pepper. Add the chopped basil and toss gently to combine, taking care not to smash the beans. Taste and adjust the seasoning. Transfer to a serving platter.

Remove the albacore from the oil, flake it into large pieces, and arrange over the bean salad. Garnish with the basil leaves. Serve surrounded with the halved cherry tomatoes and hard-cooked eggs if you like. A dab or two of aïoli would be welcome too.   MAKES 4 TO 6 SERVINGS

Slow-cooked albacore tuna with shell beans (previous page).

DRIED BEANS & LEGUMES

Too often regarded as the vegetarians' protein, or as fodder only for the poor, beans deserve praise, not prejudice. But I'm a little bean-biased. Or perhaps a lot. Beans make me unapologetically euphoric. I'm always ready to proselytize for the humble bean; for that matter, I'm also a lentil lover, a chickpea enthusiast, a split pea booster, and a fool for fava beans.

Dried beans are incredibly versatile—hot or cold; in salads and soups; long-cooked, baked, stewed, or mashed; on their own, anointed with olive oil; or simmered with ham hocks and eaten with cornbread. Beans done right are a nourishing meal at any time of the year.

The main thing to know about cooking dried beans is that new-crop beans taste fresher and cook more evenly than beans of uncertain vintage, like the beans sold at the supermarket, where they have lain for who knows how long. It's better to buy dried beans at a farmers' market or online from specialty growers. They cost a little more—many are heirloom varieties—but they are well worth the price.

Old World cooks knew only lentils, peas, chickpeas, and fava beans, which date back to ancient Greek and Roman times. It seems remarkable that the world has only relatively recently come to know the kidney bean family, *Phaseolus vulgaris*—New World varieties that include pinto, navy, black, cranberry, lima, and a host of others. All beans and legumes—much like every food that we have—were once wild, then subsequently cultivated, traded, transported, and grown on a mass scale.

Tiny Lentil Salad

Large flat brown lentils can be fine for soup, but for a great lentil salad, you want the tiny ones, such as the black lentils called beluga, gray-green *lentilles du Puy*, or Castelluccio lentils from Umbria. These lentils keep their shape and a somewhat firm texture when cooked.

FOR THE LENTILS

1 pound (about 2 cups) black lentils

1 small onion, stuck with a clove

A large thyme sprig

A bay leaf

Salt and pepper

2 tablespoons olive oil

2½ cups diced onions

1½ cups diced carrots

1¼ cups diced celery

FOR THE VINAIGRETTE

3 tablespoons sherry vinegar

½ teaspoon salt, or to taste

2 teaspoons chopped thyme

1 teaspoon grated orange zest

5 tablespoons extra virgin olive oil

FOR GARNISH

1 cup sliced scallions

½ cup chopped chervil

¼ cup chopped mint

To make the lentils, pick them over for stones or debris. Rinse them and put them in a medium saucepan. Add the onion, thyme, bay leaf, and 1 teaspoon salt. Cover with 8 cups water and bring to a boil over high heat. Reduce the heat to a gentle simmer and cook until the lentils are tender but still firm, 25 to 30 minutes. Drain the lentils—discard the onion, thyme, and bay leaf but save the cooking liquid for another purpose (such as a soup or a pasta dish)—and spread them on a platter or baking sheet to cool to room temperature.

Put the olive oil in a wide skillet over medium-high heat. Add the onions and cook until translucent, about 2 minutes; adjust the heat as necessary to keep the onions from browning. Add the carrots and celery, season with salt and pepper, and cook until the vegetables have softened, about 5 minutes more. Transfer to a bowl and add the cooled lentils.

To make the vinaigrette, mix together the vinegar, salt, thyme, and orange zest in a small bowl, then whisk in the olive oil. Adjust the seasoning to taste.

To finish the salad, season the lentil mixture generously with salt and pepper. Add the dressing and toss well. Allow to sit for at least 15 minutes, or up to an hour, for the flavors to meld.

Taste the salad for acid and salt (lentils tend to need a lot of vinegar). Transfer to a serving bowl and scatter the scallions, chervil, and mint over the top. Serve.   MAKES 6 TO 8 SERVINGS

White Bean Crostini with Rosemary

Good for snacks with drinks, these Tuscan-inspired white bean toasts are unassuming but addictive. (Even bean-o-phobes agree.) There's really nothing to it—the important part is making sure the bean puree is assertively seasoned. It's a good use for leftover cooked beans. It's quite good made with chickpeas too. For extra credit, grill the toast over coals.

2 cups warm cooked cannellini beans or
    other white beans, drained
2 tablespoons extra virgin olive oil, plus
    more for brushing the bread
1 tablespoon lemon juice
2 garlic cloves, grated or minced
Pinch of cayenne

½ teaspoon fennel seeds, toasted and
    crushed
2 teaspoons chopped rosemary
2 tablespoons chopped flat-leaf parsley,
    plus more for garnish
Salt and pepper
1 baguette, sliced into thin rounds
Crushed red pepper

Put the beans, olive oil, lemon juice, garlic, cayenne, and fennel seeds in a food processor and process until smooth. Transfer to a bowl. Add the rosemary, parsley, and salt and black pepper to taste. Set aside for a few minutes to allow the flavors to meld, then taste and adjust the seasoning. (The bean puree can be prepared to this point up to a day in advance and refrigerated. Rewarm in a small saucepan over medium heat, thinning with a little bean cooking liquid as necessary.)

Heat the oven to 400 degrees (or, if you have your grill going, use that to toast the bread). Brush the baguette slices with olive oil and toast on a baking sheet in the oven (or over medium-hot coals), turning once, until golden.

Spread each toast with about 1 tablespoon white bean puree, warm or at room temperature. Garnish with chopped parsley and crushed red pepper.
MAKES ABOUT 2 CUPS

Biblical Brown Lentils

I call these Biblical brown lentils after the Old Testament story, in which Esau sells his birthright to his brother Jacob for a bowl of porridge, which was likely a pot of soupy lentils. A fanatic lentil lover myself, I understand the temptation completely. Some say my "love" for lentils borders on obsession.

2 tablespoons olive oil

1 large onion, chopped

Salt and pepper

1 teaspoon cumin seeds,
   toasted and ground

1 teaspoon coriander seeds,
   toasted and ground

1 tablespoon paprika

1/8 teaspoon cayenne

4 garlic cloves, finely chopped

A large thyme sprig

A bay leaf

1 short cinnamon stick

1 pound (about 2 cups) brown lentils,
   picked over for stones and debris
   and rinsed well

8 cups Blond Chicken Broth (page 460)
   or water

Heat the olive oil in a large heavy-bottomed soup pot over medium heat. Add the onion and cook until softened, about 5 minutes. Season generously with salt and pepper, then add the cumin, coriander, paprika, cayenne, garlic, thyme, bay leaf, and cinnamon stick and cook for 1 minute.

Add the lentils, then cover with the stock and bring to a boil. Reduce the heat to low, skim any rising foam, and simmer until the lentils are very tender, about 1 hour. Monitor the liquid level, making sure the soup doesn't get too thick; add more broth or water if necessary.

Adjust the seasoning and serve the lentils.   MAKES 6 TO 8 SERVINGS

There's really nothing better than lentils stewed slowly with onion, garlic, and Middle Eastern spices.

Red Lentil Dal

Dried legumes (lentils, chickpeas, split peas), known as *dal*, are consumed daily by most Indians. Dal, whether served as a soup or a thicker stew, is truly, deeply delicious. The secret of great dal lies in a technique all Indian cooks know: Sizzle a handful of spices in hot ghee or oil to make a *tarka*. This dal features cumin seeds, or *jeera*, along with the near-obligatory turmeric, chopped garlic, chiles, and finely diced onion. The tarka transforms a pot of lentils into something rich-tasting, buttery, and shot through with flavor.

FOR THE DAL

2 tablespoons ghee (see page 440) or
   unsalted butter

1 medium onion, finely diced

Salt and pepper

1 tablespoon ground turmeric

1/2 teaspoon cumin seeds, toasted
   and ground

1/8 teaspoon cayenne

1 pound (about 2 1/4 cups) red lentils, rinsed

10 cups water

FOR THE TARKA

2 tablespoons ghee or unsalted butter

1 serrano chile, finely chopped

3 garlic cloves, grated or minced

1/2 teaspoon cumin seeds

Melt the ghee in a large heavy-bottomed pot over medium heat. Add the onion and season generously with salt and pepper, then add the turmeric, cumin, and cayenne. Cook, stirring, until the onion is softened, about 10 minutes. Add the lentils and water and bring slowly to a boil. Skim and discard any rising foam—there may be a lot—and stir diligently, because sometimes the mixture can overflow the pot during the first few minutes of cooking.

Turn the heat down to low, partially cover the pot, and simmer gently for about 45 minutes, until the lentils are quite soft. When the lentils are cooked, taste and adjust the salt. For a smooth, velvety consistency, puree the dal in a blender, then return to the pot. Or, if you prefer some texture, just beat with a whisk for a minute or two. If the dal is very thick, thin with a little water. (I prefer it on the soupy side.)

To make the tarka: Heat the ghee in a small skillet over medium-high heat. Add the serrano, garlic, and cumin seeds and cook until the cumin is fragrant and the garlic is lightly colored, about 1 minute. Immediately pour the contents of the skillet into the pot and stir into the dal. Taste again and correct the seasoning if necessary. MAKES 6 TO 8 SERVINGS

Serve the dal with
a dollop of yogurt
or Spicy Yogurt Raita
(page 382).

Pasta e Ceci

The hearty Italian dish called *pasta e ceci* is traditionally a thick chickpea soup with a little pasta added at the end as a garnish. But this take on it, which may just be my own, reverses tradition: It's a pasta in a savory sauce made from the chickpea broth, chock-full of ceci beans (chickpeas) and seasoned with rosemary and a fruity olive oil. I always cook more chickpeas than I need for this dish and then use the extra to make a soup or to add to a salad.

You could make this pasta dish with any type of dried bean. Add some chopped pancetta or bacon to cook with the onions if you wish.

FOR THE CHICKPEAS
2 cups chickpeas, soaked overnight in cold water to cover
1 medium onion, halved
1 medium carrot
A bay leaf
A small rosemary sprig
Salt

FOR THE PASTA
2 tablespoons extra virgin olive oil
1 medium onion, finely chopped
Salt and pepper
½ teaspoon crushed red pepper
½ teaspoon chopped rosemary
4 garlic cloves, minced
½ pound orecchiette or other short dried pasta
¼ cup roughly chopped flat-leaf parsley
Grated pecorino for serving

Put the drained chickpeas, the onion, carrot, bay leaf, and rosemary in a large saucepan and add cold water just to cover. Bring to a boil, reduce the heat to maintain a simmer, skim any rising foam, and cook gently for 30 minutes. Add 1 tablespoon salt and continue cooking until the chickpeas are tender, about 30 minutes more. Remove from the heat and let the chickpeas cool in their liquid. (The chickpeas can be cooked up to 2 days in advance, cooled, and refrigerated in their liquid.)

Put the olive oil in a wide skillet over medium-high heat, add the chopped onion, and cook until softened, about 5 minutes, letting the onion brown slightly. Season generously with salt and black pepper, then stir in the crushed red pepper, rosemary, and garlic.

Drain the chickpeas, reserving their liquid. Add 2 cups of the chickpeas and 1 cup of the cooking liquid to the onion, stir to coat, and simmer over medium heat for 2 to 3 minutes. (Reserve the extra chickpeas and liquid for another purpose.) Taste and adjust the seasoning if necessary—the mixture should be highly seasoned.

Meanwhile, bring a pot of well-salted water to a boil. Add the pasta and cook just until quite al dente. Drain the pasta, reserving about ½ cup of the pasta water, and add to the chickpeas. Raise the heat to medium-high and cook for about 2 minutes more, stirring to make a beany-starchy sauce in the bottom of the pan; add a little pasta water as necessary to keep the pasta moist.

Turn off the heat and stir in the parsley, then transfer to shallow soup bowls. Serve with freshly grated pecorino and a cruet of good fruity olive oil.

MAKES 4 TO 6 SERVINGS

Jamaican Split Pea Stew

My friend Michael came back from Jamaica with the happy memory of a savory stew he had eaten there, made with yellow split peas, some salted pigs' tails, and a few spices. He cooked it for me, knowing it was right up my alley, and it was spectacular. Here is my version of his dish. Since the salted pigs' tails were not an option, I used fresh pork belly and a fresh pig's foot instead—most butchers here have these. These gelatinous cuts give the stew its desired creamy consistency.

1 pound fresh pork belly, skin on
1 fresh pig's foot (about 1 pound)
Salt
2 cups yellow split peas, picked over for stones and debris and rinsed
1 large onion, halved
2 bay leaves
4 whole cloves
½ teaspoon pepper

6 allspice berries
1 Scotch bonnet pepper
A large thyme sprig
1 tablespoon grated or minced garlic
6 cups water
2 cups coconut milk
4 large russet potatoes, peeled and cut into 2-inch chunks
4 large carrots, cut into 2-inch chunks
4 scallions, chopped

Season the pork belly and pig's foot generously with salt and put them in a large soup pot. Add water just to cover and bring to a boil, then lower the heat and simmer for 30 minutes.

Add the split peas to the pot. Press a bay leaf against each onion half and secure it with 2 cloves. Add the onion, black pepper, allspice berries, Scotch bonnet pepper, thyme, garlic, water, and coconut milk to the pot and bring to a boil. Skim any rising foam, then reduce the heat to a gentle simmer, partially cover, and simmer for about 1 hour, or until the meat is tender and the split peas are mushy and falling apart. Fish out the pork belly, chop it into rough 2-inch pieces, and return it to the pot.

Add the potatoes and carrots (and a little more water if the stew seems too thick) and cook for 20 minutes more, or until the vegetables are tender. Check the seasoning and add salt if necessary.

Serve the stew in large soup bowls, sprinkled with the scallions.

MAKES 6 TO 8 SERVINGS

The stew is even better the next day, but it will have thickened substantially. Add a little water to the pot when reheating it.

Cowboy Beans with Bacon

Pinto beans are good, cheap, hearty fare—cowboy food. But they are actually some of the best-tasting dried beans, with a natural sweetness. These plain ones make a great meal on a plate with a chunk of cornbread, the way I first had them years ago while working on a cattle ranch. It was deliberately a plate, not a bowl, and they were meant to be eaten with a fork, not a spoon. So said the cook. Always cook your beans at a bare simmer, and be sure to keep the liquid level no more than 1 inch above the level of the beans. This keeps the beans from falling apart and concentrates the flavor of the "gravy," or bean broth, so it's not thin or watery.

1 pound (about 2 cups) dried pinto beans, picked over for stones and debris and rinsed
1 small onion, halved
A bay leaf

¾ pound slab bacon
1 tablespoon salt
1 tablespoon paprika
¼ teaspoon cayenne

Put the beans in a soup pot and add the onion, bay leaf, and bacon. Add water to cover by 1 inch and bring to a boil. Skim any rising foam, then reduce the heat to maintain a bare simmer, partially cover the pot, and cook for 1 hour, stirring occasionally.

Stir in the salt, paprika, and cayenne and continue simmering until the beans are soft and creamy and the broth is lightly thickened, 30 minutes to 1 hour more.

Remove the bacon and roughly chop, then return it to the pot. Taste and adjust the seasoning.   MAKES 4 TO 6 SERVINGS

NOTE: The beans can be prepared up to 2 days ahead, cooled, and refrigerated in their liquid; reheat to serve, adding a little water if necessary.

Greetings from the
Clean Plate Club.

Black Beans with Chorizo and Squid

This spicy dish of black beans and squid is both dramatic-looking and whimsical. I've always been fond of white beans and calamari in salads and pastas. Having only black beans on hand one day was serendipitous. It turns out that black bean broth has a richness (and color) uncannily similar to squid ink—a sensational discovery. Chorizo, garlic, olive oil, and hot pepper also play an important role in this success story.

FOR THE BEANS

1 cup dried black beans, picked over for stones and debris and rinsed

1 medium onion, halved and each half stuck with a clove

1 medium carrot

A bay leaf

A small rosemary sprig

Salt

FOR THE SQUID

1 pound cleaned squid bodies and tentacles

Salt and pepper

2 tablespoons extra virgin olive oil

¼ pound Spanish chorizo, cut into ½-inch dice

2 garlic cloves, thinly sliced

½ teaspoon crushed red pepper, or more to taste

¼ cup thinly sliced scallions

2 tablespoons chopped flat-leaf parsley

½ teaspoon grated lemon zest

2 tablespoons lemon juice

½ cup herbed bread crumbs (see page 205; optional)

Put the beans, onion, carrot, bay leaf, and rosemary in a large saucepan, add cold water just to cover, and bring to a boil. Reduce the heat to maintain a simmer, skim any rising foam, and cook gently for 30 minutes. Add 1 tablespoon salt and continue cooking until the beans are tender, about 30 minutes more. Remove from the heat and let the beans cool in their liquid. (The beans can be cooked up to 2 days in advance and refrigerated in their liquid.)

When ready to serve, reheat the beans by combining them in a saucepan with 1 cup of their cooking liquid and simmering them over medium heat to reduce and thicken the bean broth. Taste and adjust the seasoning. Keep warm.

Slice the squid bodies crosswise into 1-inch pieces; split any larger clusters of tentacles in half. Rinse the squid, drain in a colander, and pat dry. Spread out on a plate or baking sheet and season generously with salt and black pepper.

continued

Squid sizzling with
chorizo, garlic, and
hot pepper.

Heat the olive oil in a large skillet over medium-high heat. Add the chorizo and cook for a minute or so to release some of the (tasty) fat, then add the garlic and crushed red pepper and let sizzle for 10 seconds. Raise the heat to high, add the squid, and cook, stirring constantly, until the squid is puffed and just cooked through, about 2 minutes. Remove from the heat and stir in the scallions, parsley, and lemon zest and juice.

Spoon the warm beans onto a platter. Top with the squid and all the juices from the pan. Garnish with the bread crumbs if you like.   MAKES 4 TO 6 SERVINGS

TOMATOES

In places where tomatoes are part of a daily ritual—Italy, for instance—they are grown to full sweetness instead of harvested early for better transport, as they so often are here. In Sicily, farmers and home gardeners take their tomatoes seriously enough to make *estratto*—the divinely concentrated sun-dried tomato paste—and to can enough tomatoes to last the whole family until the following season.

Sadly, too few people today know what a ripe, just-picked summer tomato tastes like. The demand for tomatoes year-round has meant the proliferation of hothouse tomato horticulture. A multitude of tomato varieties, all of which look shiny and perfect on the outside, with true tomato color, are sold in clusters as vine-ripened. But cut one open, and the interior is pale, mushy, and tasteless—an imitation. A *faux-mato*. Even the colorful heirloom varieties that command exorbitant prices are now often grown in hothouses.

So, I may just be spitting into the wind, but I'd like to encourage people to join the expanding ranks of fellow diners who have learned (or never forgot) that real tomatoes are at their best for a splendid but fleeting moment at the end of the summer. Is there anything more disappointing—even in Italy—than a Caprese salad of good mozzarella paired with a pitiful excuse for a tomato?

August may seem like too long to wait, but you should. If it sounds like I'm saying you can only have truly great tomato salads in late summer, and for only a few weeks, well, yes. I am.

But off season, when you need tomatoes for a sauce, choose organic ones packed in jars rather than cans.

Iced Tomato Soup

Perfectly beautiful tomatoes may not always be the best ones. Often it's the gnarly, misshapen, split-topped tomatoes that are the sweetest. You can also seek out the nearly overripe must-sell-today tomatoes that can often be found discounted at farmers' markets. These are perfect for this kind of chilled soup, a no-cook delight that is best made at the end of summer, when tomatoes are at their sweetest. It's so good you could drink it by the glass, but for a more substantial version, I float an avocado toast topped with a colorful pepper relish in the center of each bowl.

FOR THE SOUP

3 pounds ripe red tomatoes,
    cored and diced
4 large garlic cloves, sliced
1 tablespoon salt, or to taste
1/4 cup extra virgin olive oil
2 tablespoons sherry vinegar
Pepper
Generous pinch of cayenne

FOR THE PEPPER RELISH

1 cup finely diced bell peppers,
    preferably a mix of colors

1/2 cup finely diced sweet onion,
    such as Vidalia
Salt and pepper
2 tablespoons extra virgin olive oil
1 tablespoon sherry vinegar

6 thin slices baguette
    (cut on a long diagonal), toasted
1 garlic clove
1 firm but ripe avocado, halved,
    pitted, peeled, and thickly sliced
Salt and pepper
2 tablespoons chopped flat-leaf parsley
2 tablespoons chopped chives

To make the soup, put the tomatoes and garlic in a nonreactive bowl and sprinkle with the salt. Add the olive oil, vinegar, black pepper to taste, and the cayenne and mix well. Leave to macerate for at least 15 minutes, or up to an hour.

Pulse the tomatoes in a food processor or blender until just crushed. Pass through a strainer or food mill into a bowl to remove the skins and seeds, pressing well to obtain all the juices. You should have about 5 cups. Add enough

ice water to make 6 cups. Stir well, taste, and adjust the seasoning. Chill the bowl in a larger bowl of ice for 15 minutes, or refrigerate for up to several hours.

About 30 minutes before serving, make the pepper relish: Put the bell peppers and onion in a small bowl and season with salt and black pepper. Add the olive oil and vinegar and mix well; set aside.

To serve, rub each toast lightly with garlic. Top the toasts with thick slices of avocado and season with salt and black pepper. Place an avocado toast in each bowl and ladle in about 1 cup of chilled soup. Garnish each toast with a generous spoonful of the pepper relish and a sprinkling of the parsley and chives.

MAKES 6 SERVINGS

Just-Picked Tomatoes with Salt

I know a family that has a small vegetable garden in an allotment outside the city. In the shed where they keep essential gardening tools is a saltshaker. The recipe is fairly obvious: Pick a tomato still warm from the sun, cut it in half equatorially, and sprinkle the cut sides with salt. Eat with your hands. First one half and then the other. Repeat. Then put the saltshaker back on the shelf.

Turkish Spoon Salad

This classic Turkish salad is designed to be eaten with a spoon, hence the name. A welcome part of any mezze offering, or very nice served alongside grilled meat, this spicy salad finds its acidity in three ways—a Turkish trinity, if you like—lemon juice, sumac (a sour ground seasoning used thoughout the Middle East), and pomegranate molasses (which sounds as though it would be sweet, but in fact is predominantly sour). Crumbled dried mint is actually preferred in Turkey, but some cooks like to add fresh leaves too. The salad is traditionally made with walnuts; my twist also includes pistachios. My friend Gamze from Istanbul insists that each ingredient in this salad be chopped very fine.

1½ pounds ripe tomatoes
1 small red onion, finely chopped
½ cup chopped fresh mint
½ teaspoon crumbled dried mint
1 tablespoon sumac
½ teaspoon crushed red pepper
Salt
¼ cup pomegranate molasses

Juice of ½ lemon
¼ cup olive oil
1 cup walnuts, soaked in ice water for
    10 minutes, drained, and finely chopped
3 tablespoons pistachios, toasted and
    chopped
½ cup pomegranate seeds

Halve the tomatoes, remove the centers and seeds, and save for another use. Finely chop the tomato flesh and place in a serving bowl. Add the onion, fresh and dried mint, sumac, crushed red pepper, and salt to taste and mix together.

To make the vinaigrette, whisk together the pomegranate molasses, lemon juice, and olive oil in a small bowl. Stir into the tomato mixture. Taste and adjust the seasoning.

Top the salad with the walnuts, pistachios, and pomegranate seeds and serve.

MAKES 4 SERVINGS

Tomato Chutney

I have learned about all kinds of chutney from my friend and cooking companion Niloufer, who has a sublime recipe for Parsi Tomato Chutney, chock-full of tomatoes, spices, and hot pepper, in her book *My Bombay Kitchen*. She makes an enormous batch of it annually, enough to fill a hundred jars. It is like a savory tomato marmalade with a kick, sweet and hot. Of course, there are many more uses than just with traditional Indian fare. A spoonful will enhance almost any Western dish you can think of. Here is my version of her recipe.

3 pounds ripe tomatoes, chopped
1/2 cup finely slivered ginger
1/4 cup thinly sliced garlic
1 1/2 cups apple cider vinegar
1 cup golden raisins
1 cup packed brown sugar
1 cup granulated sugar

6 small dried hot red chiles
1/2 teaspoon cayenne
1/2 teaspoon ground cloves
12 black peppercorns
1 teaspoon kalonji (nigella) seeds
1 teaspoon black mustard seeds
1 teaspoon salt

Put everything in a nonreactive heavy-bottomed pot and bring to a boil. Reduce the heat and simmer, stirring vigilantly, until the mixture has thickened to the consistency of a thick jam or marmalade, about 1 hour. Let cool.

Store the chutney, well sealed, in the fridge. It keeps for months, but you'll no doubt employ some immediately and give some away. Or, if you like, ladle the chutney into sterilized half-pint jars and go through the process of canning the old-fashioned way.   MAKES 3 PINTS

Cherry Tomatoes and Angel Hair Pasta

This may be one of the easiest dishes imaginable, but it's worth making only if you've got truly sweet, ripe cherry tomatoes. Often cherry tomatoes are colorful yet flavorless. If you get them at a farmers' market, you can ask for a taste before committing. Backyard cherry tomatoes, grown in a hot sunny spot, usually have an intense sweetness. Angel hair pasta cooks in a bare few minutes, so you can make this on the spur of a summer moment. There are a couple of ways to approach the dish. You can simply dress the halved tomatoes and toss them raw with the hot pasta (they will stay firmish and salad-like), or sauté them briefly before adding them. Both ways are lovely.

Cut a pound of cherry tomatoes into halves or quarters and combine with 2 minced small garlic cloves, a good pinch of crushed red pepper, and a handful of roughly chopped basil, then add 3 to 4 tablespoons fruity extra virgin olive oil and mix together. Add a drop of red wine vinegar if you like. Let the mixture sit for 5 to 10 minutes.

Cook 3/4 pound angel hair pasta in boiling salted water, then drain and toss with the seasoned cherry tomatoes. Or, if you prefer to cook the cherry tomatoes, just heat the dressed tomatoes in a skillet for 3 to 4 minutes and toss with the pasta. Garnish the pasta with a little more chopped basil. If you want cheese, sprinkle with coarsely grated ricotta salata.   MAKES 4 SERVINGS

I like to use angel hair pasta for its delicacy. Fresh linguine would be another choice.

Tomato Salad Sandwich

I can appreciate the classic tomato sandwich on white bread with Hellmann's or Miracle Whip, but given the choice, this is what I really want. It is essentially my version of that Provençal favorite, *pan bagnat*. If you want a good one, you've got to make it yourself. Prepare a well-seasoned salad with ripe tomatoes, olive oil, garlic, capers, anchovy, and basil, then put it on a split roll. The sandwich is quickly made, but it must stand for at least an hour. That way the tasty juices permeate the bread in a soggy, heavenly way. Eat it outside on a sunny day—on a grassy knoll, on the beach, on a park bench. Of course, this sandwich could be deconstructed to become a salad on a plate instead of a roll.

1 pound ripe tomatoes, preferably assorted colors and sizes

Salt and pepper

2 garlic cloves, finely minced

2 anchovy fillets, rinsed and roughly chopped

1 teaspoon small capers, rinsed

3 tablespoons extra virgin olive oil

2 teaspoons red wine vinegar

Pinch of crushed red pepper

12 basil leaves

A few tender flat-leaf parsley leaves

4 French rolls or 1 long baguette

Cut larger tomatoes into thick slices or wedges and smaller ones into halves, and put in a salad bowl. Season with salt and black pepper.

Add the garlic, anchovies, capers, olive oil, vinegar, crushed red pepper, and half the basil leaves, torn or chopped. Gently toss with the tomatoes and leave for 5 to 10 minutes.

Split the rolls or baguette lengthwise. Spoon the tomato salad, with its juices, onto the bottoms of the rolls or the bottom half of the baguette. Lay the remaining basil leaves and the parsley leaves over the tomatoes. Replace the top(s) and press lightly. If using a baguette, cut it into 4 pieces.

Cover the sandwiches with a clean dishtowel and leave for an hour or so before serving. MAKES 4 SERVINGS

Multicolored Heirloom Tomato Tian

In the south of France, the word *tian* is the name of an earthenware baking dish. But it also refers to the contents of the baking dish—for example, the traditional Provençal tian of summer vegetables. Eggplant, zucchini, onion, and tomato slices are arranged in the dish like overlapping roof tiles, anointed with garlic and olive oil, and baked so the flavors mingle and concentrate.

One day I returned from the market with ripe tomatoes of every color, so I decided to make an all-tomato tian. If you can't get multicolored ripe tomatoes, you can use all red ones, but don't attempt to make this out of season.

A tomato tian tastes good paired with all kinds of things. Serve alongside whatever you are grilling: a lovely piece of grilled fish, some spicy sausages, or a platter of lamb chops. Or simply by itself, with a drizzle of the oily, garlicky pan juices, or with a few arugula leaves, perhaps a few black olives, and a bit of feta cheese.

Cut 4 pounds of ripe heirloom tomatoes into ½-inch slices. Spread the slices in a single layer on a large cutting board or a baking sheet and season with salt and pepper. Pour ¼ inch of olive oil into an earthenware baking dish, approximately 9 by 12 inches. Scatter some chopped garlic over the the oil, about 6 medium cloves; scatter over a dozen basil leaves as well. Beginning at one end of the dish, make a row of overlapping tomato slices, standing them upright on edge, not flat (once you get a few rows going, it's easier to accomplish this). Continue adding slices, alternating colors at random, until the baking dish is full.

Put the tian on a baking sheet, place it on the top shelf of a 375-degree oven, and bake, uncovered, for 45 to 60 minutes, until the top is nicely colored and the tomatoes have collapsed. Allow the tian to cool completely. (Sometimes a tian will throw a lot of juice. Spoon off the excess and save it for another cooking use.) The tian should be eaten at room temperature; it actually tastes best a few hours out of the oven, or even the next day. Keep it in a cool spot, but don't refrigerate it.   MAKES 8 TO 10 SERVINGS

Shrimp with Tomatoes and Feta

This take on a traditional Greek recipe is sensational prepared in summer with sweet ripe tomatoes and wild-caught fresh shrimp from Georgia, North Carolina, or the Gulf. Elemental flavors—olive oil, garlic, feta, and oregano—carry the dish. Some add a little ouzo, but I'd rather drink it on the side. Serve as a main course or in small portions as an appetizer, taverna-style.

5 tablespoons extra virgin olive oil
3 large shallots, finely diced
4 garlic cloves, grated or minced
Salt and pepper
2 pounds large ripe tomatoes
½ teaspoon crushed red pepper

1½ pounds large shrimp, peeled and deveined
¼ pound Greek feta cheese
½ teaspoon dried oregano
2 tablespoons roughly chopped mint

Put ¼ cup of the olive oil in a wide skillet over medium heat. When the oil is hot, add the shallots and garlic, season with salt and black pepper, and cook, stirring, until softened, 5 to 8 minutes; lower the heat as necessary to keep the mixture from browning. Remove from the heat and set aside.

Fill a pot with water and bring to a boil. Add the whole tomatoes and cook for about 1 minute, just until the skins loosen. Immediately plunge the tomatoes into a bowl of cold water to cool, then drain. With a paring knife, core the tomatoes and slip off the skins. Cut into thick wedges.

Heat the oven to 400 degrees. Set the skillet of shallots and garlic over medium-high heat. Add the tomato wedges and season with salt, pepper, and the crushed red pepper. Cook, stirring, until the mixture is juicy and tomatoes have softened, about 10 minutes. Transfer to a shallow earthenware baking dish.

Put the shrimp in a medium bowl. Add the remaining tablespoon of olive oil, season the shrimp with salt and pepper, and stir to coat. Arrange the shrimp over the tomato mixture in one layer. Crumble the cheese over the top and sprinkle with the oregano.

Bake for 10 to 12 minutes, until the tomatoes are bubbling and cheese has browned slightly. Remove from the oven and let rest for 5 minutes. Sprinkle with the mint and serve.   MAKES 4 TO 6 SERVINGS

Fast Fresh Tomato Sauce

Long-simmered tomato sauces have their place, but this one tastes much brighter, and a lot more like fresh tomatoes. You must use dense, sweet, late-summer specimens here. This makes a manageable small batch of sauce that is ready to use in less than 30 minutes. It has a lightness that complements delicate pastas and vegetable dishes, flavorful but not overwhelming.

5 pounds tomatoes

¾ teaspoon salt

2 tablespoons olive oil

1 tablespoon tomato paste

1 garlic clove, halved

A basil sprig

A bay leaf

Cut the tomatoes horizontally in half. Squeeze out the seeds and discard, or save for another purpose (like making beef broth). Press the cut side of each tomato against the large holes of a box grater and grate the tomato flesh into a bowl. Discard the skins. You will have about 4 cups of dense tomato pulp.

Put the tomato pulp in a wide saucepan over high heat and add the salt, olive oil, tomato paste, garlic, basil, and bay leaf. Bring to a boil, then lower the heat to a brisk simmer and reduce the sauce by almost half, stirring occasionally, for 10 to 12 minutes; you should have a medium-thick sauce that coats a spoon. Taste and adjust the salt. Remove from the heat and let cool.

The sauce will keep for up to 5 days in the refrigerator, or it can be frozen.

MAKES ABOUT 3 CUPS

A handy low-tech method for a fast, fresh tomato sauce.

SWEET PEPPERS

What we call sweet peppers are a nonspicy cultivar of the species *Capsicum annuum* (native to Central and South America, where they predominantly exist as hot chiles). They are often called bell peppers, owing to their shape, but are also known simply as capsicums in a number of English-speaking countries. The bell peppers we encounter now have no capsaicin (the stuff that gives hot chiles their bite), or very little; they are fleshy, juicy, and sweet, delicious raw, sautéed, or roasted. Bells come in assorted colors—you can find bright red, orange, and yellow ones at most supermarkets. Green (unripe) bell peppers have mostly crunch to offer, but some people enjoy them cooked. The supermarket hothouse peppers from Holland and elsewhere are usually waiting for you year-round; perfect specimens, yes, but with flavor a secondary consideration.

The true season for peppers is late summer, just as for tomatoes. They do best in a hot climate, standing up to the harsh sun, taking their time. Some of the best, sweetest peppers are harvested in August and September. All peppers are green in their infancy, turning red or orange as they begin to ripen. At the farmers' market these days, other quite colorful varieties of sweet pepper are available—long Italian types like Corno di Toro, some with playful names like Gypsy, Lipstick, Orange Blaze, and Carmen. Some are the palest green, others are violet, brick-hued, or even dark as chocolate.

Sweet peppers in season are simply delightful—thinly sliced for salads and pastas, or stuffed and baked. It's no trouble at all to roast and peel sweet peppers for antipasti, a worthwhile habit to acquire. A freshly roasted sweet pepper, simply paired with good fresh mozzarella or ricotta, is welcome and gorgeous.

For perfect roasted
peppers, use a
clever tool like this
asador, a stovetop
grill, which fits
over a gas burner.

Fire-Roasted Peppers

Roasting peppers on a stovetop burner or over hot coals is easier than you might think, and a much fresher-tasting alternative to those from a can or jar. Get out your tongs and place your peppers straight on the flame (or over the coals) or on an asador, then cook, turning them, until the skin is completely blackened and blistered all over—it should take 10 minutes. Put them on a plate to cool. (Some recommend putting the blackened peppers in a bag or covered container to steam, but I never do, because the residual heat cooks them too much for my taste.) Once they are cool, cut them lengthwise in half, remove the stems, and scrape away the seeds with a paring knife; then flip them over and scrape away the skin. Don't worry about a few charred flecks, and don't even think about rinsing them: You'd lose all the tasty juices and smoky aroma, and have waterlogged peppers to boot. Once roasted, they will keep for a week, refrigerated, so you can slice them on demand for salads, antipasti, and pizzas.

Roasted Pepper Salad

For the simplest roasted pepper salad, cut the pepper flesh into strips and sprinkle with salt and pepper. Toss with a drizzle of fruity olive oil and a few drops of red wine vinegar. Add torn basil leaves and serve at room temperature.

Roasted Pepper and Walnut Spread

This is a rendition of the spicy Middle Eastern dip called *muhammara*, marrying roasted peppers with toasted walnuts and a touch of pomegranate molasses for its puckery sour flavor. I keep a little jar of the rust-colored stuff in the fridge, ready to spread on crisp grilled flatbread. Pair this spread with the equally savory Smoky Turkish Eggplant (page 268) for a cocktail party.

2 medium red bell peppers,
    roasted, seeded, and peeled
    (see Fire-Roasted Peppers, page 253)
½ cup walnuts, lightly toasted
1 garlic clove, minced
1 teaspoon pimentón
1 teaspoon sweet paprika
½ teaspoon cumin seeds,
    toasted and ground

½ teaspoon coriander seeds,
    toasted and ground
½ teaspoon salt, or to taste
⅛ teaspoon cayenne
2 tablespoons extra virgin olive oil
1 tablespoon walnut oil (optional)
1 tablespoon pomegranate molasses

Cut the peppers into long thin strips, then cut them crosswise into very small dice. Chop the pepper flesh with a large knife (as if chopping parsley) as fine as possible, almost to a puree. Transfer to a bowl.

Chop the walnuts as fine as possible and add to the peppers. Add the garlic, pimentón, paprika, cumin, coriander, salt, and cayenne. Whisk in the olive oil, walnut oil, if using, and pomegranate molasses and continue beating for a minute or so to meld the ingredients. (Or, if you're in a hurry, put everything in a food processor and give it a whirl. Do keep the texture rough. The color won't be as vibrant.) Leave to rest for a few minutes, then taste and adjust the seasoning.   MAKES 1½ CUPS

NOTE: To store, pack the mixture into a small jar and drizzle a film of olive oil over the top. It keeps refrigerated for up to a week.

Pepper Salad with Feta

A fine rustic snack is a good piece of sheep's-milk feta cheese anointed with olive oil. There is something primal about the two combined flavors. Sometimes I make a little meal of it. Not much else is needed other than bread and wine. But in season, sliced ripe peppers, sweet onions, and cherry tomatoes are a welcome addition, seasoned aggressively with garlic, hot pepper, and oregano. That's my idea of a simple Greek salad.

1 red bell pepper, very thinly sliced
1 yellow bell pepper, very thinly sliced
1 large red onion, very thinly sliced
A handful of cherry tomatoes, halved
2 garlic cloves, minced
Pinch of crushed red pepper
Salt and pepper

3 tablespoons extra virgin olive oil
2 tablespoons red wine vinegar
1 tablespoon chopped flat-leaf parsley
1 tablespoon chopped basil
1 tablespoon chopped mint
3 ounces feta cheese, in rough chunks
Pinch of dried oregano, wild if possible

Put the bell peppers, onion, tomatoes, garlic, and crushed red pepper in a large salad bowl. Season generously with salt and black pepper. Add the olive oil and vinegar and toss well. Add the parsley, basil, and mint and toss again. Scatter the feta cheese over the top of the salad, sprinkle with the dried oregano, and serve.

MAKES 4 SERVINGS

Peperonata

Similar to eggplant caponata flavorwise, this is a savory stew of colorful sweet peppers and red onion, slowly cooked in olive oil, spiked with vinegar and capers. Usually served at room temperature, peperonata can be part of an antipasto, paired with fresh mozzarella or good canned tuna, but it can also be a perky accompaniment to just about any kind of fish, meat, or fowl.

2 tablespoons extra virgin olive oil
1 red bell pepper, very thinly sliced
1 yellow bell pepper, very thinly sliced
1 large red onion, very thinly sliced
Salt and pepper
2 garlic cloves, finely chopped
1 teaspoon capers, roughly chopped

Pinch of crushed red pepper
2 tablespoons red wine vinegar
1 tablespoon chopped flat-leaf parsley
1 tablespoon chopped basil
Pinch of dried oregano
A handful of good olives (optional)

Put the olive oil in a large skillet over medium-high heat. When the oil is hot, add the bell peppers and onion, season generously with salt and black pepper, and cook, stirring frequently, until softened, about 5 to 7 minutes. Add the garlic, capers, crushed red pepper, and vinegar and cook for 1 minute more. Taste and adjust the seasoning.

Transfer the peperonata to a serving platter and sprinkle with the parsley, basil, and dried oregano. Serve at room temperature, garnished with the olives if desired.   MAKES 4 TO 6 SERVINGS

NOTE: It's a good idea to make peperonata a day or two in advance of serving so the flavors can meld.

Baked Peppers with Feta and Bread Crumbs

Sweet peppers seem destined for stuffing, given their shape and hollow interior. Cooks around the globe fill them with cheese, meat, or rice. Some versions are highly seasoned and complex, while others are dull and stodgy—I was raised on the latter, sad to say. But now there are all kinds of delightful sweet peppers available, in every color and size. I found some diminutive, colorful Gypsy peppers at the market one day and came up with this dish, which actually qualifies as dainty and delicate. They're especially nice served with Melted Spinach (page 178).

6 thick slices day-old French bread, crust removed

3 tablespoons olive oil

3 garlic cloves, grated or minced

3 tablespoons chopped flat-leaf parsley

2 teaspoons chopped thyme

1 teaspoon chopped rosemary

1 ounce Parmesan, grated

Salt and pepper

6 very small sweet peppers (see headnote; about 1 pound)

6 ounces mild feta cheese, crumbled

Heat the oven to 350 degrees. Cut the bread into 1-inch cubes and pulse in a food processor in batches to make coarse, soft crumbs. (It should yield about 3 cups.)

Toss the crumbs with the olive oil and spread on a baking sheet. Bake, stirring often, until the crumbs are crisp and barely browned, about 15 minutes.

Put the baked crumbs in a bowl and add the garlic, parsley, thyme, rosemary, and Parmesan. Season with salt and black pepper and toss well. Set aside.

Cut the peppers lengthwise in half and remove the cores and seeds. Place skin side down in a shallow baking dish in one layer. Season lightly with salt. Fill each pepper half with about 3 tablespoons crumbled feta and press in the cheese with your fingers. With a spoon, divide the seasoned crumbs evenly among the pepper halves.

Bake for about 30 minutes, until the crumbs are golden and the cheese is softened. Serve warm from the baking dish.   MAKES 6 SERVINGS

EGGPLANTS

Eggplant is cooked and cherished throughout Asia, the Mediterranean, and the Middle East, and no wonder: it has wonderful versatility, whether miso-glazed, crumbed and fried, or smoked over hot embers and pounded to a creamy paste. It has long been admired by vegetarians, who are lured by its substantial "meaty" texture, its ability to both absorb and contribute flavor, its mushroom-like qualities. And many an erstwhile carnivore has subsisted on eggplant sandwiches, cutlets, and pasta sauces during times of scarcity or impoverishment.

At the height of the season, eggplants arrive at the market in all shapes, sizes, and hues. Some are pear-shaped, fat, shiny, and black; others are snakelike, a foot long and deep purple or shocking bright fuchsia. There are eggplant skins with magenta and white striations (one such variety is called Graffiti). Some are pale violet, some pale green, some mustard yellow. Some are truly egg-shaped and ivory white. And there are tiny round pumpkin-colored ones no bigger than an inch in diameter, used for curries or pickles.

The large purple-black generic eggplant stocked at most supermarkets will get the job done, but smaller ones will likely be sweeter and contain fewer seeds. In any case, with whatever type of eggplant you choose, unblemished, firm, and shiny is what you want; this signifies freshness.

Japanese Eggplant with Miso

Japanese eggplants are long and slender. I like them split down the middle and smeared with a nutty, salty miso glaze, then baked until soft and nicely browned. The flavors play well together, like old friends.

4 small Japanese eggplants
Salt
1 tablespoon white miso
1 tablespoon red miso
1 tablespoon sake
1 tablespoon mirin
2 teaspoons soy sauce

1 teaspoon toasted sesame oil
2 teaspoons grated fresh ginger
1 tablespoon sugar
2 large egg yolks
2 scallions, thinly sliced
Toasted sesame seeds for garnish

Heat the oven to 450 degrees. Split the eggplants lengthwise in half, leaving the stems attached. Sprinkle the cut sides lightly with salt and place cut side up on a baking sheet.

In a small bowl, stir together the white miso, red miso, sake, mirin, soy sauce, sesame oil, ginger, sugar, and egg yolks. The mixture will have the consistency of a thick batter. Spread it generously over the entire surface of the cut sides of the eggplants.

Place the pan on the top rack of the oven and bake for 15 to 20 minutes, until the eggplants are tender and the miso coating has begun to bubble and brown. If necessary, run the eggplants under the broiler for a minute or two. Garnish with the scallions and toasted sesame seeds.   MAKES 4 TO 6 SERVINGS

Italian Grilled Eggplant

While this is one of the simplest, most direct of recipes, it couldn't be more satisfying. The catch, if there is one, is that you want eggplants that are firm and on the smaller side, as these will have sweeter flesh and be less likely to have big fully formed seeds. Look for them at farmers' markets and Asian produce stands.

Making this dish is just a matter of painting eggplant slices (not too thick, not too thin) with olive oil, seasoning them with salt and pepper, and grilling them over coals until golden. The fire beneath them should be brisk so the slices really sear and brown beautifully. Alternatively, use a stovetop grill pan. The heat should be such that it takes no more than 2 minutes per side. Serve these as a first course with a squeeze of lemon and finely chopped basil and parsley.

Fried Eggplant "Sandwich"

To make these sandwiched treats, peel an eggplant and slice into ½-inch rounds. Season the slices with salt and pepper, then coat them lightly in flour, dip in beaten egg, and coat in bread crumbs. Fry them gently in ½ inch of olive oil, turning once. Remove and drain briefly on paper towels.

Tuck a bit of mozzarella between pairs of fried slices and place on a baking sheet. Pop the sandwiches into a hot oven for a few minutes to melt the cheese. Sprinkle with salt and crushed red pepper. Eat the sandwiches while hot, holding them in a napkin. Or, for a fancier rendition, spoon some Fast Fresh Tomato Sauce (page 249) onto each plate, set a sandwich on top, and sprinkle with grated Parmesan and chopped basil.

Smoky Turkish Eggplant

I call this Turkish delight (though I'm also a fan of *leokum*, the famous Turkish sweet). Start by placing eggplants directly over a gas flame or hot coals and mercilessly charring the skin all over. This traditional technique guarantees creamy, slightly smoky eggplant flesh, perfect when paired with tahini, garlic, and yogurt for a savory spread. Olive oil, cumin, cayenne, and lemon will take care of the rest. Serve with pita or crudités.

3 medium eggplants (about 2 pounds)
Salt
½ cup plain yogurt
¼ cup tahini
2 tablespoons lemon juice
4 garlic cloves, smashed to a paste with a
   pinch of salt
⅛ teaspoon cayenne

½ teaspoon cumin seeds, toasted and
   coarsely ground
3 tablespoons olive oil
½ teaspoon paprika
1 tablespoon finely chopped flat-leaf
   parsley
1 tablespoon finely chopped mint
Warm pitas, for serving

Pierce the eggplants in several places with a fork or skewer. Place each one directly on a stovetop burner turned to high (or cook over a bed of hot coals) and allow the skin to blister and char, turning the eggplants with tongs, until the entire surface is blackened and they are completely soft, 10 to 12 minutes. Set aside until cool enough to handle.

Slice the eggplants lengthwise in half and lay cut side down on the cutting board. With a paring knife or your fingers, carefully remove and discard the burnt skin. Do not rinse the eggplant flesh—a few bits of remaining char are fine. Salt the flesh lightly, transfer to a colander, and let drain for 5 to 10 minutes, then squeeze gently to get rid of extraneous juices.

Transfer the eggplant to a food processor or blender. Add ½ teaspoon salt, the yogurt, tahini, lemon juice, garlic, and cayenne and blitz to obtain a creamy puree. (Or, for a more rustic spread, first chop the eggplant and then beat the mixture with a sturdy whisk instead.) Taste and adjust the seasoning. Transfer the mixture to a shallow serving bowl. Just before serving, stir together the cumin and olive oil and drizzle over the surface of the spread. Sprinkle with the paprika, parsley, and mint. Serve with warm pitas, cut into triangles.

MAKES ABOUT 3 CUPS

POTATOES

If I had to choose just one edible tuber (not that I would want to), it would have to be the potato. I am ever thankful to the ancient peoples of the Andes for domesticating this magnificent vegetable thousands of years ago. Although in North America only a few varieties are found to be commercially profitable, in Peru, the types of potato still number in the hundreds. It pleases me to think that when I finally make a pilgrimage there, I will never run out of a new potato to try, even if I stay a year.

It is startling to realize that, like so many New World foods we now take for granted, potatoes were unknown in Europe five hundred years ago. In their journey to the heart of so many cuisines and holiday meals, they have long been perceived as cheap, filling peasant food—as if that's a bad thing. But they're packed with nutrition and can be stored to eat throughout the year, making them a staple of sustenance. They are also completely, utterly delicious and comforting. And where would we be without potato salad, mashed potatoes, home fries, latkes, hash browns, or baked potatoes? Not to mention French fries and their mass appeal. Potatoes have simply become part of our genome. Contrary to their general usage as a side dish, I recommend potatoes on their own for a wonderful meal. Think steak and potatoes—just replace your steak with a nice green salad, and you have a perfect supper. Or have a potato gratin or Spanish tortilla, or perhaps new potatoes boiled in water as salty as the sea. Suffice it to say, in all spud-related matters, simplicity rules the day.

The Glorious Spanish Tortilla

A Spanish tortilla is a savory cake made of potatoes and onions stewed in olive oil, then bound with egg and fried in a pan. (The ratio of potato to egg sets this apart from a frittata, but not by much.) Although it might be pushing it to call a tortilla ethereal, it certainly is to me. A good fresh tortilla is hard to find in tapas bars these days, even in Spain, where more often than not they get reheated in the microwave. It's a great bite to have with friends and drinks, with other tapas or not, or you can serve a wedge for lunch with a salad.

4 large russet potatoes
2 medium onions
2 cups olive oil

Salt and pepper
8 medium eggs

Peel and slice the potatoes and onions into ⅛-inch rounds.

Warm the olive oil in a large deep skillet over medium-high heat. Add the potatoes and onions and simmer gently, without letting them brown, until soft, about 10 minutes. Carefully drain them in a colander set over a bowl, reserving the olive oil. Spread out the potatoes and onions on a baking sheet, season well with salt and pepper, and cool to room temperature.

Beat the eggs in a large bowl. Add the cooled potato-onion mixture and stir gently to incorporate. Let sit for 15 to 20 minutes to allow the flavors to meld.

Put 2 tablespoons of the reserved olive oil in a large cast-iron skillet over medium heat. When the oil is hot, pour in the egg mixture and cook gently for 5 minutes, tilting the pan now and then and lifting the edges to help the eggs set. Put a dinner plate over the top of the pan and carefully invert the tortilla onto the plate.

Add a little more oil to the pan, then slip the tortilla back into the pan to cook for 5 minutes on the second side. Flip the tortilla once more and cook for a few more minutes. Insert a small knife into the center of the tortilla to check for doneness—the knife should emerge clean. Put the tortilla on a serving platter and cool to room temperature. To serve, cut the tortilla into small wedges or squares.   MAKES 4 TO 6 SERVINGS

NOTE: The cooked potato and onion mixture is so good on its own, you will no doubt find other uses for it. The leftover olive oil can be saved and used again.

If you want a good tortilla, you'll have to make it yourself.

French Potato Salad

Generic mayo-based potato salad thrills me not one bit, but a French salad of warm sliced potatoes dressed with a good vinaigrette is a thing of beauty. For that matter, vinaigrette potato salads are also common in Germany, Italy, and Spain, and other places as well.

Salt and pepper
2 pounds medium yellow-fleshed potatoes, such as Yukon Gold or German Butterball
A bay leaf
A large thyme branch
1 small shallot, finely diced

2 garlic cloves, smashed to a paste with a little salt
¼ cup red wine vinegar
1 teaspoon Dijon mustard
2 anchovy fillets, pounded to a paste
⅓ cup olive oil
2 tablespoons thinly sliced chives

Bring a large pot of well-salted water to a boil. Add the potatoes, bay leaf, and thyme branch and cook at a brisk simmer until the potatoes are easily pierced with a skewer but still firm, about 30 minutes. Drain and let cool slightly.

While the potatoes are cooking, make the vinaigrette: Put the shallot and garlic in a small bowl and add the vinegar and a pinch of salt. Add the mustard and anchovies, then whisk in the olive oil.

Peel the potatoes and carefully cut into ¼-inch slices. Put the potatoes in a wide bowl and season with salt and pepper. Pour over the vinaigrette and gently toss, using your fingers to coat the potatoes well. Transfer the salad to a serving dish and sprinkle with the chives. MAKES 4 SERVINGS

Oh-so-versatile yellow-fleshed potatoes—good for salads and gratins; equally good panfried, boiled, or baked.

Classic Potato Gratin

I think it's a good idea to keep a sack of potatoes on hand so you can make a gratin whenever you get the urge. It's not so hard to do, simply a matter of slicing potatoes thin, layering them in a baking dish, and adding cream. Once you have the technique up your sleeve, you'll find the gratin a very useful addition to your dinner party repertoire. It's a dish with near-universal appeal, and there are virtually limitless variations, such as adding ham and cheese to this classic French *gratin dauphinois*; see the variation below.

3 pounds medium baking potatoes,
such as russets, Bintje, or
German Butterball

4 tablespoons butter, plus more for the
baking dish
Salt and pepper
2½ cups heavy cream, or as needed

Heat the oven to 375 degrees. Peel the potatoes and put them in cold water.

Smear a baking dish thickly with butter. My favorite gratin dish is a circular pan 14 inches in diameter and 2 inches deep. If you don't have a large dish, make 2 smaller gratins. Just make sure the dish is not too deep.

To assemble the gratin, place a cutting board on the counter between the bowl of potatoes and the baking dish. Using a mandoline or a very sharp knife, slice a few potatoes at a time as thin as possible. Quickly lay the potato slices in the bottom of the baking dish, overlapping them to make an even layer. Sprinkle lightly with salt and pepper. Slice a few more potatoes and make another layer. Continue in this fashion, seasoning each layer, until all the potatoes are used.

Pour the cream over the potatoes and tilt the pan to distribute it well. With your hands, push down on the top layer to even out the pile. The cream should just barely cover the potatoes; add a little more if necessary. Dot the surface with the butter.

Cover the dish tightly with foil and put it in the oven. Bake for 30 minutes. Remove the foil and return the pan to the oven for another 30 minutes or so to finish cooking the potatoes and turn the top of the gratin a crispy, deep golden brown. Let the gratin rest for 10 minutes before serving. (The gratin can also be cooled and left at room temperature for several hours, then reheated in a moderate oven.)　MAKES 6 TO 8 SERVINGS

Potato Gratin with Cheese and Ham

Obviously there are many other delicious ways to make a gratin. For a ham and cheese version, or a cheese-only version, sprinkle grated assertive cheese, such as Swiss Gruyère or raclette, or even Fontina, between each layer of potatoes, with or without some bits of ham. You'll need about 2 cups grated cheese and 1 cup diced ham.

Jansson's Temptation

A Swedish version, or a reasonable facsimile, can be achieved by scattering a few chopped anchovy fillets over each layer. The anchovy melts into the cream and adds a touch of umami. The flavor is fantastic. Not fishy at all.

Salt-Boiled New Potatoes

These extremely special spuds must be cooked in water as salty as the sea. Rather than penetrate them, the salt leaves a thin, white, flavorful film on the skins and gives the flesh a luscious creamy texture. The dish has been attributed to Irish salt miners working near Syracuse, New York, who would bring potatoes for their lunch and boil them in a salty brine. (My kind of lunch.) However, salt-boiled potatoes surely originated elsewhere. I reckon it may have been somewhere on the Peruvian coast.

You want small round "creamer" potatoes, 1½ inches in diameter, whether they are "new" or not. First get your salted water boiling. For a gallon of water, use about 2 cups kosher salt, and stir over the heat with a wooden spoon until it dissolves. Put in 3 to 4 pounds of potatoes and let them simmer briskly until they are tender when probed with a skewer. Drain the potatoes and put them back in the pot. Cover with a towel and leave them to steam for a few minutes. A lovely salt film will form. Eat the potatoes warm with melted butter or olive oil or with a spicy salsa. In the unlikely event you have potatoes left over, peel and slice them for a great potato salad.   MAKES 4 SERVINGS

Garlicky Pork and Potatoes

This is essentially a potato gratin topped with pork chops (or a roast). The potatoes are seasoned simply with salt, pepper, and a generous amount of chopped garlic and arranged neatly in an earthenware baking dish. Instead of cream, I use broth or water to moisten the potatoes; the fat from the pork adds sufficient richness. The long, slow roasting in the garlic-saturated pan juices makes potatoes that are beautifully crisp on the outside and tender on the inside. There's no denying that this is a hearty meal. Make sure you also have a crisp green salad.

4 thick pork shoulder chops
    (about 3 pounds), or a 3-pound
    pork shoulder roast
Salt and pepper
3 pounds medium yellow-fleshed potatoes,
    such as Yukon Gold, peeled and sliced
    ⅛ inch thick

2 tablespoons extra virgin olive oil
6 garlic cloves, chopped
About 4 cups Blond Chicken Broth
    (page 460) or water

Heat the oven to 450 degrees. Place the pork on a baking sheet and season generously all over with salt and pepper.

Put the sliced potatoes in a large bowl, add the olive oil, garlic, and salt and pepper to taste, and toss to coat. In a large shallow baking dish (big enough to hold the pork chops, if you are using chops, side by side), arrange the potato slices as for a gratin, overlapping them. Arrange the pork chops on top, or set the roast on the potatoes. Add enough broth to come halfway up the sides of the baking dish.

Cover the dish tightly with foil and bake for 20 minutes. Reduce the heat to 350 degrees and cook for 20 minutes more. Take off the foil and bake for 20 minutes, or until the potatoes have browned on top and the pork has crisped (see Note). Let rest for 10 minutes before serving.   MAKES 4 SERVINGS

NOTE: If necessary, remove the chops when done and let the potatoes brown a bit more on top. If using a pork shoulder roast, the interior temperature should be 130 degrees before resting (residual heat will cook it a bit more).

Mashed Potato Variations

The whole world loves mashed potatoes. Mention potato puree to a French person, and you'll hear them moan with pleasure. (Seriously, try it.) The French version is as good as that moan suggests—as smooth as satin and somewhat of a national obsession. In the south of France, you may find potatoes mashed with simmered garlic cloves and enriched with fruity olive oil rather than butter. Irish cooks add a quantity of chopped scallions in addition to good Irish butter for the mashed potatoes they call "champ." Classic American mashed potatoes are made with just salt, pepper, butter, and milk, but an elevated version adds sharp Cheddar. There are, of course, other ways to glorify the mash. One is to include other root vegetables along with the potatoes, such as celery root, turnips, or parsnips, in whatever proportion you prefer. I don't know how I feel about wasabi mashed potatoes, though.

Basic Mashed Potatoes

*2 pounds yellow-fleshed potatoes,
    such as Yukon Gold, peeled and
    cut into 1-inch chunks*
A bay leaf

Salt and pepper
4 tablespoons unsalted butter
½ cup heavy cream or half-and-half

Boil the potatoes wih the bay leaf in a large pot of well-salted water until tender, about 15 minutes. Drain the potatoes well, reserving 1 cup of the cooking liquid, and return to the pot. Cover and let stand for 10 minutes.

Pass the potatoes through a food mill or mash them by hand, and put them in the bowl of a stand mixer fitted with the whisk attachment (or put them in a large bowl and use a hand mixer). Beat for a minute or two to allow steam to escape, then beat in the butter and cream. Add enough of the reserved cooking liquid to achieve the desired consistency. Adjust the salt if necessary, add pepper to taste, and serve.   MAKES 4 SERVINGS

Scallion Mashed Potatoes

Add in ½ cup sliced or chopped scallions along with the butter and cream.

Olive Oil and Garlic Mashed Potatoes

Boil 8 peeled garlic cloves (or more, to taste) with the potatoes. Use ¼ cup good fruity extra virgin olive oil instead of the butter, and potato cooking water instead of the cream. (The soft garlic cloves are mashed along with the potatoes.)

Golden Panfried Potatoes

It is not so easy to make proper French fries at home, but these crispy, shallow-fried potatoes will satisfy the craving. Parboiling the potatoes is key to perfect potatoes without the need for the excessive amount of oil required for deep-frying. A sprinkle of sea salt and pepper is totally sufficient, but I like to finish these with persillade, the classic French garlic-and-parsley mixture.

3 pounds baking potatoes (any type), peeled and cut into 1-inch cubes or wedges
About 2 cups clarified butter (see page 440), olive oil, or duck fat
Persillade (page 20; optional)
Salt and pepper

Boil the potatoes in a large pot of well-salted water for 10 minutes, or until cooked through but still firm. Drain the potatoes, spread them on a baking sheet, and allow them to cool to room temperature (you can—and in fact should—do this well ahead of time).

Put two large cast-iron skillets over medium-high heat (or work in batches if you have only one pan) and add ½ inch of clarified butter to each one. Carefully add the potatoes to the pans in one layer and adjust the heat to keep them frying briskly. Resist touching them until they begin to brown on the bottom and loosen from the pan, about 8 minutes. Gently turn them with a slotted spoon or spatula and let them cook for another 8 minutes, or until they're beautifully golden. Lift the potatoes from the cooking oil and blot them on paper towels. Repeat with any remaining potatoes.

Put the potatoes in a large bowl. Add the persillade, if using, season generously with salt and pepper, and toss well. Transfer to a warm serving dish. MAKES 6 SERVINGS

BEETS

I know I'm not the only one who grew up on waterlogged canned beets, which definitely predisposes a person to dislike the vegetable. The vacuum-packed, shelf-stable cooked beets are not much better, flavor-wise. But oh, the joy of just-pulled garden beets! Sweet and earthy, there really is no comparison. It's a shame they don't sell already-cooked beets at farmers' markets here as they do in France, a great convenience. Here we just have to roast them to perfection at home. A little water in a covered roasting pan essentially steams them, so you can peel off the skins with ease. You'll know they're done just as you do with potatoes, when a paring knife slips in easily. There's nothing wrong with boiling (peeled) beets in salted water, but roasting them skin-on imparts a more robust flavor. I find it very convenient to roast and peel a half dozen beets to keep on hand in the fridge, to use one way or another throughout the week. When tomatoes are out of season, beets are a natural addition to green salads—and a salad of sweet beets and ripe tomatoes is a winning combination.

Now consider the myriad beet possibilities: sliced yellow beets in a mustard-infused vinaigrette; ice-cold beet-enhanced gazpacho or a cool glass of creamy pink borscht; hot roasted beets dressed up like baked potatoes. Or a steaming bowl of beet-stained vegetables bobbing in a rich beef broth.

Spicy Beet Gazpacho

Refreshing and fortifying just like traditional gazpacho, a pitcher of beet gazpacho can be perfect for hot summer nights. You might wonder whether to call it a chilled soup or a vegetable smoothie. Spicy and nutritious, it may resemble cold borscht, but to me it's got Spanish written all over it.

1 medium beet, peeled and coarsely chopped

1 small tomato, coarsely chopped

2 cups chopped peeled cucumber

1/2 teaspoon salt, or to taste

1/4 teaspoon black pepper, or to taste

1 garlic clove, grated or minced

Pinch of cayenne

1/2 teaspoon chopped jalapeño chile

3 tablespoons olive oil

1 cup cold water

Chopped flat-leaf parsley, mint, and scallions for garnish

Lime wedges

Put everything but the herbs (and lime wedges) in a blender and blend at high speed to make a smooth puree. Taste and adjust the seasoning, then whizz once more. Strain the soup and ladle into bowls. Sprinkle with chopped herbs and serve with lime wedges.   MAKES 4 TO 6 SERVINGS

A perfect chilled soup for a summer's night, made with raw beets, tomato, and cucumber.

Beets Roasted in Their Skin

I sometimes like to treat beets like baked potatoes, roasting them whole, skin on, and serving them hot with "all the fixings."

Choose small to medium-sized beets and wash them well. Trim them, but leave a bit of root and stem so they look as natural as possible. Put them in a pie pan with ½ inch of water and a thyme sprig, cover tightly with foil, and pop them into a hot oven. They'll take at least an hour at 375 degrees, sometimes a bit longer. Serve the beets with their skin on, split top to bottom. Lavish them with butter, crème fraîche, and snipped chives, and finish with some fleur de sel and a twist of the pepper mill. You can upgrade the presentation with a dab of caviar or trout roe for a special occasion.

When roasting beets, always throw in a few extra so you'll have enough for several days of salads.

Yellow Beet Salad with Mustard Seeds

If you're beet-phobic because you fear the inevitable crimson stains, try golden yellow beets instead. Yellow beets, nearing orange on the color spectrum, are slightly milder than red ones and make a beautiful winter salad. First cook your beets (see Beets Roasted in Their Skin, opposite). While they're in the oven, make a vinaigrette with Dijon mustard, grated horseradish, lemon juice, and a mild vegetable oil.

Cool, peel, and slice the beets. Season with salt and toss with the dressing to coat well. Roast a teaspoon of black mustard seeds or *kalonji* (nigella) seeds in a tiny bit of oil in a small pan over medium-high heat. When the seeds begin to pop, pour the contents of the pan over the dressed beets. Serve at room temperature, with a spoonful of thick yogurt on the side if you wish.

PARSNIPS

A parsnip's flavor is beguiling. A touch of carrot, a hint of chestnut, a whiff of winter squash, and its own unique aroma. The ancient Romans revered the parsnip, and so do I. It's a great vegetable to keep in supply throughout the colder months, useful for soups, gratins, or stews—not to mention mashed parsnips.

The best time to eat parsnips is late fall, winter, and early spring, when they are at their sweetest. Browned in a roasting pan is the easiest and perhaps best way to cook them, but there are dozens of others. Their innate sweetness can also be used to advantage in modern desserts. My friend Ignacio uses parsnip puree (a little salt too) to make ice cream at his restaurant Estela in New York City. The result is remarkable. You can also use parsnips to replace pumpkin for a praiseworthy (and, I think, more seductive) Thanksgiving pie.

Pan-Roasted Parsnips with Coriander

These parsnips are browned on the top of the stove in a wide cast-iron skillet, which concentrates their sweetness as they cook. They can be cooked several hours in advance and reheated before serving.

Salt

2 pounds parsnips, not too large

2 tablespoons butter

1 large onion, finely chopped

$\frac{1}{2}$ teaspoon coriander seeds, toasted and coarsely ground

Pinch of cayenne

1 small bunch cilantro

Sea salt for finishing

1 lime, halved

Bring a large pot of well-salted water to a boil. Peel the parsnips, quarter lengthwise, and remove the tough cores, then cut into 3-inch batons. Add to the boiling water and simmer for 5 minutes, or until cooked through but still firm. Drain and spread on a baking sheet to cool.

Set a wide cast-iron skillet over medium-high heat and melt the butter in it. Add the onion and cook until softened and beginning to color, 5 to 8 minutes. Season with salt and add the ground coriander and cayenne. Add the parsnips and cook, stirring every few minutes with a wooden spoon, until they are browned here and there and fork-tender, about 10 minutes. Transfer to a serving dish.

Roughly chop the cilantro, both leaves and tender stems, and scatter over the parsnips. Sprinkle lightly with sea salt and squeeze the lime juice over the top.

MAKES 4 TO 6 SERVINGS

Parsnip Soup

Make a soup by adding some chicken or vegetable broth once the parsnips have browned. Simmer for a few minutes, then puree. Garnish as above, with chopped cilantro and lime juice.

Parsnips with Turmeric and Feta

These baked parsnips are savory and belly-warming, and colorful to boot. It's an unusual combination of ingredients that works quite wonderfully.

Salt and pepper

3 pounds parsnips

2 tablespoons butter, softened

2 cups heavy cream

$^1/_2$ teaspoon ground turmeric

$^1/_2$ teaspoon cumin seeds, toasted and ground

Small pinch of cayenne

4 ounces feta, crumbled

Bring a large pot of well-salted water to a boil. Peel the parsnips and quarter lengthwise. With a paring knife, remove the tough central cores. Cut the parsnips into 3-inch batons. Parboil for 2 minutes, then drain and spread out on a baking sheet to cool briefly.

Heat the oven to 400 degrees. Use the softened butter to butter a 9-by-12-inch earthenware baking dish. Arrange the parsnips in the dish.

Whisk together the cream, turmeric, and cumin. Season with salt and pepper and the cayenne. Pour the cream mixture over the parsnips and sprinkle with the feta. Bake the parsnips for about 30 minutes, until bubbling and nicely browned. MAKES 4 TO 6 SERVINGS

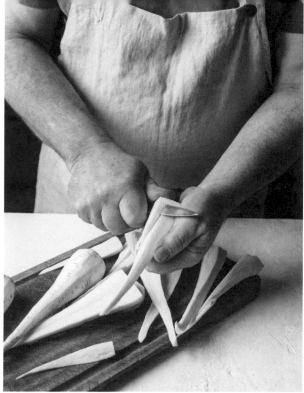

Use a paring knife
to remove the
tough cores of large
parsnips.

Parsnip Mash with Sesame Oil

Parsnips are good mashed, and unlike mashed potatoes, they don't require a lot of butter and cream. I often veer toward sesame oil and dried red chiles to offset their sweetness. Like mashed winter squash, parsnip mash is a perfect side dish for nearly any kind of cold-weather meal. For a more Italianate mash, substitute olive oil for the sesame oil and crushed red pepper for the whole chiles. Add lemon juice to taste.

Peel 2 pounds medium parsnips and quarter lengthwise. With a paring knife, remove the tough central cores. Cut into rough 1-inch chunks and transfer to a saucepan. Add water just to cover and a good pinch of salt. Bring to a boil, then simmer over medium heat for 15 to 20 minutes, until the parsnips are very tender. Drain and keep warm.

Put 2 tablespoons toasted sesame oil in a small skillet over medium heat. When the oil is hot, add 2 dried red chile peppers and 2 smashed garlic cloves and let them sizzle for about 1 minute, or until fragrant. Pour over the parsnips and mash roughly with the back of a large spoon. Adjust the salt to taste, transfer to a warm serving dish, and sprinkle with scallions.   MAKES 4 SERVINGS

CARROTS

What started out long, long ago as a slim, slightly bitter, woody purple root in Southeast Asia eventually developed, only relatively recently, into the ubiquitous crunchy sweet orange carrots we now know. Our ancestors had both yellow and white carrots; in Japan today, most carrots are red. Here we call big fat ones horse carrots or winter carrots, and horses really do love them. But they're also great for making stock, and sometimes even the big ones can have their charm, slow-roasted or long-simmered in a chicken stew. It stands to reason that carrots with their green tops attached are the freshest.

Those peeled "baby" carrots sold everywhere are to be avoided— they're actually just junk commodity carrots shaved down into homogeneity, detached from their carrotness, and dipped in lord knows what to keep them from spoiling in their little plastic bags. And they give kids the wrong idea about food, even if they seem convenient. Real carrots, no matter their size, are something to celebrate, be they raw, roasted, or braised.

North African Carrot Salad
with Preserved Lemon

I never tire of this type of Moroccan-spiced carrot salad. It doesn't take long to hand-slice the carrots into fine julienne, and I enjoy that quiet, pleasant task, but it's quicker to use a mandoline or a food processor fitted with a julienne blade. Preserved lemons have a delightful aroma and flavor. They're easy to pick up at Middle Eastern groceries and some supermarkets, usually near the olives, where you can buy just one or two. (When you get hooked on them, you can make your own, but it takes a month for them to be ready.) They are pickled in salt so they must be well rinsed and finely diced to avoid a too-salty salad. Scrape out the interior pulp and use just the skin.

1 small shallot, finely diced

2 tablespoons lemon juice

1/2 teaspoon grated or minced garlic

2 tablespoons diced preserved lemon (from about 1/4 preserved lemon)

Pinch of ground cinnamon

Pinch of cayenne

3 tablespoons extra virgin olive oil

3/4 pound medium carrots

Salt and pepper

1/2 teaspoon cumin seeds, toasted and coarsely ground

2 tablespoons thinly sliced chives

To make the vinaigrette, combine the shallot, lemon juice, garlic, and diced lemon in a small bowl. Add the cinnamon and cayenne. Stir in the olive oil. Set aside for at least 10 minutes for the flavors to mingle.

Meanwhile, peel the carrots and cut into fine julienne. You should have about 3 cups. Put in a medium bowl.

Season the carrots with salt and black pepper, add the vinaigrette, and toss well. Let marinate for 5 to 10 minutes. Taste and adjust the seasonings.

Pile the carrots onto a serving platter. Sprinkle with the cumin and chives.

MAKES 4 SERVINGS

Yellow Carrots à la Crème
(Creamy Buttered Carrots)

With the abundance of multicolored carrots available at the market, you might think it was always thus. In fact, the common orange-colored carrot is a relatively recent member of the species, developed in the Netherlands about two hundred years ago. Previous to that, most carrots in the Western world were white or yellow, while carrots in Asia were mostly red. Even if you can't find yellow ones, this is a good way to cook all kinds of carrots, though purple carrots are better candidates for roasting.

1½ pounds small to medium yellow
*   carrots*
1 cup water
1 teaspoon salt
2 tablespoons unsalted butter

¼ cup crème fraîche
Tarragon leaves
Fresh dill
Black pepper

Peel the carrots and cut them into 3-inch batons (if the carrots are small, halve them lengthwise). Rinse well and drain. Larger carrots may need quartering.

Put the water and salt in a heavy saucepan over high heat. Add the carrots, cover, and bring to a boil. Reduce the heat to a brisk simmer and cook, covered, for 5 minutes. Remove the lid, add the butter, and cook, uncovered, for 3 to 5 minutes more, until tender.

Raise the heat and boil away most of the remaining liquid. Stir in the crème fraîche and cook for 1 minute more. Transfer to a warm serving dish and garnish with tarragon leaves, snipped dill, and freshly ground black pepper.

MAKES 6 SERVINGS

Other Carrot Thoughts

This easy recipe and method may be used as a template. Substituting other flavors, you can change the personality of the dish at will. For instance, season them with the spices from the North African Carrot Salad on the previous page. Another choice could be a squeeze of lemon and a fistful of chopped fresh herbs.

Roasted Coconut Carrots

For a dish of carrots with brilliant flavor, roast them (which will concentrate their natural sweetness) with aromatic coconut oil. Cilantro, mint, hot pepper, and lime ensure there is nothing one-dimensional about this dish. Chop the herbs just before serving for the freshest flavor.

1½ pounds medium carrots
Salt and pepper
2 tablespoons coconut oil, melted
1 red Fresno or green serrano chile, finely chopped (seeds removed if desired)

2 tablespoons chopped mint
1 cup roughly chopped cilantro leaves and tender stems
1 lime, halved
Fresh coconut slivers (optional)

Heat the oven to 400 degrees. Peel the carrots and cut into 2-inch batons. Put them on a baking sheet, season well with salt and pepper, and drizzle with the coconut oil. Spread out the carrots and roast, uncovered, until they are lightly browned and tender when pierced, 20 to 25 minutes. (The carrots can be roasted up to 3 hours in advance and held at room temperature, then reheated.)

Transfer the hot carrots to a serving dish. Add the chile and mint and toss to distribute. Sprinkle with cilantro and a squeeze of lime juice and top with the coconut slivers, if using.   MAKES 6 SERVINGS

TURNIPS

Turnips are terrific if you take the time to get to know them. Which you should. They seem sadly forgotten. At the very least, they deserve to be in a mixture of roasted root vegetables, or turned into pickles. Tender young baby turnips are sweet enough to eat raw and hardly need any cooking or dressing up, but steamed with their tender green tops, they are insanely delicious. Larger purple-top turnips benefit from a more aggressive approach, such as the stovetop turnip confit (see page 311). My British friend Caroline and I have always been at loggerheads regarding the turnip. For her, turnips evoke dreary boarding-school meals and the jumbo yellow turnips they call "swedes," tragically (and shamelessly) cooked to watery smithereens. But if they're not too large, yellow turnips—which have a slightly grainy texture—are very good just boiled and buttered.

Young Turnips with Greens

A lot of so-called baby vegetables are immature, harvested too young, before they've had a chance to really develop any character. Not so with young turnips, one of the early spring crops. At the market, look for walnut-sized ones with their vibrant greens still attached and perky. Or, better yet, pull them straight from the garden.

Cut the greens from 2 bunches of young turnips (about 2 pounds), leaving a bit of green stem attached to each turnip. Wash the greens twice in cold water, then drain. Roughly chop the greens or, if small, leave them whole. Set aside.

Trim the roots from the turnips with a paring knife. Unless they are quite small, halve or quarter them. Soak in a bowl of warm water to remove any grit.

Put 2 tablespoons butter or olive oil in a large saucepan, add the turnips, and season with salt and pepper. Add ½ cup water and bring to a simmer over medium-high heat. Cover and steam until the turnips are tender, 3 to 4 minutes. Add the turnip greens and a pinch more salt and continue cooking, covered, to wilt the greens, about a minute more. Serve hot.   MAKES 4 SERVINGS

Tender young spring turnips, simmered with butter, salt, and their very own bright green tops.

Pan-Roasted Purple-Top Turnip

Perhaps you've seen these large, rough-looking roots, sometimes called winter turnips (or clip-top, since they're sold without their greens) in the supermarket. Though they may not look very inspiring, and they really must be peeled, they're the perfect candidate for roasting, cut into wedges or cubes. Oven roasting is fine, but I'm fondest of this stovetop method taught to me by my friend Michael, who learned it as a young cook while working in a restaurant kitchen in France, where it was known as turnip confit. This technique produces incredibly flavorful turnips, easily cooked in advance and reheated.

Take 6 purple-top turnips about the size of a tennis ball and peel them. Cut them crosswise into ⅛-inch slices (use a mandoline or a large knife). Melt a knob of butter in a large skillet over medium-high heat. When the butter foams, put in the turnip slices and season well with salt and pepper. Listen for the sound of sizzling, then move the slices at the bottom of the pan to the top using a small spatula. Continue in this fashion, repeatedly ferrying the bottom slices to the top, until all are tender, 15 to 20 minutes. (You'll notice that the bottom slices will caramelize at first but then lose their browned edges somewhat as they continue to cook and the turnip sugars dissolve.) MAKES 4 SERVINGS

RADISHES

I always serve a plate of radishes at dinner parties. I set it out with the hors d'oeuvres, then bring it to the table for nibbling during the meal. Crisp and peppery, a radish is always welcome. Do look for the best radishes, though, with fresh green leaves, not the sad topless ones in plastic bags at the supermarket. And go for other varieties along with round reds: French breakfast, icicle, or Easter egg. There are also long or round black radishes and colorful watermelon radishes (these must be very thinly sliced, as they are hard and dense and would be unpleasantly chewy otherwise). And daikon radish, which is delicious raw, cooked, pickled, or turned into kimchi. The green leaves of any radish can be cooked like spinach or added to a mixture of cooking greens. My French friends love to eat bright red radishes with a dab of good butter and crunchy sea salt. That's fine, but I'd rather have thinly sliced salted radishes on buttered bread.

Shaved Radish Salad

Only four ingredients—radishes, salt, pepper, and crème fraîche—and yet this makes an extremely tasty raw vegetable first course. If you can, use the wonderfully sharp black radishes, still relatively scarce in the States but available at some farmers' markets. Or try a combination of red radishes, daikon, and/or pink-and-green-striped watermelon radishes. You can even use some tender young turnips. The only work is in the slicing. A mandoline is the best tool to ensure the slices are uniformly thin.

½ pound radishes of your choice, well rinsed
Coarse sea salt
½ cup crème fraîche, or a little more if you like
A few drops of milk (optional)
Pepper

With a mandoline or a sharp knife, slice the radishes as thin as possible. Arrange the slices on a platter. Sprinkle lightly with salt—use a sea salt with texture.

If the crème fraîche is quite thick, beat it with a spoon for a minute to loosen it, or thin with a few drops of milk or water. Spoon it generously over the sliced radishes. Finish with as much freshly ground pepper as you like.   MAKES 4 SERVINGS

Other Embellishments

A drizzle of fruity olive oil, about 1 tablespoon, is a delicious indulgence spooned over the crème fraîche at the last minute. Or garnish this with spicy radish sprouts and chopped chives. You can also serve the radish salad on toasted thinly sliced rye bread for great little open-faced sandwiches.

A stunning mix of red-, white-, and violet-hued radishes.

Butter-Stewed Radishes with Dill

Round red radishes, when braised, resemble little turnips in flavor and texture and are surprisingly good seasoned just with salt and pepper. They're done in the blink of an eye and turn pale pink or violet when cooked.

> *1½ pounds red radishes (about 3 bunches)*
> *Salt and pepper*
> *4 tablespoons butter*
> *1 cup water*
> *2 tablespoons chopped dill or flat-leaf parsley*

Trim the tops from the radishes, leaving ¼ inch of the green stems. Cut off the root at the base of each radish, then cut each radish in half or quarters from top to bottom. Radishes can be sandy, so soak them in a large bowl of lukewarm water, agitating them to loosen any clinging sand. Remove, drain, and rinse briefly.

Put the radishes in a wide skillet and season well with salt and pepper. Add the butter and water and bring to a boil over high heat. Cover, reduce the heat to a brisk simmer, and cook the radishes until just tender when pierced with a paring knife, about 5 minutes. Remove the lid, raise the heat, and boil to evaporate most of the liquid.

Adjust the seasoning to taste and serve the radishes in the buttery juices, sprinkled with the dill.　MAKES 4 SERVINGS

Above: Kombu seaweed and dried bonito flakes are the simple ingredients for making the Japanese broth known as dashi.
Right: Daikon slices simmered in dashi.

Daikon Radish in Dashi Broth

Daikon is considered a radish and it can be sliced thinly for a salad, but in most instances it's treated more like a turnip and cooked. (You can substitute daikon for turnips in any restaurant dish too. In fact, the traditional turnip cakes you find in dim sum parlors are actually daikon cakes.) Japanese cooks like to simmer daikon in dashi, the delicious broth made with kombu, a type of seaweed. The simmered daikon makes a light, genteel appetizer or snack. Simply place a few slices in small bowls with a ladle of broth. Serve warm or cold.

1 medium daikon radish, about 2 inches in
    diameter, peeled and cut into 3/4-inch
    slices
2 cups Dashi (page 461)
1/2 teaspoon salt

1 teaspoon soy sauce
1 teaspoon mirin or sherry
2 tablespoons katsuobushi
    (dried bonito flakes; optional)
Greens from 1 scallion, cut into thin rings

Put the daikon in a saucepan, add the dashi, salt, soy sauce, and mirin, and bring to a simmer over medium-high heat. Reduce the heat and simmer gently for 30 to 40 minutes, until the daikon is tender when probed with a chopstick.

To serve, put 2 or 3 slices daikon in each of six small bowls and spoon a little broth over. Garnish each serving with a pinch of the *katsuobushi*, if using, and a few scallion rings.   MAKES 6 SERVINGS

CELERY & CELERIAC

Celery, with its attendant fresh crispness, is an ordinary vegetable with many fans. A jar of celery sticks in the refrigerator gives weight watchers a virtuous treat. Kids love upturned celery canoes filled with peanut butter. Mid-twentieth-century cocktail parties usually featured grown-up versions piped with cream cheese or pimento cheese spread. I think the idea is trending again, with more creative fillings.

Celery has myriad uses in the kitchen. The usual aromatic group of vegetables chosen for seasoning broths, soups, and stews is a combination of celery, carrot, and onion, left in large chunks or turned into little cubes with a sharp knife. Known as *mirepoix*, it is a classic French pillar that every young entry-level cook learns to master.

But celery functions quite well as a soloist, too, in addition to the customary role it plays in the production of a Bloody Mary. Celery makes a beautiful salad, thinly sliced and lightly dressed in something lemony, and adorned with the chopped pale inner leaves. Such a salad may be served on its own or as part of an antipasto, or spooned over salmon steaks, for example.

Celeriac, branch celery's cousin, also called celery root, is from a different varietal, cultivated to be all root with barely any stalk. When it emerges from the earth, gnarled and knobby, it hardly looks like dinner. A celery root cleans up real nice, though, with a scrub in warm water and a rinse. Once peeled, it must be held in an acidulated bath of water and lemon juice; otherwise it will oxidize and blacken like a peeled potato exposed to air.

Combine chopped celery root with potatoes, leeks, and onions for a stunning pureed soup with a haunting floral aroma. Or cut it into a fine julienne and indulge in the ritual of transforming it into the classic French bistro hors d'oeuvre *céleri-rave rémoulade*.

Celery Salad with Pistachios

Thinly sliced celery with a lemony dressing makes a crisp, refreshing cool-weather salad that won't wilt. Use only the light green and paler green inner stalks—save the tougher outer stalks for another use. You'll need 2 heads of celery. Cut them into long diagonal slices.

3 tablespoons lemon juice

¼ teaspoon grated or minced garlic

Salt and pepper

5 tablespoons extra virgin olive oil

6 cups sliced celery stalks, plus a few
    tender inner leaves, roughly chopped

1 cup flat-leaf parsley leaves

¼ cup slivered scallions

¼ cup roughly chopped toasted
    pistachios

Pinch of crushed red chile pepper,
    such as gochugaru (Korean crushed
    red pepper)

To make the vinaigrette, put the lemon juice and garlic in a small bowl. Add ¼ teaspoon salt and a little freshly ground black pepper. Whisk in the olive oil.

Put the sliced celery in a salad bowl. Season with salt and black pepper and dress lightly with half the vinaigrette. Add the parsley and celery leaves, and toss gently. Top with the scallions, pistachios, and red pepper and dribble over the remaining dressing.   MAKES 6 SERVINGS

Celery Root My Way

Céleri-rave rémoulade is a classic French salad, sold in most French charcuteries and delicatessens, rather like potato salad is here. It's one of the best ways to enjoy celery root and not difficult at all to prepare at home. Allow time for the julienned strips to rest with the salt and lemon juice, an hour or two, or even overnight, for the best flavor and texture. It is often dressed with a mustardy mayonnaise, but my version calls for crème fraîche, mustard, and horseradish.

1½ pounds celery root
Salt and pepper
Juice of 1 large lemon
½ cup crème fraîche

3 tablespoons Dijon mustard
2 tablespoons grated horseradish
Small pinch of cayenne
1 tablespoon snipped chives

Peel the celery root's rough craggy skin with a paring knife (it's too tough for most vegetable peelers) and cut into matchsticks about 3 inches long. (I do this with a knife or a mandoline, but a food processor equipped with a julienne blade makes the job a bit easier.) Put the celery root in a bowl. Salt lightly, add the lemon juice, and toss well. Cover the celery root with parchment or plastic wrap, then set a plate and a heavy weight on top and refrigerate for at least an hour, or overnight.

Drain the celery root and blot with towels. Mix together the crème fraîche, mustard, and horseradish in a small bowl. Add salt and pepper to taste and the cayenne. Put the celery root in a bowl and dress liberally, then transfer to a serving bowl. Sprinkle with the chives.   MAKES 4 TO 6 SERVINGS

CAULIFLOWER

A moment of silence, if you please, for all the cauliflowers that have been boiled to death—and the folks who had to eat them. The good news is that cauliflower does not have to be bland. Treat it right, and you'll win over the unconverted. It's ideal for roasting, and it takes on an especially rich, sweet dimension when crisped, browned, and caramelized.

Of course, cauliflower does well with aggressive seasoning, but it's also good when perfectly steamed, shining subtly on its own, with just a dab of warm butter and salt. Whatever Italian first paired cauliflower with anchovy should be sainted. I would gladly take it up over lunch with the current pope.

The old standby Cauliflower Cheese, in which a whole cauliflower is baked until quite tender and napped in a cheesy white sauce, is still a worthwhile dish. Now trending in cooking magazines is a more Italianate version of roasted whole cauliflower, with tomatoes and capers. But if a whole cauliflower seems too daunting, slice what you need for a simple pan roast and save the rest for another meal later in the week. Remember, too, you can collect any crumbly bits, cores, and odd trimmings to make a lovely pureed soup.

Clockwise from top left: Tiny florets, medium-sized florets, and slices for pan-roasting.

Seared Cauliflower
with Anchovy, Lemon, and Capers

It seemed for a while that every fine-dining restaurant in New York City was offering a thick "cauliflower steak" as a playful, rather high-priced vegetarian main course. Crisp, caramelized, and juicy, it is awfully good. But it's more practical for a home cook to achieve the same delightful effect with smaller slices.

To make the sauce, heat ½ cup olive oil in a small saucepan. Add 3 or 4 chopped anchovy fillets and cook slowly over medium heat until the anchovies have dissolved. Add a pinch of crushed red pepper and 2 or more minced garlic cloves. Turn off the heat and stir in some grated lemon zest and chopped capers. Set aside. (The sauce is also good with boiled or steamed cauliflower florets.)

Halve and core a cauliflower and cut into small ½-inch thick slices. (Save the little crumbly bits for another time.) Put two large cast-iron skillets over medium-high heat. Add 2 tablespoons olive oil per pan. Slip the slices carefully in the pans in a single layer. Season with salt and pepper and let them brown on the first side, 4 to 5 minutes. Carefully turn them over and cook for about 2 minutes more, until tender but still firm. Don't crowd the slices or they won't crisp well. Transfer to a platter, spoon the anchovy sauce over the cauliflower, and sprinkle with roughly chopped flat-leaf parsley. Serve with lemon wedges.   MAKES 4 SERVINGS

Cauliflower "Couscous" with Spiced Butter

The idea here is to cut a cauliflower into the tiniest florets possible. It's not difficult, but it takes a little time. Of course, the cauliflower morsels are not really quite as small as couscous, but they are small enough to cook very quickly. A delicate, flavorful side dish.

Salt
1 large cauliflower (about 3 pounds)
4 tablespoons butter
½ teaspoon ground turmeric
Pinch of cayenne
¼ teaspoon pepper

⅛ teaspoon grated nutmeg
⅛ teaspoon ground cloves
2 teaspoons grated fresh ginger, or
    ½ teaspoon ground ginger
2 tablespoons snipped chives
1 tablespoon lime juice, or to taste

Heat the oven to 400 degrees. Bring a large pot of well-salted water to a boil. Meanwhile, with a paring knife, cut the cauliflower into tiny florets, as small as possible. (Save the stems and other trimmings for making soup.) You should have about 8 cups.

Working in batches, cook the florets in the boiling water for 1 to 2 minutes, until just tender but still firm. Scoop them from the pot with a small strainer or a spider, blot on kitchen towels, and let cool.

Melt the butter in a small saucepan. Stir in the turmeric, cayenne, black pepper, nutmeg, cloves, and ginger. Put the cauliflower in a large bowl and season lightly with salt. Drizzle the butter over it and toss gently. (The seasoned cauliflower can be kept at room temperature for up to 3 hours or covered and refrigerated overnight.)

Transfer the cauliflower to an ovenproof serving dish. Put in the oven and heat through, 10 to 15 minutes. Sprinkle with the chives and lime juice and serve.
MAKES 6 TO 8 SERVINGS

Indian Panfried Cauliflower

To get sweet caramelized cauliflower, panfried is the way to go. Some cooks make this dish with grated cauliflower, but I prefer to make irregular thin slices, which brown beautifully. Make it as spicy as you wish.

3 tablespoons ghee or clarified butter
  (see page 110) or vegetable oil
1 small cauliflower (about 1½ pounds),
  cored and cut into ¼-inch slices
Salt and pepper
1 teaspoon cumin seeds
1 teaspoon black mustard seeds
2 teaspoons grated fresh turmeric, or
  1 teaspoon ground turmeric
2 or 3 kaffir lime leaves (optional)

A 1-inch piece fresh ginger, peeled and
  slivered or finely grated
3 garlic cloves, finely chopped
2 serrano chiles, or to taste, finely chopped
1 pound fresh English peas, shucked
  (about 1 cup), or 1 cup frozen peas
  (optional)
2 or 3 scallions, slivered
Cilantro sprigs for garnish

Put a large sauté pan or cast-iron skillet over medium-high heat. Add the ghee, and when it is hot, add the cauliflower. Stir occasionally as the cauliflower begins to color, 1 to 2 minutes. Season with salt and pepper and continue stirring until the cauliflower is half-cooked, about 5 minutes; lower the heat if necessary to keep it from browning too quickly.

Tilt the pan to expose a small pool of hot ghee and add the cumin, mustard seeds, turmeric, and kaffir lime leaves, if you have them. When they begin to sizzle in the oil, add the ginger, garlic, and chiles, stir well, and then add the peas, if using, along with a sprinkle of salt. Cover to let the cauliflower (and peas) steam until tender, 3 to 4 minutes.

Transfer the cauliflower to a serving bowl, sprinkle with the slivered scallions and cilantro, and serve. MAKES 4 TO 6 SERVINGS

CABBAGE & CO.

Pity the poor misunderstood cabbage with its enduring PR problems. Many people don't recognize its abundant culinary possibilities. It's one of the oldest domesticated food crops, having kept sailors from scurvy and Russian peasants from starvation. We have essentially co-evolved with cabbage along with its many cruciferous cousins.

And there is at least one story of cabbage as a hangover cure, eaten raw like an apple (evidently you need to eat a whole cabbage). I do enjoy it raw, with its crisp broccoli-crossed-with-radish undertones, and you should too—hungover or not—sliced into wide ribbons, with a pinch of salt and a squeeze of lime.

Cabbage is also nearly synonymous with the history of fermentation, from kraut to kimchi. So let's pay homage: It should be celebrated— raw, cooked, or fermented—in all its beautiful varieties, from the common firm Dutch green and red to the intricately frilly leaved savoy to the stout, juicy napa.

Green Cabbage with Caraway

The goal is to cook these wide ribbons of cabbage to just the right stage: firm but not crunchy, and still green. Bring a pot of salted water to a boil. Cut ½ pound of cabbage into 1-inch-wide ribbons and drop them in. Simmer for just 2 or 3 minutes, then transfer the cabbage to a serving bowl. Add 2 tablespoons butter, a pinch of caraway seeds, and a little chopped parsley. Season with salt and pepper, toss, and serve. This is a good way to cook savoy cabbage too.

MAKES 2 SERVINGS

Lime and Chile Slaw

I've never been a fan of the sort of slaw that's oversweetened and drowned in mayo, nor of soggy slaw. I love this fresh, crunchy version for its bite. If they made coleslaw in Mexico, it might be something like this: super-tasty, super-easy, and super-spicy. To me this tastes best about an hour after it's made. It softens a bit after that but it's still good eating, especially with fried chicken or on a fish taco.

1 small firm green cabbage, cored and shredded
1 small red onion, very thinly sliced
1 jalapeño or serrano chile, minced
Juice of 3 limes, or to taste
Salt and pepper

Put the cabbage, onion, chile, and lime juice in a bowl, season generously with salt and pepper, and toss well. Cover and refrigerate for at least an hour; after an hour, the cabbage will have wilted slightly. Taste the slaw, adjust the seasonings if necessary, and serve.   MAKES 6 SERVINGS

Napa Cabbage Kimchi

Traditional Korean kimchi, a naturally fermented product, is prized for its probiotic health benefits as well as its flavor. No proper Korean meal is complete without it—it is served as an appetizer or as a condiment and used as an ingredient in soups and stews. As American palates have become more globally adventuresome, kimchi now mixes with Western fare as well—on burgers and ham sandwiches, for example, or in Chef Roy Choi's brilliant Los Angeles kimchi tacos. Kimchi is actually fun to make at home. The following recipe is adapted from the one in Lauryn Chun's *Kimchi Cookbook*.

2 heads napa cabbage (about 4 pounds), cored and cut into 2-inch squares

¼ cup salt

SEASONING PASTE
½ cup thinly sliced onion
1 tablespoon grated or minced garlic
1 tablespoon grated fresh ginger

2 tablespoons jeotgal (Korean anchovy sauce)

2 tablespoons salted shrimp (sold in small jars at Korean groceries and online)

2 teaspoons sugar

½ cup gochugaru (Korean crushed red pepper)

6 scallions, cut into 2-inch pieces

¼ cup water

Layer the cabbage in a large bowl, sprinkling each layer with some of the salt. Set aside for 1 hour.

Drain the cabbage in a colander, rinse with cold water, and drain well. Blot with kitchen towels.

To make the seasoning paste, put the onion, garlic, ginger, anchovy sauce, salted shrimp, and sugar in a food processor and grind to a paste. Transfer to a small bowl and stir in the crushed red pepper and scallions.

Wearing rubber gloves, layer the cabbage and seasoning paste in a large bowl, then mix well with your hands to distribute the seasoning. Pack the kimchi into a 2-quart jar. Rinse the bowl with the ¼ cup water to get every drop of seasoning paste and add the water to the jar. Set the jar in a bowl (to catch any overflow as the kimchi ferments), cover loosely, and leave at room temperature for 3 days to ferment. Then store the kimchi in the refrigerator for up to 6 months.

MAKES 2 QUARTS

Kimchi Soup with Pork Belly

Kimchi is the main ingredient in this easy traditional Korean dish, *kimchi jigae* (*jigae* meaning soup or stew). It rather amazing how cooking the kimchi transforms it. Kimchi jigae tastes a lot like a good vegetable soup. For a richer version, use chicken, pork, or beef broth, but I find that making it with plain water is just fine.

1 pound fresh pork belly, cut into 1-inch pieces, or use thick pork shoulder chops

4 garlic cloves, minced

1 tablespoon grated fresh ginger

2 tablespoons soy sauce

1 teaspoon toasted sesame oil

1 teaspoon fish sauce

2 tablespoons unsalted butter

1 medium onion, chopped

2 cups kimchi, drained (reserve the juice), squeezed dry, and chopped

3 tablespoons gochujang (Korean red pepper paste)

1 tablespoon gochugaru (Korean crushed red pepper)

1 cup reserved kimchi juice

8 cups water

½ pound soft or silken tofu, cut into large cubes

6 scallions, slivered

Put the pork belly (or chops) in a bowl, add the garlic, ginger, soy sauce, sesame oil, and fish sauce, and toss or turn well to coat. Let marinate for 10 minutes.

Melt the butter in a heavy-bottomed soup pot over medium heat. Add the pork belly mixture. If using chops, cut in half, leaving bones intact, and let cook gently for 5 minutes. Add the onion and cook, stirring, until softened, about 5 minutes. Turn the heat to medium-high, add the kimchi, red pepper paste, and crushed red pepper, and let the mixture simmer for 2 minutes.

Add the kimchi juice and water and bring to a boil. Reduce the heat to a brisk simmer and cook for 20 minutes. Taste the broth and adjust the seasoning. (The soup can be prepared to this point up to 2 days ahead, cooled, and refrigerated. Reheat before proceeding.)

Just before serving, add the tofu, stir gently to combine, and simmer just until heated through. Ladle the soup into bowls and garnish with the scallions. MAKES 4 TO 6 SERVINGS

Stir-Fried Brussels Sprout Petals

I'm a fan of Brussels sprouts, the tiniest member of the cabbage family, but not if they are stodgy and bland, which they always seem to be unless they're cut small. To me, even a halved sprout can seem disappointingly dense (I know, cue the violins). The solution is more than a bit time-consuming, but it's worth it. Turn each Brussels sprout into a pile of "petals" by deconstructing it leaf by leaf using a paring knife, discarding the tough outer leaves. (If you are making this for more than a party of two, get a helper.) Separating the leaves makes it possible to cook them quickly in a hot pan, rendering them succulent but still bright green and fresh tasting. (A somewhat easier alternative, and nearly as satisfying, is to slice the whole sprouts as thin as possible with a sharp knife or mandoline.)

For the stir-fry, choose Western or Eastern flavors, depending on the rest of your menu. For a Mediterranean version, as below, go with olive oil, garlic, and chopped sage (a little pancetta too, if you like); or use ginger, garlic, hot pepper, and sesame oil for an Asian inflection. You'll need about 1½ pounds of sprouts.

Put 3 tablespoons olive oil in a wide cast-iron skillet over medium-high heat. When the oil looks wavy, add 3 to 4 cups Brussels sprout petals and season with salt and pepper. Stir-fry the petals for 2 to 3 minutes, letting them brown a bit. Add 2 minced garlic cloves, 2 teaspoons chopped sage, and 1 tablespoon chopped flat-leaf parsley. Cook for a minute more, then serve.   MAKES 4 SERVINGS

WINTER SQUASH

Though related to cucumbers, melons, and zucchini, and planted in the fields at the same time, winter squash take all summer to ripen. By harvesttime, they display their various sturdy decorative skins. Some have smooth skins, like butternut squash, while others display more rusticity with warts and craggy dimples. Hubbard squash can range in color from bright orange to celadon blue-green. Sweet, starchy kabocha squash, a Japanese favorite, is a rough, dark green with the occasional tinge of orange and widespread vertical stripes.

The small, ridged Delicata squash is hollow, containing a thin layer of sweet golden flesh, and its skin is edible so no peeling is necessary. The list goes on: Sweet Dumpling squash, small and green-speckled, resembles a cute mini-pumpkin. Acorn squash comes in a range of autumnal colors now. Check out the variety of tasty pumpkins at the market.

Every type of winter squash has a particular pronounced flavor of its own, but all are good roasted solo, mashed, or turned into well-seasoned soups and stews.

To crack open a large squash (it's really more like splitting wood), use a long, heavy chef's knife or cleaver. If necessary, find a tall person or stand on a box so you tower over it a bit as you push down. Once the squash is split, dividing it into smaller pieces is easier. At the market, some vendors sell thick slices of large squash and pumpkin so you don't have to lug an entire squash home. I'll confess, I sometimes buy pre-peeled cut-in-chunks squash at the supermarket—it's easy and convenient.

Butternut squash is easily peeled with an ordinary sharp vegetable peeler if you are making slices or cubes. But for the simplest way to make mashed butternut, split the squash lengthwise and bake skin side up for an hour. When the squash is completely soft, you can easily lift the skin away in one piece.

Hubbard Squash
with Parmesan and Brown Butter

I can't think of much that wouldn't be good with Parmesan and brown butter, actually, but the combination is especially good with roasted winter squash. This makes a warm first course in small portions or a substantial meatless main. Use leftovers for a baked pasta—layer the squash with rigatoni or penne cooked firmly al dente, and then shower with grated cheese and bread crumbs.

2 pounds peeled Hubbard or other winter squash, cut into $1/2$-inch slices or a bit thinner	Pinch of crushed red pepper
Salt and pepper	12 large sage leaves, roughly chopped, or a handful of smaller sage leaves
Olive oil	Arugula or chopped parsley for garnish
3 tablespoons butter	A chunk of Parmesan for shaving
	Lemon wedges

Heat the oven to 400 degrees. Put the squash slices in a large bowl, season with salt and black pepper, and drizzle with enough olive oil to coat. Toss the squash with your hands to distribute the seasoning, then transfer to two baking sheets and spread out the slices. Roast until the squash is cooked through and the edges are browned here and there, about 15 minutes. (You can roast the squash up to 3 hours in advance and hold it at room temperature.)

Arrange the squash on a warm platter or on individual plates, then quickly make the brown butter sauce: Melt the butter in a small skillet over medium-high heat. Add the crushed red pepper and sage, season with a little salt and black pepper, and whisk the butter and aromatics as the butter begins to bubble and brown. When the butter is foamy and nutty-smelling, in a minute or so, spoon it over the squash. Garnish with a few arugula leaves or chopped parsley and use a sharp vegetable peeler to shave Parmesan over the squash. Serve with lemon wedges.

MAKES 6 TO 8 SERVINGS AS A MAIN COURSE, 10 SERVINGS AS AN APPETIZER

Sake-Steamed Kabocha with Miso

Cooked in this light-handed way, kabocha squash, a Japanese varietal with a lovely, starchy, chestnut-like texture, is delectable straight from the pan, at room temperature, or cold the next day. I prefer it as a snack, with drinks or tea, savored one piece at a time. This recipe is adapted from one by Nancy Singleton Hachisu, author of *Japanese Farm Food*.

1 pound kabocha squash (about ½ medium squash), seeds removed	*3 tablespoons vegetable oil*
3 tablespoons white miso	*2 small dried red chile peppers*
6 tablespoons sake	*Salt*
	1 teaspoon toasted sesame oil

Using a vegetable peeler, peel the squash very lightly, exposing the green flesh just beneath the skin. Cut the squash lengthwise into 1-inch-wide wedges, then cut the wedges crosswise into ¼-inch slices.

In a small bowl, combine the miso and 3 tablespoons of the sake and stir well; set aside.

Put the oil in a wide skillet over medium-high heat. When it is hot, add the chile peppers and let them sizzle for half a minute, then add the squash and stir to coat. Sprinkle lightly with salt, spread out the squash slices, and cook gently without browning for about 3 minutes. Add the remaining 3 tablespoons sake, cover, and allow the squash to steam for about 2 minutes, until it is just cooked through.

Add the miso-sake mixture and the sesame oil, stirring carefully to coat the squash slices without smashing or breaking them. Serve hot, at room temperature, or cold.   MAKES 6 TO 8 SMALL SERVINGS

MUSHROOMS

There's a difference between cultivated and foraged foods that often corresponds to depth of flavor. This is certainly the case with mushrooms. A wild mushroom tastes deep and earthy in a way no ordinary mushroom can. Although many kinds of mushrooms can be cultivated, the mushrooms we prize the most, like chanterelles, morels, and porcini, must be collected by hand in the wild. Lest you think mushroom foraging is a simple idyllic walk in the woods, basket in hand, take it from me that this is most often not the case. Wild mushrooms pop up according to their own rules, when conditions are correct and the sunshine-moisture ratio is just so. Hence the price: You're paying an expert to roam the forest at the right time and bring back the goods.

However, there is nothing wrong with more affordable cultivated button mushrooms, portobellos, and shiitake, or a beautiful tuft of oyster mushrooms. If you're making a mushroom soup or stew, though, it's a good idea to goose it up with some dried wild mushrooms.

About washing mushrooms: Most cultivated mushrooms just need a little wiping with a paper towel or a dry pastry brush, since they are usually fairly clean. If, however, your button mushrooms or cremini look especially dirty, give them a quick swish in a bowl of lukewarm water, let them drain in a colander, and then blot them immediately with a kitchen towel. Generally speaking, wild mushrooms should only be cleaned using a paring knife or brush to scrape away grit or debris. But sometimes wild mushrooms can be extremely sandy, in which case a very brief dunk in lukewarm water is permissible. Wild mushrooms are apt to get waterlogged, so avoid this step if at all possible.

Royal trumpets are a lovely meaty type of cultivated oyster mushroom, perfect for grilling.

Raw Porcini Mushroom Salad

When you have freshly harvested, very firm porcini, make this exquisite salad. You'll need one small mushroom per person. Peel the stems with a paring knife and thinly slice the porcini. Arrange on individual plates. Add a little shaved fennel if you wish. Season with salt and pepper, drizzle with your best olive oil, and squeeze over a few drops of lemon juice. Garnish with parsley leaves or arugula and a few curls of shaved Parmesan. If wild porcini are not available or within your budget, you can make the salad with firm white button mushrooms instead.

Tagliatelle with Wild Mushrooms

If you are lucky enough to land some gorgeous porcini mushrooms—the prized *Boletus edulis*—or morels or chanterelles, go all out and make this decadent pasta. Break out the cream, butter, and Parmesan. The meaty, perfumed scent of the wild mushrooms permeates the dish. Serve in luxurious small portions. This sauce is also excellent spooned over soft polenta (see page 169).

Salt and pepper
½ pound porcini, chanterelles, or morels
2 tablespoons butter
2 cups (8 ounces) crème fraîche or heavy cream

½ teaspoon grated lemon zest
10 ounces fresh egg tagliatelle or fettuccine
1 ounce Parmesan, grated
2 tablespoons chopped flat-leaf parsley
1 tablespoon snipped chives

Bring a large pot of well-salted water to a boil. Meanwhile, trim the mushrooms and thinly slice. Put a wide skillet over medium-high heat and add the butter. When it foams, add the mushrooms and let them brown a bit. Season well with salt and pepper, stir, and cook for about 5 minutes, until somewhat colored and softened. Add the crème fraîche and bring to a simmer, then turn off the heat and stir in the lemon zest.

Add the pasta to the boiling water and cook until nearly al dente. Drain, reserving about 1 cup of the pasta water. Add the pasta to the skillet, turn the heat to medium-high, and let the pasta simmer in the sauce for a minute or so, stirring occasionally. Thin the sauce with the pasta water as necessary. Add the grated cheese.

Using tongs, divide the pasta among heated shallow soup bowls. Spoon the sauce remaining in the pan over the pasta, sprinkle with parsley and chives, and serve.

MAKES 4 TO 6 SERVINGS

This luscious pasta features fresh, wild porcini and chanterelles.

Grilled Royal Trumpets
with Garlic, Parsley, and Rosemary

Royal trumpet mushrooms may look something like wild porcini at first glance, but they are a cultivated member of the oyster mushroom family, sometimes called king oyster or king trumpet mushrooms. Their meaty stems are perfect for slicing into thick uniform planks for grilling. It's simply a matter of giving them an herby marinade. Royal trumpets are more budget-friendly, but large porcini are wonderful grilled this way too.

Grate a garlic clove into ½ cup olive oil (or finely mince the garlic and add to the oil). Add a bit of roughly chopped rosemary (or thyme or marjoram). Cut 4 large royal trumpet mushrooms lengthwise into ⅛-inch slices. Paint them with the olive oil mixture. Grill the slices over hot coals for 2 minutes on each side. They should sizzle when they hit the grill and brown nicely. Sprinkle the slices with chopped parsley and serve warm. (Alternatively, cook the mushrooms on a cast-iron stovetop grill or in a cast-iron skillet.) MAKES 4 SERVINGS

Glazed Shiitake Mushrooms with Bok Choy and Sesame

Shiitake mushrooms, first cultivated in Japan, have a lot of flavor and work well, naturally, with elemental Asian flavors—ginger, sesame, and soy. In the United States, most shiitakes are grown in Pennsylvania and Washington State.

Salt and pepper

2 pounds baby bok choy

3 tablespoons vegetable oil

3 small dried red chile peppers

1 pound shiitake mushrooms, stems removed

4 garlic cloves, grated or minced

1 tablespoon grated fresh ginger

1 tablespoon sugar

1 teaspoon toasted sesame oil

3 tablespoons tamari or soy sauce

6 scallions, sliced on the diagonal

1 tablespoon toasted sesame seeds

Bring a large pot of well-salted water to a boil. Meanwhile, cut off and discard the tough stem ends of the bok choy. Separate the leaves, rinse, and drain.

Drop the bok choy leaves into the boiling water and blanch for 1 to 2 minutes, until barely cooked. Drain and spread out on a towel-lined baking sheet to cool, then arrange the leaves in one layer in a shallow baking dish and set aside.

Put a large wok or cast-iron skillet over high heat. Add the vegetable oil and heat until nearly smoking, then add the chiles and shiitake caps, stirring to coat. Season lightly with salt and black pepper and stir-fry for 2 minutes. Reduce the heat slightly, add the garlic, ginger, sugar, sesame oil, and tamari, and stir-fry for 1 minute.

Spoon the shiitakes and pan juices over the bok choy. Serve at room temperature or, if you prefer, reheat, covered with foil, for 10 to 15 minutes in a 400-degree oven. Garnish with the scallions and sesame seeds. MAKES 4 SERVINGS

Mushroom Ragout

This mushroom stew uses mostly cultivated mushrooms, with help from an infusion made with a handful of dried porcini, which adds deep flavor. (You may want to add some dark chicken broth too.) But do try to add at least a few fresh wild mushrooms. A half pound of chanterelles won't break the bank. As it simmers, the herbaceous mushroom stew gains character. Serve it as a sauce for pasta or polenta, or on its own with garlic toast.

1½ pounds cultivated brown mushrooms, such as cremini, shiitakes, or portobellos

½ pound pale wild mushrooms, such as chanterelles (or use cultivated king trumpet or oyster mushrooms)

¼ cup extra virgin olive oil

1 large onion, diced

Salt and pepper

1 teaspoon chopped thyme

1 teaspoon chopped sage or rosemary

Pinch of crushed red pepper or cayenne

1 tablespoon tomato paste

3 small ripe tomatoes, peeled, seeded, and chopped

1 tablespoon all-purpose flour

2 cups Porcini Mushroom Broth or Dark Chicken Broth (page 460)

1 tablespoon butter

3 garlic cloves, grated or minced

3 tablespoons chopped flat-leaf parsley

Clean the mushrooms, keeping the two colors separate, and trim the tough stems; or, if using shiitakes, remove the stems entirely. (Save the stems for broth.) Slice the mushrooms about ⅛ inch thick.

Put 2 tablespoons of the olive oil in a wide skillet over medium-high heat. Add the onion, season with salt and black pepper, and cook, stirring, until softened and browned, about 10 minutes. Remove from the pan and set aside.

Add 1 more tablespoon of oil to the pan and turn the heat to high. Add the brown mushrooms, season lightly, and stir-fry until nicely colored, about 3 minutes. Lower the heat to medium and add the thyme, sage, crushed red pepper, and tomato paste. Add the tomatoes, stir well, and cook for 1 minute. Season again with salt and black pepper. Sprinkle with the flour, stir to incorporate, and cook, stirring, for 1 minute. Stir in the onion.

Add 1 cup of the broth and stir until slightly thickened, about 1 minute. Gradually add the remaining 1 cup broth and cook for 2 minutes. The sauce should have a

gravy-like consistency; thin with more broth if necessary. Adjust the seasoning. (The stew can be prepared to this point several hours, or a day, ahead and refrigerated. Reheat before proceeding.)

Put the butter and remaining 1 tablespoon olive oil in a wide skillet over medium-high heat. When the butter begins to brown, add the chanterelles, season with salt and black pepper, and sauté for about 2 minutes, until cooked through and beginning to brown. Add the garlic and parsley, stir to coat the mushrooms, and cook for 1 minute more.

Add the chanterelles to the mushroom stew and serve.   MAKES 4 TO 6 SERVINGS

A bounty of wild mushrooms: golden chanterelles, small, firm porcini, and black trumpets.

THE ART OF SEASONING

Simply put, we season our food to make it more delicious, to enhance it, to make it a rounder, brighter, better, happier version of itself. For starters, look to salt, spices, and chiles. You need them in your kitchen.

The word *spice* is now used colloquially to describe nearly any seasoning or flavorful substance that's used to make food more savory, so defining exactly what a spice is can sometimes seem a bit ambiguous, or an exercise in semantics. Cilantro, for example, is an herb when fresh and green, but its dried seeds are the spice called coriander. Still, most spices are not herbs. Let's agree that spices are more apt to be dried seeds, barks, pods, and resins, and that herbs (see page 94) are more likely leafy and plantlike.

We use spices in both understated and exuberant ways, depending on what we happen to be cooking. A little freshly ground pepper. A teaspoon of caraway seeds. A pinch of cinnamon. At the other end of the spectrum are customized multiple-spice mixtures that may become pungent Indian curries or fragrant North African stews. There are thousands of spices, of course, and here I offer the tiniest tip of the iceberg, with a few techniques for using them. You'll find other examples throughout the book.

Hot chiles are welcome in most kitchens around the world, and certainly in mine. Used judiciously, even in minuscule quantities, they add a rich vegetal kick wherever they are employed. I heartily endorse them. The result can range from zippy to medium-hot to *muy picante*, to match the cook's palate—or toned down to please guests who can't handle too much heat. Chiles are represented here in all forms: fresh green chiles of all sorts, used raw or roasted, and an assortment of dried red chiles, whole, flaked, and powdered.

SALT TO TASTE

Of course, there's more to the art of seasoning than using salt, but that is quite often the first step in the process. When using salt, the goal is to bring out an ingredient's inherent flavor, not necessarily to make it salty. Without salt, most foods—even desserts—taste lackluster.

Salt (the noun) is necessary for good cooking; knowing how to salt (the verb), and when, is key to becoming a good cook. A green salad, for instance, calls for a tiny dash of salt just before tossing, as well as the right amount in the dressing. Meat often benefits from advance salting, an hour or sometimes even a day ahead. A vegetable stew or a soup needs to be salted at the beginning and then again throughout the cooking process. Pasta requires both well-salted cooking water and salt in the sauce.

Sea salt is, obviously, evaporated from seawater. Salt is also harvested from ancient inland deposits, mined like gold; hence it is known as rock salt. Although we take it for granted, salt has been prized throughout much of history as a luxury—hoarded, rationed, and cherished.

What kind to use? Some cooks prefer fine salt, but I usually go for a flakier, larger-grained salt. Kosher salt is one such option for general use, simply because it's a mild, pure salt and widely available. It was used to test the recipes in this book. Unrefined salt with a similar coarse texture is another good choice—and it contains trace minerals, which add flavor and nutrients.

For daily cooking, I stick with the same salt for the sake of consistency—even some brands of kosher salt, for example, taste saltier than others. This way, you'll know from experience how much to use, how big a pinch. Aside from your "house salt," it's lovely to have a few special salts for a final crunchy sprinkle or for the saltcellar you set out on the table. Flaky Maldon salt from

England and crunchy fleur de sel or moist sel gris from France are among the many kinds of artisanal sea salts to choose from. You might also consider pink rock salt from Hawaii or Utah. Or sulfury black salt from India or the famous salt from Trapani, on Sicily's northwest coast.

It's possible to buy all manner of unusual flavored or smoked salts in designer packaging. If I want flavored salt, however, I make my own; it's easy, fresher tasting, and cheaper. (See Cumin Salt, page 392, and chile salt, page 130.)

A SAMPLING OF FRAGRANT SPICES

Many of the spices we think of as everyday ingredients—cinnamon, cloves, and nutmeg, for instance—were once both precious and exotic. Now we take spices, right down to the notion of salt and pepper, for granted. We expect them to be in any supermarket— nearly any variety waiting for us in the spice section. But something about seeing those pristine little jars, neatly packaged and labeled, blurs any vestigial collective memory of the spice market. I usually prefer to buy spices whole and grind them as necessary, so I patronize shops that cater to Asian, Latino, and Middle Eastern communities, where high turnover means spices are likely to be fresher and more flavorful.

Consider first how long humans have been using spices: thousands of years. The Bible is replete with references to spices. The ancient Romans knew all about spices (or many of them). And consider that, like everything else that we eat, spices were found in the wild long before they were ever cultivated.

I find it hard to resist buying spices whenever I see them in a spice shop. I usually come home with a giant bagful of them—some to use today and some to have on hand. My spice cupboard tends to be full to overflowing. We jokingly call it "Spice World"—but that's not so far off base, because spices do transport you to other worlds. And they can inspire you to explore unfamiliar cuisines.

It's important to store spices in airtight containers in a cool, dark place so that their volatile oils, which give them their flavor, don't diminish. Open containers of spices can quickly lose their potency. The best advice is to purchase spices in small quantities and to replenish them only as needed.

Clockwise from top left: Tellicherry black peppercorns, fennel seed, saffron strands, cayenne powder, Vietnamese cinnamon, turmeric (fresh and dried), black and yellow mustard seeds, Sichuan pepper, coriander seed, star anise. *Center:* Allspice berries, fresh bay leaves, smoky pimentón.

As you become more comfortable cooking with spices, you may be inclined to grind your own, as you would do with coffee beans. The same principle applies—grinding spices releases the flavorful oils, and buying spices whole rather than preground prevents their flavors and fragrances from dissipating over time. Many recipes suggest toasting the spices in a dry pan until fragrant before grinding them because this helps unleash their essence. The Indian technique of sizzling spices in butter or oil, referred to as *tarka*, can be invaluable as well (see Spicy Yogurt Raita, page 382).

For the most part, Western cooks (though this is certainly an overgeneralization) are satisfied with only a few different spices, or they may even shy away from them altogether (other than pepper). But an Indian cook, for example, is culturally predisposed to understanding the use of many spices, including half a dozen or more in a single dish. Even if it's a dish of humble potatoes or lentils, a hint of spice can make a world of difference.

The possibilities for using spices in your cooking are boundless, and the examples that follow are by no means an encyclopedic list. They are only the tiniest tip of the iceberg.

Spices of the Souk

Given the opportunity, it's still exciting to buy spices in a souk-like setting. In Morocco, the spice merchant welcomes you to the shop with a cup of mint tea and chats for a while. Then he commences weighing out spices on an old bronze scale, wrapping each purchase in paper. Once I was served an infusion made with pure saffron and gold leaf, suitable for fancy occasions.

Moroccan Lamb Tagine

The shank is the best cut for this Moroccan-spiced lamb stew. Its natural gelatin gives a melting, unctuous quality to the dish. (Even when I make this tagine with meaty neck bones or lamb shoulder chops, I like to add at least one shank to the pot.) The meat is simmered to sticky tenderness with buttery saffron-flecked onions, soft prunes and apricots, and a spice mixture with just enough cayenne. Interestingly, Moroccan food is often spice-laden, but rarely spicy-hot.

FOR THE TAGINE
6 lamb shanks (about 1 pound each),
    trimmed of fat
Salt and pepper
2 tablespoons butter
2 medium onions, thickly sliced
Pinch of saffron threads
6 garlic cloves, finely chopped
A 2-inch chunk fresh ginger, peeled and
    slivered
1 small cinnamon stick
2 teaspoons cayenne
1 teaspoon coriander seeds

1 teaspoon cumin seeds
1 cup golden raisins
2 cups pitted prunes
2 cups dried apricots
4 cups Blond Chicken Broth (page 460)
    or water
1 cup tomato puree

FOR THE GARNISH
1 tablespoon butter
1 cup blanched whole almonds
Salt
Sugar

Preheat the oven to 325 degrees. Season the lamb generously with salt and pepper.

Melt the butter in a large skillet. Add the onions, sprinkle with a little salt, and crumble in the saffron. Stew the onions gently for 5 minutes, or until slightly softened. Remove from the heat and stir in the garlic, fresh ginger, and all the spices, then stir in the raisins, half the prunes, and half the apricots.

Put the lamb in a Dutch oven and top with the onion mixture. Add the broth and tomato puree and bring to a simmer over medium heat. Cover the pot with foil and the lid, transfer to the oven, and cook for about 2 hours, until the meat is meltingly tender. Remove the lid and foil, add the remaining prunes and apricots to the pot, and submerge them in the liquid.

Raise the heat to 400 degrees and return the lamb to the oven, uncovered, for 15 minutes. Remove from the oven and let rest for 10 minutes or so.

continued

Skim off any surface fat. (The tagine reheats perfectly, so you can make it up to 2 days ahead.)

Just before serving, melt the butter in a small skillet over medium heat. Add the almonds and gently fry until golden. Drain on paper towels and sprinkle with salt and sugar.

Transfer the tagine to a large platter, sprinkle with fried almonds, and serve.

MAKES 6 TO 8 SERVINGS

Earthy, aromatic lamb tagine.

Aromatic Peppercorns

If you go to a spice store, you can choose between Tellicherry or Malabar *Piper nigrum* (black pepper) from South India, both of which have a bright, fruity quality. Or you can try other varieties from Brazil, Vietnam, Indonesia, and beyond; some are quite floral in flavor. Good black peppercorns provide more than just heat; they can add a note of sweetness as well as a woodsy background flavor.

Sichuan pepper is not actually pepper but rather the dried fruit of a shrub native to northern China's Sichuan Province. In addition to being "peppery," it's also musky and aromatic. Sichuan pepper is also famous for the pleasant tingly sensation it creates in your mouth.

Chicken Breasts au Poivre

The term *au poivre* usually refers to some kind of beef steak, but there's something really pleasing about making this dish with chicken breasts instead of beef. I like the contrast of the very peppery crust against the sweet, mild flavor of the chicken. You could use just black peppercorns, but Sichuan pepper gives this another dimension. Crushing the peppercorns releases their flavorful oils. Use a mortar and pestle, or a heavy rolling pin or cast-iron skillet, to obtain the coarsest texture possible.

2 large skinless, boneless chicken breasts
(8 ounces each)
Salt
3 tablespoons crushed black peppercorns
1 tablespoon crushed Sichuan pepper
2 tablespoons extra virgin olive oil or butter

FOR THE SAUCE
1 cup Dark Chicken Broth (page 460)
1 tablespoon butter
1 teaspoon chopped flat-leaf parsley

Lay the chicken breasts on a baking sheet and season on each side with salt. Combine the black and Sichuan peppers. Coat the chicken with the peppercorns on each side. Let rest for at least 1 hour at room temperature or refrigerate for a few hours; bring back to room temperature before proceeding.

continued

Put the olive oil in a heavy-bottomed skillet set over medium-high heat. When it is hot, add the chicken and cook for about 3 minutes on each side, until lightly browned and just cooked through. (Residual heat will cook them more as they rest, so don't go longer.) Transfer the chicken to a plate and set aside to rest in a warm place while you make the sauce.

Add the chicken broth to the pan, bring to a simmer over medium heat, and cook until reduced by one-third. Stir in the butter, then turn off the heat.

Slice the chicken breasts on an angle and arrange on a platter. Spoon the sauce over, sprinkle with parsley, and serve.   MAKES 4 SERVINGS

A coating of black peppercorns and Sichuan pepper brightens a chicken breast immeasurably.

Curry Spices

It's easy to make your own curry spice mixture using cumin, coriander, fennel seeds, nutmeg, black pepper, cayenne, and turmeric rather than resort to a commercial rendition made in a huge factory. Customize the blend to suit your own taste. Indian cooks make a *masala* (spice mixture) suited to the individual dish, not an all-purpose blend. And "curry" can be a controversial term—it lumps any type of saucy seasoned dish into a catchall category that is ultimately vague—but everybody uses it, even in India.

Soft-Shell Crabs with Curry Butter

Soft-shell crabs are delicious, no matter their preparation. I am always happy with a crispy deep-fried one. Soft-shell crabs cooked in butter and finished with garlic, parsley, and lemon are always sheer pleasure. Go one better and sauté them in a spicy curry butter. The kicky components of the spice mixture, along with ginger, garlic, and lime, add a bright boost of flavor and complement the sweetness of the crabs. Dusting them with rice flour ensures a crispier creature.

*6 tablespoons Curry Butter
   (recipe follows)
4 large soft-shell crabs
   (about 5 ounces each), cleaned*

*1 cup rice flour (optional)
1 bunch watercress
Lime wedges*

Heat a large skillet over medium-high heat. Add 2 tablespoons of the curry butter, let it melt, and swirl the pan to distribute it. Dust the crabs lightly with the rice flour, if using. When the butter is foamy, add the crabs in one layer, raise the heat to high, and cook for 3 minutes. (Be careful, as the butter may spatter.) Turn the crabs, using tongs, and cook for 3 minutes on the other side, or until crisp and cooked through. Remove the crabs and keep warm.

Add the remaining 4 tablespoons curry butter to the pan and heat until it sizzles. Arrange the crabs on a warm platter or individual plates. Spoon the melted curry butter over the crabs, garnish with the watercress sprigs and lime wedges, and serve at once. MAKES 4 SERVINGS

Curry Butter

This curry butter is wonderful with all kinds of fish and shellfish. It's also nice to have on hand for sautéing vegetables or cooking eggs. It would be delicious dabbed on grilled lamb chops or used to butter an avocado sandwich.

1/2 teaspoon cumin seeds

1/2 teaspoon coriander seeds

1/2 teaspoon fennel seeds

1/4 teaspoon grated nutmeg

1/4 teaspoon black pepper

1/8 teaspoon cayenne

1/2 teaspoon ground turmeric

1 cup (2 sticks) unsalted butter, softened

2 teaspoons grated fresh ginger

1/2 teaspoon grated or minced garlic

1/2 teaspoon salt

Grated zest and juice of 1 lime

1/4 cup unsalted roasted almonds, crushed

1/2 cup chopped scallions

Heat the cumin, coriander, and fennel seeds in a dry skillet over medium heat until lightly toasted and fragrant, a minute or so. Grind the toasted spices to a powder with a mortar and pestle or spice mill. Add the nutmeg, black pepper, cayenne, and turmeric.

Put the butter in a bowl. Add the spices, ginger, garlic, salt, and lime zest and juice and mash into the butter with a wooden spoon. Add the crushed almonds and scallions and mix until well incorporated. Cover and refrigerate until ready to use. The recipe makes more curry butter than is needed for this dish. Freeze leftovers, cut into 1-inch cubes, and wrap well.   MAKES ABOUT 1 CUP

Luscious Soft-Shell Crabs with Curry Butter.

Fresh from the frying
pan. Eat them while
they're hot.

Eggplant and Potato Pakora

Pakoras are crispy fritters that can be made from most any vegetable—chiles, corn, eggplant, or potatoes, for example—dipped in a spiced chickpea flour (*bejan*) batter. This batter contains ajwain seeds, which taste a bit like thyme or oregano and add a sweet pungency, and *hing*, or asafoetida, a strongly perfumed, resinous spice that lends a richness and flavor that some say is reminiscent of truffles. Fry a few to serve with drinks before dinner. Or, if you have help in the kitchen, these are just the thing for a cocktail party.

FOR THE BATTER
1½ cups chickpea flour
½ cup rice flour
½ teaspoon ajwain seeds
½ teaspoon sesame seeds
Pinch or two of powdered hing
  (asafoetida)
¼ teaspoon cayenne
½ teaspoon ground turmeric
½ teaspoon salt
4 to 5 cups water

Vegetable oil for deep-frying

FOR THE VEGETABLES
1 medium eggplant, sliced into ⅛-inch
  rounds
3 small potatoes, peeled and sliced into
  ⅛-inch rounds
Salt
Green Yogurt Chutney or Spicy Yogurt
  Raita (recipes follow)

To make the batter, combine the chickpea flour, rice flour, ajwain seeds, sesame seeds, hing, cayenne, turmeric, and salt in a large bowl. Whisk in 4 cups of the water to make a smooth batter, then add up to 1 cup more water if necessary; not too thin, but not too thick. When ready to cook, do a trial pakora to see if the batter needs thinning.

Pour 2 inches of oil into a wok or cast-iron Dutch oven and heat to 375 degrees. Dip little clusters of vegetable slices into the batter (2 eggplant slices and 2 potato slices held together) and slide into the hot oil; do not crowd the pan. Fry the pakoras for about 2 minutes, until nicely colored. Drain on paper towels and sprinkle lightly with salt. Repeat with the remaining vegetables and batter.

Serve the pakoras hot, as they are ready, with chutney or raita.   MAKES 6 SERVINGS

Green Yogurt Chutney

This quickly made spicy green chutney is also perfect with steamed green vegetables or grilled fish.

1 cup mint leaves

1 cup cilantro leaves and tender stems

2 serrano chiles, roughly chopped

¼ cup plain whole-milk yogurt

1 teaspoon sugar

¼ teaspoon salt, or to taste

Put the mint, cilantro, chiles, yogurt, sugar, and salt in a blender or food processor and blend well. Transfer to a serving bowl and adjust the seasoning if necessary.   MAKES ABOUT 1 CUP

Spicy Yogurt Raita

Mustard and cumin seeds roasted in hot oil until they sizzle and begin to pop—the technique is called *tarka*—infuse this raita with flavor. It's good as a dip as well as a condiment to accompany a meal.

1½ cups plain whole-milk yogurt

1 teaspoon grated fresh ginger

1 tablespoon finely diced red chile, such as Fresno or red jalapeño

½ teaspoon salt

1 teaspoon vegetable oil

½ teaspoon black mustard seeds

½ teaspoon cumin seeds

2 tablespoons chopped mint

Put the yogurt in a bowl and stir in the ginger, chile, and salt.

Put the oil in a small skillet set over medium heat and heat until hot. Add the mustard and cumin seeds and let sizzle until seeds begin to pop, about 1 minute. Carefully stir the hot contents of skillet into the yogurt. Add the chopped mint, cover, and let the flavors mingle for at least 15 minutes. The raita can be prepared several hours before serving, covered, and refrigerated.   MAKES ABOUT 1½ CUPS

A beautiful bunch of cilantro, also called green coriander, about to become chutney.

Sizzled mustard and cumin seeds flavor a raita.

Chinese Five-Spice Powder

Fragrant Chinese five-spice powder—a heady traditional mix of Sichuan pepper, fennel seeds, cloves, star anise, and cinnamon—is genius. Complex and sprightly, it's especially delectable with duck, but it also works well with roast pork or chicken.

Muscovy duck breast cooked in the French style, but seasoned with a classic Chinese five-spice blend.

Five-Spice Duck Breast

I t's easy to cook a duck breast at home once you know the technique. It's simply a matter of slowly crisping the skin and cooking the breast like a steak, until the juices start to rise. You want large Muscovy duck breasts, which weigh about a pound each. And, like steak, the duck breast should be cooked to a rosy medium-rare. Serve this with Glazed Shiitake Mushrooms (page 361) if desired.

> 2 Muscovy duck breasts (about 1 pound each)
> Salt
> 2 teaspoons Chinese five-spice powder (see Note)
> 1 tablespoon grated fresh ginger
> 2 garlic cloves, smashed to a paste with a little salt

Trim the duck breasts if necessary, removing excess fat or gristle. With a sharp knife, score the skin of each breast diagonally. Season both sides of the duck breasts with salt, then sprinkle both sides evenly with the five-spice powder. Mix together the ginger and garlic and slather over the breasts. Cover and marinate for 30 minutes at room temperature. (Alternatively, wrap the breasts and refrigerate for several hours, or even overnight; bring back to room temperature before cooking.)

Place a cast-iron skillet over medium-high heat. When the pan is hot, lay the duck breasts in it, skin side down, and let sizzle gently for about 7 minutes, adjusting the heat as necessary to keep the skin from getting too dark too quickly, until the skin is crisp and golden. Turn the breasts over and cook for 3 to 5 minutes more; an instant-read thermometer inserted into the thickest part of the breast should register 125 degrees for medium-rare. Transfer to a warm plate and let rest for 10 minutes.

To serve, slice the duck breasts thinly across the grain on a diagonal and arrange on a platter. MAKES 4 SERVINGS

NOTE: To make your own five-spice powder, grind 1 tablespoon each Sichuan pepper (or black peppercorns), star anise, crushed cinnamon stick, cloves, and fennel seeds in a spice grinder. Store in a glass jar.

Fennel Seeds

Italians love fennel seed and use it in abundance—in biscotti, taralli, and other baked goods. Fennel is also the perfect spice for all kinds of meat—chicken, duck, and lamb all pair well with it, but the sweetness of the seeds is especially brilliant with pork.

Bucatini with Homemade Fennel Sausage

Although most Italian delis sell good-quality fennel sausages, with a choice of sweet or hot, it's not at all a chore to make a little sausage at home. Buy ground pork from the butcher, and customize the seasoning, adding salt, garlic, hot pepper, and fennel seeds to taste. If you don't have the time, however, you can substitute one pound hot fennel sausage in links from the market—just remove the casings.

FOR THE SAUSAGE
1 pound coarsely ground pork shoulder,
   not too lean
1 teaspoon salt
1 teaspoon crushed fennel seeds
½ teaspoon crushed red pepper
1 tablespoon mild paprika
3 garlic cloves, grated or minced

3 tablespoons olive oil
1 large onion, diced
Salt and pepper

4 garlic cloves, minced
1 teaspoon roughly chopped rosemary
1 tablespoon tomato paste
1 pound Swiss chard (or other greens,
   such as kale or mustard), stems
   trimmed, leaves roughly chopped
   into 2-inch-wide strips
½ cup water
1 pound bucatini or other dried pasta
2 tablespoons chopped flat-leaf parsley
A chunk of pecorino or Parmesan,
   for grating

To make the sausage, put the ground pork in a bowl and add the salt, fennel seeds, crushed red pepper, paprika, and garlic. Working quickly to keep the meat cold, mix well by hand to distribute the seasonings evenly. Cover and refrigerate until ready to use. (The sausage can be refrigerated for up to 3 days or frozen.)

Fill a large pot with water and bring it to a boil. Meanwhile, put the olive oil in a wide deep skillet set over medium-high heat. Add the onion, season with salt and pepper, and cook until the onion begins to soften, about 5 minutes. Add the sausage, breaking it into small rough pieces with a wooden spoon, and cook, stirring frequently, until the onion and sausage are lightly browned and the sausage is cooked through, 5 to 6 minutes. Add the garlic, rosemary, and tomato paste and stir well to coat. Add the chard and water, and stir until wilted and tender, about 2 minutes. Check the seasoning and turn off the heat.

Generously salt the pasta water, add the pasta, and cook until al dente. When the pasta is nearly ready, quickly reheat the sausage mixture.

continued

Drain the pasta and add to the skillet. Using tongs or two wooden spoons, toss the pasta with the sauce over low heat. Transfer to a large warmed serving bowl and serve with the chopped parsley and grated cheese.   MAKES 4 TO 6 SERVINGS

Other Pork and Fennel Thoughts

To make fennel-scented pork chops, season thin-sliced pork chops with salt and pepper, a little chopped garlic, a good pinch of fennel seeds, crushed in a mortar, and a drizzle of olive oil. Cook quickly in a hot cast-iron pan. For a pork roast with a more elaborate fennel seasoning, try the Tuscan Pork Roast on page 109.

Cumin Seed

What is it about cumin? I love its earthy aroma. I like the simple act of toasting it to bring out its fragrance and grinding it coarsely with a mortar and pestle. Of course I like the taste of it too, in just about anything. It's a popular spice in countless cuisines, and for me, it is a spice that always adds interest, warmth, and depth.

Fragrant toasted cumin seeds for ground cumin and Cumin Salt (page 392).

Cumin Lamb Pitas

Lamb with cumin is a natural, a favorite throughout the Middle East. This is a quick stir-fry to be tucked into pitas and eaten immediately.

FOR THE LAMB

1 pound boneless lamb, cut against the grain into strips approximately ½ by 3 inches wide

Salt and pepper

½ teaspoon cumin seeds, toasted and ground, plus ½ teaspoon whole cumin seeds, lightly toasted

½ teaspoon coriander seeds, toasted and ground

½ teaspoon crushed red pepper

2 tablespoons extra virgin olive oil

2 or 3 garlic cloves, thinly sliced

2 tablespoons roughly chopped flat-leaf parsley

½ teaspoon grated lemon zest

FOR THE TAHINI SAUCE

2 tablespoons tahini

2 tablespoons lemon juice

½ teaspoon grated or minced garlic

Pinch of cayenne, or more to taste

1 cup plain yogurt (not Greek-style)

Salt and pepper

FOR SERVING

4 to 6 pitas, warmed

Cucumbers in Yogurt (page 128)

Put the lamb in a bowl and season generously with salt and pepper. Add the cumin, coriander, crushed red pepper, and olive oil and toss well to coat. Let marinate for 30 minutes.

Heat a large cast-iron skillet over high heat until nearly smoking. Add the lamb in one layer (no need to add oil to the pan) and let it sear for a minute to firm slightly. (If necessary, brown the lamb in batches so as not to crowd the pan.) Then stir-fry until the lamb is well browned and cooked through, 3 to 5 minutes. Turn off the heat, add the garlic, parsley, and lemon zest, and stir to coat. Transfer to a platter.

To make the tahini sauce, in a small bowl, stir together the tahini, lemon juice, garlic, and cayenne. Whisk in the yogurt and season with salt and black pepper.

Serve with the warmed pitas, tahini sauce, and cucumbers.   MAKES 4 TO 6 SERVINGS

Cumin Salt

I like to keep a little bowl of cumin salt on the table for sprinkling on all sorts of things: grilled vegetables, yogurt, buttered bread, eggs, fresh mozzarella. Or use it to season a roast chicken or grilled or braised lamb.

To make cumin salt, toast a tablespoon of cumin seeds in a dry skillet over medium heat until fragrant and just beginning to brown. Transfer to a mortar (or spice mill) and grind to a coarse powder. In a small bowl, mix the toasted cumin with 3 tablespoons flaky salt—or to taste; the proportions are flexible. For a spicy version, add a good pinch of cayenne or hot paprika.

Other spices make deliciously flavored salts too. Try coriander or fennel seeds or Sichuan pepper using the same method.

Sweet Spices

Saffron has a floral, honeyed perfume. Cinnamon is a sweet bark.
Cardamom seeds are pungent and musky. Allspice is round and bright.
Black pepper has notes of fruit and the jungle. Cumin is warm and earthy.
All are fragrant spices, but each is quite different from the other.

Glorious, decadent
Persian Jeweled Rice
(following page).

Jeweled Rice

Laced with buttery spiced onions, nuts, and dried gem-colored fruits, jeweled rice is luxurious. It's festive—typically served at weddings and banquets in Iran—but there's no reason you can't serve it at any family gathering. One goal in making this dish is to achieve a crisp buttery layer of rice, called *tahdig*, on the bottom of the pot. While it's not difficult to do, it takes a little finesse and practice. The half-cooked rice is browned gently over a moderate flame before being splashed with a little saffron-infused water. Then the lid goes on and the heat is turned very low so the rice steams slowly. With a little luck, the golden crust is achieved. To serve, you invert the rice so the crisp *tahdig* is the top.

2 cups basmati rice

Salt

6 tablespoons unsalted butter

1 large onion, finely diced

¼ teaspoon saffron threads, crumbled
    and soaked in ¼ cup hot water

Large pinch of ground cinnamon

Large pinch of ground cardamom

Large pinch of ground allspice

Large pinch of black pepper

Large pinch of ground cumin

⅓ cup chopped dried apricots

⅓ cup golden raisins or currants

⅓ cup dried barberries or goji berries,
    soaked in warm water for 5 minutes
    and drained (or substitute dried
    cherries or cranberries)

⅓ cup slivered blanched almonds

⅓ cup roughly chopped pistachios

Rinse the rice several times in cold water until the water runs clear. Drain. Bring 3 quarts water to a boil in a large pot. Add 2 tablespoons salt, then add the rice and boil, stirring occasionally, for 5 minutes; drain well in a sieve.

Melt 1 tablespoon of the butter in a small skillet over medium heat. Add the onion, season lightly with salt, and cook until softened and lightly colored, 4 to 5 minutes. Add 1 tablespoon of the saffron water, stir in the cinnamon, cardamom, allspice, black pepper, and cumin, and cook for 1 minute. Stir in the apricots, raisins, and barberries. Remove from the heat.

Melt 4 tablespoons of the butter in a enameled or nonstick Dutch oven over medium heat. Spread half the parcooked rice over the bottom of the pot. Spoon over the onion-fruit mixture, then spread the remaining rice over the top. Cook, still over medium heat, uncovered, for 10 to 12 minutes to gently brown the rice; do not stir or move the rice—you will need to rely on your nose to know when the rice has browned.

Drizzle the remaining saffron water over the rice, put on the lid, reduce the heat to very low, and cook, undisturbed, for 30 minutes. Turn off the heat and let stand for about 10 minutes.

Meanwhile, melt the remaining 1 tablespoon butter in a small skillet over medium-low heat. Add the almonds and pistachios and gently toast for a minute or so, taking care not to let the nuts get too brown. Remove from the heat.

To serve, invert the pot onto a platter or over a wide bowl, so the crisp bottom is on top. (If you don't succeed, just spoon out the rice, then carefully lift out the bottom crust with a spatula and place it crisp side up on top of the rice.) Sprinkle with the toasted nuts.   MAKES 6 TO 8 SERVINGS

Everyday Spiced Rice

You can also use whole spices to lend subtle flavor to everyday rice. Toss whole cardamom pods, peppercorns, and cloves into the pot to perfume the rice as it steams.

HOT CHILES

Though chiles were known in Central and South America long before Columbus, his "discovery" voyage and other similar voyages are responsible for transporting chile peppers to the rest of the planet. Portuguese and Spanish explorers took chiles to Asia and merchant traders distributed chiles throughout the Western world.

Because of the mingling of so many chile-loving cultures in North America and elsewhere, today most supermarkets here carry at least a few kinds of fresh chiles: jalapeño, serrano, Fresno, and poblano, maybe Anaheims or yellow wax. You'll find more variety in Latino or Asian stores, where the chiles likely will be fresher, and cheaper too.

I always have some on hand, and not just because of a fondness for spicy food. I have long been a firm believer that chiles—fresh and dried—can elevate even the most traditional Western dishes. A classic omelette, or a homely pot-au-feu, or butter-glazed carrots can benefit from a pinch of pimentón or cayenne or some slivered Thai chile—even today's French chefs would agree.

I buy fresh chiles whenever I see them. For me, the thought of having chiles on hand is a consoling one. Chiles are a simple way to improve the flavor of a dish, and they're more than just *hot*. The peppers have rich, vegetal qualities and a sweetness as they ripen. We usually see green jalapeños, green serranos, and green poblanos, so it's easy to forget that green chile peppers are immature, harvested early. That means they have more of a bite than riper chiles—they can be sharper and noticeably less sweet.

When used with moderation, chiles can serve to brighten a dish rather than overwhelm it; to enhance the other flavors rather than complicate them. But sometimes too much restraint is a pity.

There are many more types of chiles than can be represented in this chapter—we haven't touched on the very hot chiles, like Scotch bonnets, habanero, or the aptly named Trinidad scorpion chile.

Clockwise from bottom left: Red and green jalapeños, New Mexico chiles, Thai bird chiles, ripening poblanos, Indian chiles, more Thai bird chiles, green poblanos, and serranos.

Jalapeño Chiles

Probably the most well known chile in the United States, jalapeños are fleshy and juicy, and they can range from mildly to wildly hot. (Sometimes you get some that are off-the-charts hot, and sometimes with barely any heat at all—more likely an accident of cross-pollination and random irrigation than not.) I think of them as multipurpose. They're good raw, charred, smoked, or pickled. (When smoked, they are chipotle chiles—which you'll find packed in small cans in adobo sauce, dried whole, or powdered—quite different from fresh ones.) Look for plump, shiny jalapeños at the market.

Jalapeño Butter

In French cooking, herbs or spices are often incorporated into butter to use as a topping or spread, or to finish a sauce or glaze vegetables. Jalapeños and butter complement each other. The butterfat tempers and softens the heat of the chile, at least somewhat. Uses for this butter are many—certainly a natural with corn, it's also luscious added to a vegetable stew at the end to add richness and spice. For that matter, you can stir it into many dishes as a finishing touch—soup, rice, eggs, pasta—or enhance grilled fish or steak with a knob of it. Or spread it on a baguette when making a ham sandwich.

½ cup (1 stick) unsalted butter, softened
1 jalapeño chile, finely chopped
½ teaspoon grated lime zest
1½ tablespoons lime juice

½ teaspoon cumin seeds,
   toasted and ground
½ teaspoon salt, or to taste
3 tablespoons minced cilantro

Put the butter in a bowl, add the jalapeño, lime zest and juice, cumin, salt, and cilantro, and mash together with a wooden spoon until well incorporated. (Alternatively, blend the butter in a food processor.) Taste and adjust the seasoning. The butter will keep for a week refrigerated, or longer frozen, but it is at its best the day it's made.

Taqueria Pickles

Pickled jalapeños can be bought in cans at any Mexican grocery, but they're better homemade. It's simply a matter of simmering them in a salty, vinegary brine. Keep a jar of them in the fridge at all times—to be served with drinks as a snack or as a side to fish tacos. The carrots and onions in the pickle take on the heat of the jalapeño, which makes for a colorful mix.

3 medium carrots, sliced into
    ½-inch chunks

6 large jalapeño chiles, sliced into
    ¼-inch rounds

1 medium red or white onion, sliced
    crosswise into ¼-inch rings

4 garlic cloves, halved

2 teaspoons salt, or more to taste

A few black peppercorns

½ teaspoon coriander seeds

An epazote sprig (optional)

A bay leaf

½ cup cider vinegar

1 tablespoon olive oil

4 cups water

½ teaspoon dried oregano,
    preferably Mexican

Put the carrots, jalapeños, onion, garlic, salt, peppercorns, coriander seeds, epazote (if using), bay leaf, vinegar, and olive oil in a large saucepan and add the water. Bring to a boil, then reduce to a simmer and cook until the carrots are just cooked through, 8 to 10 minutes. Transfer to a bowl to cool.

Add the oregano to the pickles, taste, and add salt if necessary. The pickles will keep for a month or more in the refrigerator.   MAKES 1 QUART

Serrano Chiles

Serranos—slender and spicy—are the green chile of choice in Mexico for any number of salsas, and are generally used raw. They can just be sliced thinly, but if you're chopping them, you might want to remove some of the seeds to lessen the heat. I use them often in Asian cooking too, especially when I don't have access to Asian chiles.

Green Salsa with Tomatillos and Serranos

Tomatillos (sometimes called "husk" tomatoes, though they are not tomatoes at all) are often simmered to make a green salsa, but this bright emerald version uses them raw. Together with the lime juice, the tomatillos provide acidity and sweetness, while the serranos give the salsa sharp lingering heat.

2 serrano chiles, roughly chopped
12 tomatillos, husked, rinsed, and
    quartered
1 cup cilantro leaves

¼ cup flat-leaf parsley leaves
Juice of 1 lime
2 teaspoons salt, or more to taste

Put the serranos, tomatillos, cilantro, parsley, lime juice, and salt in a food processor and blend until pureed. Taste and adjust the seasoning. (Alternatively, finely chop the serranos, tomatillos, and herbs and combine with the lime juice and salt in a bowl.) This keeps for several days in the refrigerator, but with diminshing returns.   MAKES 2 CUPS

Salsa Mexicana

This *salsa cruda*, meaning "raw salsa," is best made just before serving because it tends to get soggy after sitting, but you can chop the onions and tomatoes in advance and then put the salsa together at the last moment.

1½ cups diced red or white onions
1½ cups diced firm but ripe tomatoes
2 small serrano chiles, finely chopped
1 teaspoon salt, or to taste

Juice of 2 limes, or more to taste
1 cup roughly chopped cilantro
½ cup roughly chopped flat-leaf parsley

Soak the onions in ice water for 15 minutes; drain well.

In a serving bowl, toss together the onions, tomatoes, serranos, and salt. Add the lime juice and toss again. Adjust the seasoning to taste. Mix in the chopped cilantro and parsley and serve.   MAKES 3 CUPS

Poblano Chiles

Poblano chiles are larger and fleshier than many other chiles and are used more like a vegetable, either stuffed for *chiles rellenos* or cut into the strips called *rajas*. They're on the mild side, but once in a while you will bump into a batch of somewhat spicy ones.

Poblanos are always fire-roasted and peeled before using. To roast them, put the chiles directly on a gas burner or over hot coals and turn them occasionally until they are blackened and blistered all over. You want to accomplish this quickly, so make sure the heat is high—if they stay too long over the fire, they will be overcooked. Some cooks like to steam the chiles in a bag or closed container after roasting, but that also cooks the peppers too much. I prefer to let them cool on a plate or cutting board. To peel the roasted chiles, first slice them in half lengthwise (unless you intend to stuff them), then use a paring knife to scrape away the seeds. Turn them over and use the knife to scrape away the charred skin. Don't rinse them; it's fine if some bits of the charred skin remain.

Poblano Chile Rajas in Crema

Roasted poblano chiles sliced into ribbons are called *rajas*. A traditional and delicious way to eat them is to dress them lightly in crema, Mexican-style sour cream, and serve them warm or at room temperature. There are many different versions; this one is dead easy. You can use them as a vegetable side dish or a filling for tacos, or serve alongside scrambled eggs for breakfast.

Slice 2 or 3 roasted and peeled poblanos into ½-inch-wide strips, place in a bowl, and season with salt to taste. Add just enough crema or crème fraîche to lightly coat, about ½ cup. Serve as is, or heat briefly.

Some versions add sautéed onion and corn kernels, also quite good. Or skip the cream and sauté the rajas in olive oil with some sliced onions and a little oregano.   MAKES 2 SERVINGS

NOTE: Unfortunately, some brands of commercially available crema contain stabilizers and preservatives, so they don't have a fresh creamy flavor. So I usually use crème fraîche instead, which, store-bought or homemade (page 438), has no additives.

Poblano Chile Torta

Torta is the word for "sandwich" in Mexico. I first tasted this vegetarian beauty in Oaxaca one sunny afternoon years ago, and it remains one of my favorite snacks.

You need a freshly baked crusty *bolillo* (a kaiser roll would also do), a couple of tablespoons of refried or smashed black beans, several strips of roasted and peeled poblano, a few slices of slightly firm avocado, and a slice of queso Oaxaqueño (or fresh mozzarella). Split the roll and layer everything inside. It's phenomenal. If you wish, tuck in a few Taqueria Pickles (page 400) and some cilantro sprigs too.   MAKES 1 SERVING

New Mexico Green Chiles

New Mexican cuisine is anything but subtle. It has roots in Spanish peasant fare and simple Mexican and Native American cooking. At the center of it all is the state vegetable: the beloved New Mexico chile. It is used both in its immature green stage, roasted and peeled, and after it has ripened and dried to a beautiful deep earthy red. In restaurants there, the first question is always: Red or green? Meaning, what color do you want your unapologetically fiery sauce?

The green chile harvest takes place during late August or early September. People buy the chiles in bulk—enough to last the year—from entrepreneurial chile roasters who set up in parking lots or at roadside stands. Twenty-pound sacks of fresh chiles are emptied into large perforated iron baskets that rotate over hot flames. Five minutes of high-heat roasting blackens and blisters the chiles' tough skins so they can be peeled. It also cooks them and brings out their flavor. Everyone takes their roasted chiles home and packs them into zippered plastic bags to freeze (some traditionalists still can them) for use throughout the year in green chile stew and other traditional dishes. The pungent aroma of roasting green chiles is a seasonal cultural touchstone.

Classic New Mexican Green Chile Sauce

If you have roasted New Mexico green chiles on hand (thawed frozen chiles are fine), it's a simple matter to make a batch of this traditional green chile sauce. You need only a few ingredients besides the chiles—onion, garlic, a little cumin, and a touch of oregano. Most people thicken the sauce with a little flour, as I do here. You'll find this useful for all sorts of things, from quesadillas or enchiladas to tacos or burgers, or spoon some over your breakfast eggs. It's always served warm.

2 tablespoons butter, lard, or vegetable oil
1 small onion, finely diced
Salt
4 garlic cloves, minced
2 tablespoons all-purpose flour
2 cups Blond Chicken Broth (page 460)
  or water

2 cups chopped roasted, peeled, and seeded
  New Mexico or Anaheim green chiles
  (about 2 pounds fresh chiles)
½ teaspoon cumin seeds, toasted and
  coarsely ground
½ teaspoon dried oregano, preferably
  Mexican

Melt the butter in a heavy-bottomed saucepan over medium heat. Add the onion, season lightly with salt, and cook, stirring, until softened but not browned, about 5 minutes. Add the garlic and cook for 1 minute. Sprinkle in the flour and stir to coat.

Add the broth a little at a time, whisking constantly, and cook, whisking, until the sauce is thickened, about 2 minutes. Add the chopped chiles, cumin, oregano, and ½ teaspoon salt, lower the heat, and simmer, stirring occasionally, for 15 to 20 minutes, until you have a medium-thick sauce. The sauce can be prepared in advance and refrigerated for up to 5 days; reheat gently before serving.

MAKES ABOUT 3 CUPS

Roasted New Mexico
green chiles, frozen
after the harvest for
year-round use.

A fine pot of
Green Chile
Sauce improves
any breakfast.

Green Chile Breakfast Quesadillas

A Southwestern breakfast is (arguably) not complete without chiles. These quesadillas are hot, hearty, and satisfying. It's another good reason to have cooked potatoes on hand, although the quesadilla is good even without them.

4 large flour tortillas, plain or whole wheat	*Salt and pepper*
8 ounces cheese, such as Oaxaca string cheese or Monterey Jack, grated	*1 cup Green Chile Sauce (page 408), warm*
2 tablespoons butter	*¼ pound queso fresco or cotija cheese, crumbled*
2 medium potatoes, cooked and cut into small cubes (about 1½ cups; optional)	*A handful of cilantro sprigs*
8 large eggs	*1 firm but ripe avocado, halved, pitted, peeled, and sliced*
	Radishes for garnish (optional)

Heat the oven to 350 degrees. Set a large cast-iron skillet over medium-high heat. One at a time, warm the tortillas on both sides in the hot skillet, without allowing them to crisp or brown much.

Place the tortillas on a large baking sheet and sprinkle each with one-quarter of the grated cheese. Put in the oven for a few minutes to melt the cheese.

Meanwhile, melt the butter in a small skillet over medium heat. Add the potatoes, if using, and heat them through, letting them lightly brown. Beat the eggs in a bowl and season with salt and pepper, then pour over the potatoes (or pour into the pan of melted butter if not using potatoes) and quickly stir until the eggs are soft-scrambled.

Remove the tortillas from the oven and place one-quarter of the egg mixture at the center of each. Add a small spoonful of sauce. Fold the tortillas in half and transfer to four warm plates. Spoon ¼ cup warm chile sauce over each quesadilla. Sprinkle with the queso fresco and top with the cilantro sprigs and avocado slices. Garnish with whole or halved radishes if desired and serve immediately. MAKES 4 SERVINGS

New Mexico Red Chiles

The ruddy, leathery dried red New Mexico chiles start out as fresh green ones. Once they have ripened in the field to a bright crimson, they are harvested for drying. They are typically ground into a fine powder to be used in cooking or coarsely crushed into flakes. Some batches of red chiles are medium spicy, while others are flaming hot. Red chiles are emblematic of New Mexican cuisine, if not of the whole Southwest region.

New Mexican Red Chile Sauce

Simply known as "red chile" by locals, this pungent sauce is a major ingredient in daily cooking. To make it, whole dried red chiles are lightly toasted to revive them, then simmered in water and pureed. The chile puree is seasoned, thickened slightly, and simmered further, then makes its way into stewed beef *guisados*, other meat dishes, and marinades. Of course it also graces breakfast dishes like huevos rancheros, tamales, and enchiladas, and it is stirred into pots of pozole. Red chile is always served warm.

½ pound dried New Mexico red chiles (about 30), rinsed and patted dry
1 onion, coarsely chopped
6 garlic cloves, minced

½ teaspoon cumin seeds, toasted and ground
Salt

Heat the oven to 350 degrees. Spread the chiles on two baking sheets and put them in the oven for about 10 minutes, or until they smell fragrant and are lightly toasted. Remove and let cool.

Snip off the stems with scissors, cut the chiles in half lengthwise, and shake or scrape out the seeds. Transfer the chiles to a heavy-bottomed soup pot and add the onion, garlic, and cumin, then add water to cover and bring to a boil over high heat. Lower the heat and simmer for 30 minutes, or until the chiles are softened.

Working in batches, puree the chiles in a blender, using enough of the cooking liquid to make a puree the consistency of pancake batter. Pass the puree through a fine-mesh sieve into a saucepan, add salt to taste, and simmer for 15 minutes or so. Cool, then cover and refrigerate for up to a week.   MAKES 2 CUPS

Red Chile Burritos

Smothered in red chile sauce, these are the best burritos I know. They're not at all like the generic fast-food burritos, overfilled with rice and beans and guacamole. Utter simplicity rules the day: good flour tortillas filled with tender, spicy, long-simmered red chile beef. If you prefer, use pork shoulder instead.

2 tablespoons lard, beef fat, or
    vegetable oil
3 pounds boneless beef chuck,
    cut into ½-inch chunks
Salt and pepper
1 medium onion, finely chopped

4 garlic cloves, finely chopped
1 cup Red Chile Sauce (page 413)
A bay leaf
1 cup water
6 large flour tortillas

Heat the lard in a Dutch oven over medium-high heat. Add the chuck and brown lightly. Season generously with salt and pepper, lower the heat to medium, add the onion and garlic, and cook until softened, about 10 minutes.

Add the red chile sauce, bay leaf, and water to the pot, bring to a simmer, and cook until the chuck is meltingly tender and succulent, about 1 hour. Taste and adjust the seasoning.

Just before serving, set a large cast-iron skillet over medium-high heat. One at a time, warm the tortillas on both sides in the hot skillet, letting them char slightly.

Fill each tortilla with about 1½ cups of the red chile stew and roll up burrito-style. Eat immediately.   MAKES 6 SERVINGS

The quintessential
burrito experience.

Harissa

Harissa is a hot chile paste made from roasted or dried hot red peppers and often spiced with garlic, caraway, cumin, and coriander. It is popular in Tunisian, Libyan, Algerian, and Moroccan cooking. It can be used to heighten the flavor of meat braises and fish stews, or to season vegetables and bean soups. And just a dab is mighty good with a plate of fried eggs.

Quick Harissa

Rather than using whole dried chiles, this has become my preferred method for making harissa at home. It's foolproof and fast, and it keeps for quite a while in the fridge. You can also add it to a vinaigrette or turn it into a flavorful oil to spoon sparingly over pizzas, couscous, kabobs, or grilled fish.

6 tablespoons crushed red pepper

3 or 4 garlic cloves, smashed to a paste with a little salt

2 tablespoons hot paprika

1 teaspoon cumin seeds, toasted and finely ground

½ teaspoon caraway seeds, toasted and finely ground

¼ cup olive oil

Put the crushed red pepper in a small bowl, cover with hot water, and let stand for 5 minutes. Drain the crushed red pepper and return it to the bowl. Stir in the garlic, paprika, cumin, caraway, and olive oil to make a thickish paste. Store in a small jar in the refrigerator for up to 1 month.   MAKES ABOUT ½ CUP

Harissa Oil

Whisk in enough olive oil to achieve the consistency you prefer—on the denser side, or thin enough to drizzle.

Warm Chickpeas with Harissa

Chickpeas sautéed with harissa are most delectable warm or at room temperature. (Freshly cooked chickpeas—see page 221—are a hundred times better than canned.) Sometimes I serve them, along with flatbreads, as a *mezze* with drinks. They're also nice spooned over grilled fish or roasted lamb, or as part of a vegetarian main course.

Heat 2 tablespoons olive oil in a pan and sizzle 2 chopped garlic cloves in the oil, without browning. Add 2 cups cooked chickpeas and 1 tablespoon harissa and stir to coat. Season with salt and add a splash of the chickpea cooking liquid or water. Simmer for 5 minutes. Serve with lemon wedges and chopped cilantro or parsley if you wish.   SERVES 6 TO 8

Warm chickpeas enlivened with harissa.

Chinese Dried Red Peppers

Tien Tsin chiles, named for the province in China where they grow, are the little dried red peppers you see in so much of Chinese cooking. Often they're just packaged and labeled "Dried Red Chillies." You can use them sparingly—two or three—in stir-fries to add a moderate spiciness. Or toss more of them into a wok with vegetables or meat to add more substantial heat and fragrance. The hot, numbing, tingling sensation (known as *málà*) that some regional Chinese cooking is known for—especially Hunan and Sichuan cuisine—is the result of Tien Tsin chiles combined with Sichuan pepper. If you can't find them, dried chiles de árbol, sold in Latino and other groceries, are of a similar size and heat and can be substituted for Tien Tsin chiles.

Incendiary Chinese Chicken

In some Chinese dishes, a very hefty handful of whole dried red chiles is added to the wok. Left whole, they provide a kind of sneaky background heat. The dish looks frightening at first glance, and it is pretty darned spicy, but the result is not overwhelmingly incendiary as long as you remember to eat just the chicken and dodge the chiles.

4 boneless, skinless chicken thighs
   (about 1 pound), cut into 1-inch cubes
1 teaspoon cornstarch
½ teaspoon salt
½ teaspoon brown sugar
2 teaspoons sweet rice wine, such as
   Shaoxing (or substitute sherry)
1 teaspoon dark soy sauce

3 tablespoons vegetable oil
1 tablespoon Sichuan peppercorns
1 tablespoon slivered fresh ginger
6 garlic cloves, minced
24 Chinese dried red chiles
   (or substitute chiles de árbol)
2 cups Blond Chicken Broth (page 460)
4 scallions, chopped

Put the chicken in a bowl, add the cornstarch, salt, sugar, wine, and soy sauce, and toss to coat. Set aside for 20 minutes.

Put the oil in a wok over high heat and heat until hot. Add the chicken and cook for about 2 minutes, tossing constantly so it browns and crisps all over. With a slotted spoon, remove the chicken to a plate. Reduce the heat to medium.

Add the Sichuan peppercorns and let them toast for a minute or so, until fragrant. Add the ginger, garlic, and dried chiles and cook for 1 minute. Turn the heat to high, add the chicken, chicken broth, and half the scallions, and stir-fry until the liquid has reduced by half, about 2 minutes.

Transfer to a serving platter and sprinkle with the remaining scallions.

MAKES 4 SERVINGS

Star anise, cinnamon, and Sichuan pepper perfume Chinese Hot Pepper oil (*right*). For an Italianate hot pepper oil (*below*), you'll need crushed red pepper, rosemary, and garlic.

Chinese Hot Pepper Oil

Making your own hot pepper oil is a matter of steeping aromatics in a heated neutral oil.

Put 1 cup vegetable oil, 3 star anise, 1 small cinnamon stick, 2 bay leaves, and 1 tablespoon Sichuan pepper in a saucepan over medium heat and bring to a bare simmer, then reduce the heat to very low. Add 16 Chinese dried red chiles, and cook gently for 20 minutes, taking care not to let the red chiles darken or burn. Remove from the heat and let cool to room temperature.

Strain the oil if desired and pour into a jar or small wine bottle. Store in a cool place for up to 6 months.   MAKES 1 CUP

Italian Hot Pepper Oil

This is the sort of hot pepper oil you find on the table in pizzerias all over Italy, in little wine bottles with a pour spout for drizzling. It's nice to have on hand for other kinds of seasoning too.

Heat 1 cup mild olive oil in a saucepan over medium heat. Add ¼ cup crushed red pepper, 1 teaspoon fennel seeds, and a sprig of rosemary and bring to a bare simmer, then turn the heat to low and cook gently for 20 minutes, taking care not to let the red pepper darken or burn. Remove from the heat, add 1 sliced garlic clove, and let cool to room temperature.

Strain the oil if desired and pour into a jar or small wine bottle. Store in a cool place for up to 6 months.   MAKES 1 CUP

Dried Smoked Chiles

In Spain, pimentón de la Vera is the smoked chile powder of choice, made from Choricero and Ñora chiles. It is often simply called Spanish paprika, somewhat confusingly, as the more common Hungarian paprika is not usually smoked. To further confuse matters, there is also a type of Spanish pimentón (from Murcia) for which the chiles are only sun-dried, not smoked. There are three iterations of smoked pimentón—*dulce*, which is sweet and only a little hot; *picante*, which is very hot and somewhat bitter; and *agridulce*, which is slightly sweet but fairly hot. Pimentón is used in abundance in Spanish regional cuisines, both in long-cooked dishes and as a final sprinkle. Seek it out. A reasonable substitute is powdered Mexican chipotle.

Flat-Roasted Chicken with Pimentón

A flat-roasted, sometimes called spatchcocked, chicken has more exposed surface area—hence, more crisp skin and a shorter cooking time.

A flattened bird makes a fine candidate for a smoky pimentón rub. It goes without saying that one must start with the best chicken. Factory-farmed chickens, aside from the dubious politics of their overcrowded living quarters, just don't taste very good. Spend a little more for a better bird.

1 free-range organic chicken
  (3 to 4 pounds)
Salt
2 tablespoons olive oil
2 tablespoons lemon juice

4 garlic cloves, smashed to a paste
  with a little salt
½ teaspoon coarsely ground black pepper
1 tablespoon pimentón picante
1 tablespoon pimentón dulce

Flatten the bird: Cut out the backbone with a sharp knife or poultry shears. Open out the bird and make a small incision in the cartilaginous part at the top of the breastbone, then turn it over and flatten it by pushing down on the breast with your hands. Season the chicken generously with salt on both sides.

In a small bowl, mix together the olive oil, lemon juice, garlic, pepper, and pimentóns. Paint or rub the mixture thoroughly on both sides of the bird, then put it skin side up on a heavy rimmed baking sheet. Let marinate for 1 hour at room temperature, or cover and refrigerate for several hours, or overnight; bring to room temperature before cooking.

Heat the oven to 450 degrees. Roast the chicken, uncovered, for 15 minutes. Reduce the heat to 400 degrees and continue roasting for 30 to 45 minutes longer, until the chicken is well browned and the juices run clear when the thickest part of the leg is pierced. Let rest for 10 to 15 minutes.

Cut the chicken into 8 pieces with a cleaver or heavy chef's knife. Transfer to a hot platter and serve.   MAKES 4 TO 6 SERVINGS

Serve flat-roasted chicken simply with a garlicky green salad or braised dark leafy greens.

Spanish Octopus and Potatoes with Pimentón

Spanish octopus with potatoes, dusted with pimentón, is a classic menu item in nearly every Spanish tapas bar. A final drizzle of intense fruity olive oil is essential and brilliant. If octopus isn't an option, substitute roasted or grilled squid, cooked lobster, or slices of rare-grilled tuna.

Put 2 pounds small Yukon Gold or other yellow-fleshed potatoes in a pot of well-salted boiling water, reduce the heat, and simmer until tender, about 20 minutes. Drain and cool to room temperature. Peel the potatoes and cut into ¼-inch slices. Arrange the slices on a platter in a single layer. Slice about 2 pounds cooked octopus tentacles into rounds slightly thinner than the potatoes. (Some fish markets have cooked octopus for sale.) Top each potato slice with a piece of octopus. Dust with pimentón dulce, sprinkle with sea salt, and drizzle with olive oil. Serve.   MAKES 6 TO 8 SERVINGS

How to Cook an Octopus

Octopus is tricky: If you let it boil, it will toughen. Simmered slowly—really slowly—in an aromatic broth, though, it emerges succulent and savory. (Some fishmongers sell cooked octopus, but at twice the price of raw.)

Ask your fishmonger to remove and discard the head, beak, and ink sac of a 2- to 3-pound octopus. Rinse the octopus, put it in a large pot, and cover with cold water. Add a bay leaf, a thyme sprig, a halved onion, 4 garlic cloves, 1 small dried red chile, 1 teaspoon coriander seeds, a splash of olive oil, and a sizable pinch of salt. Cover the pot and bring just to a boil, then turn the heat to low. Cook for 45 minutes to 1 hour at the barest simmer, never allowing the broth to boil. Check to see if the octopus is tender by probing it with the tip of a paring knife. Remove the octopus from the broth and let cool to room temperature. (Reserve the savory broth for another use, such as a fish soup or paella.)

Separate the tentacles with a sharp knife. Rub the tentacles with your fingers to remove any loose skin, then cut into slices or chunks, as desired. The cooked octopus will keep for up to 3 days, covered and refrigerated.

Clockwise from left: Classic tapas bar octopus with potatoes, a spoonful of hot pimentón, and cooked octopus ready to slice.

KITCHEN ESSENTIALS

Collected here for reference are some annotated basic recipes and techniques I think every cook will find useful. We'll visit the egg, and I'll encourage you to make your own mayonnaise. If the thought of whisking it by hand puts you off, know that it isn't really a strenuous chore. Homemade mayonnaise is worth the effort.

Making yogurt, crème fraîche, or a mild fromage blanc is easy and fun, as well as economical. Learning these basics of home-cultured dairy may awaken your intrepid inner cheesemaker.

Electric rice cookers are great, but you don't need one to make great rice. There's a little tutorial here that's meant to demystify the process, since even very competent cooks get nervous when making rice.

Two classic, ultrasimple Italian pasta dishes are here to remind you that a delicious meal can be had in a matter of minutes, even with a mostly bare cupboard. And for a little more effort, a pair of easy Asian noodle dishes may keep you from ordering in.

When you're a long distance from a decent bakery, knowing how to produce a good loaf or a tray of biscuits will serve you well. Pizza Bianca, daubed with olive oil and seasoned with rosemary and sea salt, is eminently doable and always well received. Of course, the dough recipe can be used for any kind of pizza.

I also give you recipes for making five types of homemade broth in small batches. You'll never convince me that canned broth or the stuff in shelf-stable cartons is as good as the real deal.

OH, FOR A GOOD EGG

There is a vast and remarkable difference between the taste of conventional factory chicken eggs and that of those purchased at a farmers' market. Poultry management practices notwithstanding, most industrial eggs spend weeks languishing in cold storage, quite edible of course, but a far cry from what a good egg could be. Eight dollars or so for a dozen truly fresh, flavorful eggs is an indulgence well worth the price. You just have to look at the firm, bright golden yolks to know why, even before you taste them. I think of good eggs the same way I think about good chicken: "Spend more and eat less," as Michael Pollan puts it. Which means: Eat smaller portions of better stuff and/or enjoy it less frequently. In most parts of Europe, a single egg is considered a perfect portion at breakfast—and not every day of the week, for that matter.

How to Boil an Egg

The rule with boiled eggs is don't overdo it—greenish, dry-yolked 20-minute eggs are a sad affair. First, have your eggs at room temperature, so they won't crack when you add them to the boiling water. Find a shallow saucepan just big enough to hold them in one layer. Fill the pan with water (though not so much that it will overflow once the eggs are added), add a generous pinch of salt, and bring the water to a full boil. Carefully lower the eggs into the boiling water, then immediately reduce the heat to a medium simmer to keep them from rattling about. Set the timer the moment the eggs go in. Have a bowl of ice water ready.

The ideal "hard-cooked" large egg has a slightly moist center and is cooked for somewhere between 8 and 10 minutes. I usually aim for exactly 9 minutes, but a bit less for a softer center and a bit longer for a firmer one. (For a soft-boiled egg, or *oeuf mollet*, great on a spinach salad with bacon, cook the eggs for only 3 to 4 minutes.) When the timer goes off, remove the eggs and plunge them into the cold water bath. To make peeling easier (this is a tip from Julia Child), crack the eggs all over before you submerge them in the water, which will allow water to slip between the eggs and the shells. I also find it best to peel them underwater.

There is no comparison between the stuff in a jar (or a squeezy tube) and a genuine, properly seasoned handmade mayonnaise.

Making Mayonnaise

Why ever would you not make your own mayonnaise? It's completely baffling to me, since it is so easy to make and so divine. When I taught mayonnaise-making recently, one of the attendees asked, "Why should I do it by hand when it takes mere seconds for me to make mayonnaise with a high-speed immersion blender?" The reason: You actually learn the technique of emulsification when you make mayonnaise by hand. Besides, it's more fun, and quieter.

2 large egg yolks
1 teaspoon Dijon mustard (optional)
2 cups extra virgin olive oil

Salt and pepper
1 teaspoon lemon juice or red or white wine vinegar, or to taste

Put the egg yolks and mustard, if using, in a medium heavy bowl. Stir the yolks with a wire whisk until they thicken slightly. Slowly drizzle in the oil a teaspoon at a time while whisking in a circular motion counterclockwise, making sure the oil is thoroughly incorporated each time before adding the next teaspoon. Once the sauce begins to thicken a bit, graduate to adding the oil a tablespoon at a time, remaining vigilant to fully incorporate it each time. This is really important: Failing to do so, or adding too much oil at once, will cause the emulsion to break. (If this happens, start over with a new egg yolk, whisking in the curdled mixture as if it were oil.)

When you've added about 1 cup of the oil and the sauce is quite thick, thin it by whisking in a tablespoon or so of cold water. Then gradually whisk in the remaining cup of oil. Add a big pinch of salt, a little freshly ground pepper, and the lemon juice. Let the mayonnaise sit for a few minutes to allow the salt to dissolve. Taste and adjust for salt and acid. The finished mayonnaise should have the texture of softly whipped cream—it shouldn't be stiff or oily. Thin with more cold water as necessary.   MAKES ABOUT 2½ CUPS

NOTES: For a milder-tasting mayonnaise, use half olive oil and half vegetable oil. You can also make mayonnaise in a stand mixer with the whisk attachment or with a handheld mixer. Or make it in a food processor or with an immersion blender (for the method, see page 30). Homemade mayonnaise keeps for a week, refrigerated, but a little less if it contains garlic or herbs, which lose their fresh flavor.

French Bistro Oeuf Mayonnaise

On a bistro menu, *oeuf mayonnaise* means "hard-cooked egg with mayonnaise," and that's exactly what it is—no more, no less. It's always served in a rather unadorned fashion, just the halved egg with a spoonful of freshly made mayonnaise and a lettuce leaf. One caveat: Good egg, real mayonnaise. Once upon a time, it was a beloved bistro standard for a bite with a glass of wine or a dependable first course, and there are a few spots in Paris that still serve it—even a club of die-hard *oeuf mayonnaise* lovers.

Olive Oil–Fried Eggs with Sizzled Garlic

Though I'm inclined to cook scrambled eggs in butter, for a fried egg, it's got to be olive oil. My preferred method? Put a cast-iron skillet over medium heat and add a tablespoon of olive oil (if you're cooking more than one egg, use a tablespoon of oil per egg). When the oil is hot, crack the egg and slip it carefully into the pan. Season generously with salt and black pepper and add a pinch of crushed red pepper. Let the egg fry gently so it crisps and browns perfectly on the bottom and the white begins to form bubbles. When the egg is done, but with a still-runny yolk, 3 to 4 minutes, turn off the heat. Tilt the pan, and add a sliced garlic clove or two to the oil collected at the bottom edge. Let it sizzle briefly, just until fragrant but not browned, and then spoon the garlicky oil over the egg. Use a spatula to transfer the egg to a warm plate and drizzle with more of the oil. An egg like this also makes a superior sandwich or egg-on-a-roll.

As for accompaniments, a slice of toast (or Spanish Garlic Toast, page 18) is really all you need, though my Sicilian friend Angelo would add a sprinkle of dried oregano and a dash of red wine vinegar to his egg. Fried eggs are good with cooked vegetables too—asparagus, artichokes, and spinach are all great springtime options. During tomato season, thick ripe slices are what you want. And nearly any kind of potato will make a fried egg's day.

The finished mayonnaise has the texture of softly whipped cream.

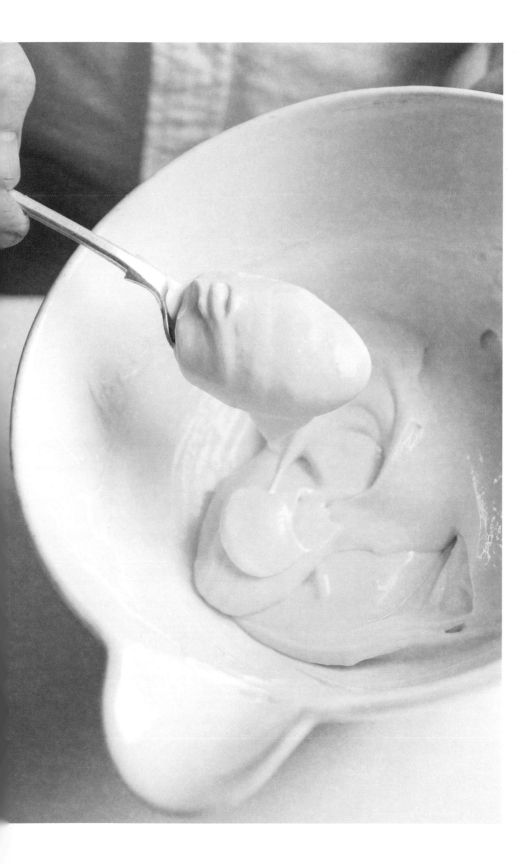

HOME-CULTURED DAIRY

There are a few cultured dairy products that are well worth making at home, and they're hardly anything you would call a major project. They mostly involve simply warming milk or cream, inoculating it with live active cultures, and waiting a day or two. The work is easy and pleasurable, and your homemade products will be tastier and cheaper than store-bought. Obviously, you'll choose the very best, freshest organic milk and cream you can get to turn into yogurt, crème fraîche, or *fromage blanc*.

Homemade is better: yogurt (*left*) and crème fraîche (*right*).

Yogurt at Home

Let's talk about yogurt. I know I'm opinionated, but I have no use for most of what is sold in supermarkets. Whole-milk yogurt tastes best to me. I'd rather have a small amount of that than a large bowl of thin-tasting, watery low-fat yogurt. Commercially made American yogurts can be bland, and are usually too thick and not sour enough—tangy yogurt just tastes better. So-called Greek-style yogurt may have the correct thickness, but it lacks the tartness of the real thing. And don't get me started on sweetened and adorned yogurt products with "fruit" on the bottom or candy on top. But I'm happy to have yogurt for dessert, topped with a spoonful of good raw honey or homemade apricot jam. Now that's delicious.

Often my preference is for yogurt sprinkled with salt and pepper and drizzled with olive oil as a snack. Yogurt seasoned in a more elaborate way can accompany a savory dish (see page 218), but sometimes a spoonful of good plain yogurt is all that's required to embellish, for instance, a beet salad or a smooth soup.

The yogurt process involves a several-hour period of incubation in a warm environment, but there is no one right way to do it. I have a friend who swears by her old-fashioned method of wrapping the jar of warm cultured milk in a thick blanket overnight (and another friend who actually sleeps with his jar of yogurt under the pillow). It can also be accomplished in a thermos or an insulated cooler. The idea is to try to keep the soon-to-be-yogurt mixture at a steady warm temperature so it will culture and thicken properly. Or you can purchase a yogurt-making kit, which gets the job done easily—you just have to plug in the incubator, fill the jars, and set the timer. For the starter, you can use a spoonful of plain commercial yogurt made with live cultures or purchase powdered yogurt cultures online from sources such as www.culturesforhealth.com.

Put 1 quart whole milk in a stainless steel saucepan set over medium heat and heat to 180 degrees. Let cool to 100 degrees, then whisk in ¼ cup plain commercial yogurt made with live cultures or a teaspoon of powdered yogurt culture. Transfer to 1-cup jars (or smaller ones) and incubate at about 100 degrees for 8 to 12 hours, until the yogurt is set and slightly tart in flavor. (As with crème fraîche, the longer you let it culture, the more tart it will become.) Refrigerate for several hours before using. The yogurt will keep for a week or more.

MAKES 1 QUART

Homemade Crème Fraîche

There are hundreds of uses for crème fraîche, the thick, tangy French version of sour cream. Use a spoonful in savory sauces, hot or cold, or to accompany desserts instead of whipped cream. One of its many virtues is that because it's made only from cultured pure cream, it won't curdle when heated and can be simmered to make a reduced sauce. For the best flavor, use organic raw or pasteurized cream (not ultra-pasteurized).

Heat 1 cup heavy cream in a stainless steel saucepan over medium heat until it reaches 110 degrees. Let cool to just below 80 degrees, then stir in 2 tablespoons cultured buttermilk. Transfer to a sterilized jar or crock and leave at room temperature, loosely covered with a clean cloth, for 12 hours, or until thickened and mildly tangy. For a thicker and more sour crème fraîche, let stand for up to 12 hours longer. Cover the crème and refrigerate overnight before using. It will keep for up to 2 weeks.   MAKES 1 CUP

NOTE: Purists may consider purchasing a crème fraîche culture from an online source instead of using buttermilk.

Homemade Fromage Blanc

Everyone seems to be jumping on the homemade ricotta train lately, but to me, it never tastes right—it's too rich and creamy compared to the Italian ideal. Instead, I prefer to make a simple kind of *fromage blanc*. Like ricotta, this is best eaten very fresh, within a day or two at most. Fromage blanc can swing both ways sweet or savory—so it goes with toast and jam for breakfast and with prosciutto on a crisp baguette, as well.

Put 1 gallon whole milk in a stainless steel saucepan set over medium heat and bring to 100 degrees. Whisk in ½ cup plain yogurt, 2 tablespoons lemon juice, and 1 teaspoon salt. Turn off the heat, put on the lid, cover with a towel, and leave for 30 minutes.

Set a fine-mesh sieve over a bowl and line it with doubled cheesecloth. Check to see if the milk has clabbered nicely—that is, separated into curds and whey. If so, carefully ladle the curds into the sieve, allowing the whey to drain off. If not, wait for another 30 minutes or so. Leave the curds to drain for about 2 hours, until spoonable. The whey makes a nutritious beverage or can be used in baking.

Gather up the edges of the cheesecloth and lay them over the top of the drained curds. Put a small plate on top as a weight and place the draining cheese in the refrigerator, where it will firm further. Chill for several hours or overnight, then unwrap and transfer to a serving bowl. MAKES ABOUT 1½ CUPS

Clarified Butter and Ghee

For adding flavor to vegetables and sauces or for making pastry, "whole" butter is ideal, but for sautéing and frying, I use clarified butter or ghee, which has been cooked to remove the milk solids (and for longer keeping). Clarified butter and ghee are interchangeable, but ghee has a pronounced lightly toasted flavor and clarified butter tastes buttery but neutral. For both, it's best to use unsalted butter. Oysters panfried in clarified butter are outrageously tasty; a drizzle of ghee gives basmati rice sparkle.

To Make Clarified Butter

Melt 1 pound unsalted butter in a medium saucepan over medium heat. Then turn the heat very low and allow the butter to simmer gently for about 20 minutes, until the water in the butter has evaporated and the milk solids have risen to the surface. Skim the milk solids from the top using a fine-mesh skimmer or slotted spoon. (You can save the skimmed solids to flavor soups and dishes such as mashed potatoes.) Ladle the clarified butter into small containers (strain through cheesecloth if you wish) and cool to room temperature. Cover and refrigerate for up to 3 months.   MAKES ABOUT 1½ CUPS

To Make Ghee

Proceed as for clarified butter, but once the water in the butter has evaporated and the milk solids have risen to the surface, continue to simmer for another 20 minutes or so, monitoring the butter closely, until the milk solids have sunk to the bottom and taken on a golden color and the butter has a toasted, nut-like aroma. Take great care during the last few minutes not to let the butter or milk solids get too dark, or the ghee will taste burnt instead of toasted. Ladle the ghee into small containers (strain through cheesecloth if you wish) and cool to room temperature. Cover and refrigerate for up to 3 months.   MAKES ABOUT 1½ CUPS

A POT OF RICE

What is it about rice that makes even otherwise good cooks tremble? Given how undemanding, really, rice is to cook, the mystery that can surround it is hard to fathom. Rice simply asks that you understand its nature. For rice to cook, it must first absorb liquid and then steam, and it can't really be rushed. The main thing you need to know is how long it takes to cook. For most white rice, that is about 15 minutes of cooking followed by 15 minutes of resting, covered, off the heat. For whole-grain rice, the time is generally double that. Never stir steamed rice as it cooks.

The ritual of preparing a pot of rice should be calming, not fretful, from the initial washing to the final fluffing. Use the following as a template and guide.

Perfectly steamed basmati rice.

Basic Steamed White Rice

This method works for nearly any kind of white rice—long-grained jasmine, Carolina, or basmati rice or short-grained Japanese. Choose the right size pot or pan for the job. For 1 to 2 cups rice, use a 2-quart saucepan. Make sure the pan has a tight-fitting lid.

First, wash your rice. This might be shocking for some people. You might think this unnecessary, but it makes for better rice and is common practice throughout Asia. (If using basmati rice, it's best to soak it first since it is fairly hard-grained. Even 20 minutes of soaking will make a difference, but you can leave the grains to soak for several hours if you wish. In a pinch, though, you'll still get good rice if you must forgo the soaking.) Wash it thoroughly by covering it with fresh water in a bowl, agitating it with your fingers, and pouring off the cloudy liquid; repeat several times until the rinsing water runs clear, then drain the rice in a sieve. It is ready to cook.

Many cooks advocate a ratio of 2 cups water to 1 cup rice and some call for a ratio of 1½ cups water to 1 cup rice. With thoroughly washed rice, however, I usually find that to be too much, so I recommend the ratio of 1 cup water to 1 cup washed rice.

Put the 1 cup washed rice in a 2-quart saucepan, add 1 cup water and ½ teaspoon salt, and bring to a boil over high heat, then immediately cover the pan and reduce the heat to the barest possible simmer. Set the timer for 15 minutes, and *do not lift the lid as it cooks*. Then turn off the heat and leave the rice to steam, covered, for 15 minutes. Voilà! Perfect rice. Drizzle with 1 tablespoon ghee or butter, fluff, and serve.   SERVES 2 TO 4

Perfumed Rice

For pleasantly aromatic rice, add 6 cardamom pods, 4 whole cloves, and 6 black peppercorns to the cooking water.

Baked Saffron Rice

Here's a method for making perfect rice for a crowd. The advantages are several. The rice can be baked ahead of time and reheated, a boon if your guests have a bad habit of arriving fashionably late. It also liberates stovetop space.

Heat the oven to 350 degrees. In a medium saucepan, warm 2 cups milk and 2 tablespoons butter with a good pinch of crumbled saffron and let steep.

Bring a large pot of well-salted water to a rolling boil. Add 2 cups soaked and thoroughly washed basmati rice and boil for 6 minutes (the rice grains will be half-cooked, with a hard center). Immediately drain the rice in a sieve, then transfer it to a 9-by-12-inch baking dish. Ladle the the milk mixture over the rice, cover tightly with foil, and bake for 45 minutes. Remove from the oven and let rest for 10 minutes, then fluff. Or, if not serving immediately, let cool to room temperature; to reheat, cover tightly with foil and bake for 30 minutes at 350 degrees.   SERVES 6 TO 8

Wash rice until the water runs clear.

TWO SUPER-SIMPLE
ITALIAN PASTAS

Spaghettata di mezzanotte, midnight spaghetti, is a marvelous thing. You (or you and a companion or two) have been out on the town, or working late, and suddenly you're famished. The idea is to make a simple delicious pasta at home out of practically nothing. Just ingredients you would always have on hand—like garlic, anchovies, cheese, and olive oil. A little hot pepper. And that's it. It's utterly satisfying—a perfect there's-nothing-in-the-cupboard meal at any time of day. There's something kind of great (isn't there?) about not caving and ordering in a so-so pizza.

Pasta Aglio-Olio-Peperoncino

Couldn't be simpler: extra virgin olive oil, garlic, and crushed red pepper. Boil ½ pound spaghetti in generously salted water until al dente. Don't trust the timing on the package; e.g., if it says "8 minutes," set the timer for 6. You can always cook it more, but you can't cook it less. (And a plate of overcooked spaghetti is so sad.) While the pasta is cooking, put 2 to 3 tablespoons olive oil in a wide skillet over medium-high heat, then add 4 minced garlic cloves and a good pinch of crushed red pepper. Cook very briefly (don't let the garlic brown), just until fragrant, and turn off the heat. Drain the pasta when it's al dente, reserving ½ cup or so of the cooking water. Add the spaghetti to the seasoned oil, along with a good splash of the pasta water, and toss with tongs until well coated. Sprinkle with a little sea salt and serve.   MAKES 2 SERVINGS

Gilding the Lily

Add chopped capers, a couple of chopped anchovy fillets, and some grated lemon zest to the oil along with the garlic. Crisp bread crumbs make a nice topping, and grated Parmesan or pecorino cheese is an option as well.

Pasta Cacio e Pepe

Cacio e pepe (literally, "cheese and pepper") has lately achieved mythic status, which is a bit surprising considering it's so basic. You can get it in any restaurant in Rome, but it's really a home dish. The trick is getting the pasta to finish cooking properly in the creamy sauce, which is just pasta water, butter, and cheese. The more peppery, the better.

Cook ½ pound linguine extra al dente (this is crucial) in well-salted water. Melt 2 tablespoons butter in a skillet over medium heat and add ½ teaspoon coarsely crushed black pepper. Drain the pasta and add to the pan, along with ½ cup of pasta water and a good pinch of salt. Stir constantly, keeping the liquid at a rapid simmer; the pasta will begin to wilt in the sauce and absorb liquid. Cook for about 2 minutes, stirring, until most of the liquid has been absorbed. Turn off the heat, add 2 cups grated pecorino, and stir until the pasta is coated with the creamy sauce. Adjust the seasoning to taste.   MAKES 2 SERVINGS

Bare-cupboard delights: Cacio e Pepe (*left*) and Aglio-Olio-Peperoncino (*right*).

EASY ASIAN NOODLE DISHES

Peanut noodles and wontons are two items from the standard Chinese takeout menu you probably crave often. Even if you're new to cooking with Asian ingredients, these standbys are not at all difficult to prepare. Not to mention, your homemade version will be cheaper and tastier than anything sent by bicycle.

Spicy Peanut Noodles (*top*) and Pork and Shrimp Wontons (*bottom*). And, in the small dish, dumplings made with the same wonton filling.

Spicy Peanut Noodles

You can't argue with good peanut noodles: They are always satisfying. What's more, they can be served hot, cold, or somewhere in between. You can make a batch of the sauce and keep it in the fridge for several days. These noodles are otherwise unadorned, but feel free to add tofu, cooked chicken, or sliced cucumbers.

¼ cup chunky peanut butter

2 tablespoons soy sauce

1 tablespoon dark Chinese vinegar
   (or substitute a smaller amount
   of red wine vinegar)

2 teaspoons toasted sesame oil

2 tablespoons Chinese hot chile paste or
   sambal oelek

1 tablespoon grated fresh ginger

2 teaspoons grated or minced garlic

2 tablespoons mirin

1 tablespoon sake

1 pound fresh Chinese noodles or
   dried udon noodles

¼ cup thinly sliced scallion greens

2 teaspoons toasted sesame seeds

Use a spoon or sturdy rubber spatula to mash the peanut butter with the soy sauce and vinegar in a bowl until thoroughly mixed. Stir in the sesame oil, chile paste, ginger, garlic, mirin, and sake. Adjust the seasoning to taste.

Cook the noodles in well-salted water until just tender. Drain well, then return to the (now empty) pot. Toss with the spicy peanut sauce and transfer to a platter or individual bowls. Sprinkle with the scallion greens and toasted sesame seeds.

MAKES 4 SERVINGS

Pork and Shrimp Wontons

Packages of high-quality wonton skins are available at any Asian grocery and many supermarkets, and then it's just a matter of filling and folding them. Once they hit the boiling water, they need only 2 minutes. This spicy pork and shrimp filling, with plenty of ginger and garlic chives, is delicious, and it can be prepared hours ahead (in fact, it must be chilled for at least half an hour). If you would rather make dumplings, buy round dumpling wrappers instead and use the same filling.

½ pound ground pork, not too lean
½ pound shrimp, peeled, deveined,
  and chopped into ¼-inch pieces
Salt and pepper
1 tablespoon sweet rice wine, such as
  Shaoxing (or substitute sherry)
1 tablespoon soy sauce
1 tablespoon sugar
1 tablespoon finely grated fresh ginger
2 garlic cloves, grated or minced
1 teaspoon spicy Chinese bean paste
  (also called chili bean sauce) or
  Chinese chile paste

2 serrano chiles, finely chopped
1 cup chopped Chinese garlic chives
  (or substitute ¾ cup chopped scallions)
About 30 wonton skins
  (about 3 by 3 inches)
1 small egg, beaten
Cornstarch for dusting
½ pound baby spinach (optional)
6 to 8 cups Blond Chicken Broth
  (page 460), heated and seasoned
  to taste
Chinese Hot Pepper Oil (page 423)
Cilantro sprigs for garnish

Put the pork and shrimp in a chilled bowl. Season with salt and pepper and mix briefly with chopsticks, wet hands, or a wooden spoon. Add the rice wine, soy sauce, sugar, ginger, garlic, bean paste, serrano chiles, and garlic chives and mix well. Panfry a small patty of the mixture to check the seasoning, and adjust if necessary. Cover and refrigerate for at least 30 minutes, or up to 24 hours.

To prepare the wontons, remove a few wonton skins from the package and lay them out on a dry work surface. Put 1 teaspoon filling in the center of each skin. Then paint the edges of each square lightly with egg, gently fold over one side to make a rectangle, and pinch the edges together. Now pull the two lower corners of each one in toward each other and pinch together to make the traditional curved wonton shape. Place the wontons 1 inch apart on a baking sheet or platter, and repeat with the remaining skins and filling; you should have about 30 wontons. Dust lightly with cornstarch and refrigerate, uncovered, until ready to cook.

Bring a large pot of well-salted water to a boil. Meanwhile, divide the spinach, if using, among deep wide soup bowls.

When the water is boiling, drop about 10 wontons into the pot and cook for about 2 minutes, until they rise to the top. Remove with a spider or a large sieve and divide among the bowls. Repeat with the remaining wontons.

Pour about 1 cup hot broth over each serving. Drizzle with hot pepper oil, garnish with cilantro sprigs, and serve.   MAKES ABOUT 30 WONTONS; 6 TO 8 SERVINGS

Clockwise from top left: Dumpling wrappers, fresh noodles, and wonton wrappers.

A FEW BAKED GOODS

Although there are more and more good bakeries now, bread
baking satisfies a primal urge for many home cooks. Here you
will find a small, eclectic collection of some of my favorites: pizza
dough, a wheaty Moroccan flatbread, a couple of biscuit recipes,
and one for scones.

Basic Pizza Dough

This pizza dough works best if it is prepared in advance and refrigerated overnight, although you can use it right away, after a brief rest. You can store it in the fridge for as long as 3 days, or portion it and wrap the dough balls individually to freeze. Each one will make a 10-inch pizza. Spread with a little tomato sauce and your favorite toppings, this dough makes a very nice pie. But just as often, I use it for almost unadorned Pizza Bianca (following page).

1 3/4 cups lukewarm water
2 teaspoons active dry yeast
4 1/2 cups 00 flour, plus a generous amount for dusting
2 teaspoons salt
2 tablespoons olive oil

Put the lukewarm water in a large bowl (you can make the dough with a stand mixer or in a food processor if you prefer). Sprinkle the yeast over the water and let stand until it dissolves, about 2 minutes.

Add the flour, salt, and olive oil and mix until the flour is well incorporated and a dough forms, about 5 minutes. The dough may look a little rough or pockmarked. Turn it out onto a well-floured work surface and knead lightly until smooth, 3 to 4 minutes. Cut the dough into 4 equal pieces (about 8 ounces each) and wrap individually in plastic wrap. Refrigerate overnight or for up to 3 days, or freeze for future use. Bring to room temperature to use.

MAKES ENOUGH FOR FOUR 10-INCH PIZZAS

NOTE: If you wish to use the dough immediately, form each piece into a ball and place on a flour-dusted or parchment-lined baking sheet. Flour the tops lightly and cover loosely with plastic wrap. Let rise at room temperature until doubled in size, about 30 minutes. Roll or stretch each piece of dough into a 10-inch circle and add your favorite topping, with a light hand. These small pizzas take only about 5 minutes to bake; see Pizza Bianca on the following page for instructions.

Pizza Bianca

Pizza bianca is the simplest pizza of all. It's a round of dough painted liberally with good fruity olive oil and sprinkled with fresh rosemary, crushed red pepper, if you like, and flaky sea salt. If you keep a batch of dough in the fridge, it's easy to make these whenever you want—to serve in small bites with drinks or family-style at dinner, passed around like bread.

Place a pizza stone or a heavy baking sheet or griddle on the top rack and heat the oven to 500 degrees. Roll or stretch a piece of risen dough into a rough 10-inch circle and lay it on a floured peel or sheet of baking parchment set on a rimless cookie sheet. Drizzle lavishly with olive oil and scatter with rosemary leaves. Carefully slip the dough from the peel or cookie sheet onto the stone and bake for 3 to 4 minutes, until puffed, golden, and crisp. Sprinkle with sea salt and crushed red pepper. Cut or tear into pieces and eat warm.

Moroccan Whole Wheat Flatbread

Paula Wolfert published a version of this delicious bread in her first cookbook, *Couscous and Other Good Food from Morocco*. I have always loved the taste of it—very wheaty and enhanced with anise seeds and sesame—and its chewy crust.

2 cups lukewarm water	2 teaspoons salt
2 teaspoons active dry yeast	1 tablespoon anise seeds
1 teaspoon sugar	1 teaspoon sesame seeds
3½ cups all-purpose flour	1 tablespoon olive or vegetable oil
1 cup whole wheat flour, preferably stone-ground	2 to 3 tablespoons semolina flour

Put the lukewarm water in a large bowl. Sprinkle the yeast and sugar over the water and let stand until dissolved, about 2 minutes.

Add the all-purpose flour, whole wheat flour, salt, anise seeds, sesame seeds, and oil and mix until the dough comes together. Turn out onto a lightly floured work surface and knead until the dough is smooth and elastic, about 5 minutes. (The dough can be prepared in advance and refrigerated, covered, overnight; bring to room temperature before proceeding.)

Sprinkle two baking sheets with semolina flour. Divide the dough in half, shape into balls, and flatten each ball into a disk about 1 inch thick. Place a loaf on each baking sheet, cover loosely with plastic wrap, and let rise in a warm place for about 1 hour, or until a finger pressed into the side of the dough leaves a deep indentation.

Heat the oven to 400 degrees. Prick each loaf deeply six or seven times with a fork. Bake for 20 to 25 minutes, until the bottom of bread sounds hollow when tapped. Remove the loaves from the oven and let cool before slicing into wedges.
MAKES 2 LOAVES

Buttermilk Biscuits

A basket of warm biscuits is always a special treat, and they're easy to make. Just follow these two basic rules: Don't overwork the dough, and use a hot oven.

2 cups all-purpose flour,
   plus more for dusting
2 teaspoons baking powder
1/2 teaspoon baking soda
1/2 teaspoon kosher salt

6 tablespoons cold unsalted butter, lard,
   or shortening, plus 3 tablespoons
   unsalted butter, melted, for brushing
1 cup buttermilk

Heat the oven to 400 degrees. In a large bowl, stir together the flour, baking powder, baking soda, and salt. Cut the cold butter into small chunks and use your fingers to work the butter into the flour mixture until it is the texture of coarse sand, with a few stray pebbles. Make a well in the center of the mixture and add the buttermilk. Stir in a circular motion with a fork until the dough forms a rough ball. It will seem a bit moist and sticky.

Turn out the dough onto a floured surface, dust lightly with flour, and knead until smooth, about 1 minute. Gently roll or pat the dough to a 1/2-inch thickness. Using a biscuit cutter, cut the dough into 2-inch circles. (Alternatively, use a sharp knife to cut the dough into diamond shapes.) Place 1 inch apart on an ungreased baking sheet. Pat the scraps together, roll or pat out, and make a few more biscuits (these scrappy ones will be somewhat less tender).

Prick each biscuit with the tines of fork and brush lightly with the melted butter. Bake until nicely browned, 10 to 12 minutes. Serve warm.   MAKES 10 TO 12 BISCUITS

Olive Oil–Rosemary Biscuits

Replace the butter with 6 tablespoons fruity extra virgin olive oil. Add 1/2 teaspoon finely chopped rosemary, 2 tablespoons grated Parmesan, and 1/2 teaspoon pepper to the dry ingredients. Paint the biscuits with olive oil instead of butter and give them a sprinkle of coarse sea salt before popping them into the oven.

Scones (*top*) and biscuits (*bottom*) straight from the oven.

Cardamom Cream Scones

The technique for making scones is exactly the same as for biscuits. The difference is that, unlike biscuits, the dough is sweetened and enriched with egg.

2 cups all-purpose flour, plus more for dusting

2 teaspoons baking powder

½ teaspoon baking soda

½ teaspoon salt

2 tablespoons sugar, plus more for sprinkling

½ teaspoon ground cardamom

6 tablespoons cold unsalted butter, lard, or shortening, plus 3 tablespoons unsalted butter, melted, for brushing

2 tablespoons currants, plumped in warm water and drained

2 tablespoons golden raisins, plumped in warm water and drained

2 tablespoons chopped candied ginger

2 large eggs, beaten

½ cup heavy cream

Heat the oven to 400 degrees. In a large bowl, stir together the flour, baking powder, baking soda, salt, sugar, and cardamom. Cut the butter into small chunks and use your fingers to work the butter into the flour mixture until it is the texture of coarse sand, with a few stray pebbles. Add the currants, raisins, and ginger and toss well. Make a well in the center of the mixture and add the beaten eggs and cream. Stir in a circular motion with a fork until the dough forms a rough ball. The dough will seem a bit moist and sticky.

Turn out the dough onto a floured surface, dust lightly with flour, and knead until smooth, about 1 minute. Gently roll or pat the dough out to a ½-inch thickness. Using a biscuit cutter, cut the dough into 2-inch circles. (Alternatively, use a sharp knife to cut the dough into wedges or diamond shapes.) Place 1 inch apart on an ungreased baking sheet. Pat the scraps together, roll or pat out, and make a few more scones (these scrappy ones will be somewhat less tender).

Prick each scone with the tines of a fork. Brush lightly with the melted butter and sprinkle with sugar. Bake until nicely browned, 10 to 12 minutes.

BASIC BROTHS

A good broth—from meat or vegetables, fish bones, or kelp—is something you must make from scratch. Chicken broth from a can, vegetable stock from a carton, or concentrated bouillon from a cube are convenient, but all of these are enhanced with "natural flavors" and not a little MSG-dosed dried onion and garlic. No commercial variety compares to homemade.

A broth can be as simple as water simmered briefly with garlic and herbs (see Provençal Garlic Soup, page 34). On the other end of the spectrum, you might brown meaty bones with vegetables for a rich three-hour "dark" stock. And then there's everything in between—a quick broth made from shrimp shells, corncobs, dried mushrooms, or Parmesan rinds, or an easy two-hour chicken stock made from raw chicken backs and necks.

Take advantage of small-scale broth opportunities too—deglazing the bottom of the roasting pan for a cupful of concentrated chicken broth, saving the "liquor" from cooked greens or garbanzo beans, or hoarding any other tasty liquids until needed to intensify a sauce, soup, or stew. An ill-considered collection of scraps will not result in a flavorful broth. But used judiciously, the carcass of that roasted chicken or the mushroom stems you might have otherwise discarded can be used to make a small pot of good broth.

All-Purpose Vegetable Broth

Put 1 halved small onion, 3 or 4 scallions, 3 sliced garlic cloves, 1 chopped celery stalk, 1 chopped carrot, 1 peeled and chopped parsnip (optional), a bay leaf, 2 thyme sprigs, and 7 cups water in a large saucepan and bring to a boil. Skim any rising foam. Reduce the heat and simmer gently for 30 minutes. Strain. Refrigerate the broth for up to 3 days or freeze for future use.　MAKES 6 CUPS

Porcini Mushroom Broth

Put ½ cup crumbled dried porcini or other dried wild mushrooms, 1 sliced small onion, 6 chopped scallions, 1 chopped celery stalk, 1 chopped carrot, a bay leaf, and 4 cups water in a large saucepan and bring to a boil. Reduce the heat and simmer for 30 minutes. Strain. The broth can be refrigerated for up to a week or frozen for future use.　MAKES 3 CUPS

Blond Chicken Broth

Put 3 pounds meaty chicken bones (a combination of wings, backs, and necks), 2 quartered medium onions, 2 chopped carrots, 1 chopped celery stalk, a bay leaf, 2 thyme sprigs, 2 parsley sprigs, 5 black peppercorns, and 6 quarts water in a large soup pot and bring to a boil. Reduce the heat to a gentle simmer. Skim off and discard any foam that has risen to the surface. Simmer, uncovered, for 2 hours, skimming frequently. Strain the broth through a fine-mesh sieve and cool to room temperature. Skim the fat from the surface and use immediately, or refrigerate for up to 3 days or freeze for future use (the fat will rise to surface and congeal).　MAKES 4 QUARTS

Dark Chicken Broth

This dark broth will be slightly jelled after chilling and a rich brown color. Follow the instructions for Blond Chicken Broth, but first roast the chicken, onions, carrot, and celery in a roasting pan in a 400-degree oven until quite well browned and caramelized. Transfer the roasted ingredients to a large soup pot and cover with 6 quarts water. Add 1 tablespoon tomato paste to the roasting pan, along with a little hot water, scraping the bottom with a wooden spoon to dissolve any flavorful brown bits. Add these deglazed juices to the soup pot. Bring to a boil, reduce the heat, skim, and then simmer for 2 hours, skimming often.   MAKES 4 QUARTS

NOTE: For a richer dark broth, substitute meaty beef shanks or turkey legs for the chicken.

Fish (or Shrimp) Broth

Put 1 tablespoon extra virgin olive oil, 2 pounds meaty halibut bones or fish heads, rinsed of blood (or shells from 2 pounds shrimp), 1 chopped medium leek, 2 thyme sprigs, and a bay leaf in a heavy-bottomed soup pot over medium-high heat. Let sizzle for a few minutes, stirring; take care not to let the mixture brown. Add 7 cups water and bring to a simmer, then reduce the heat to just under a simmer and cook for 30 minutes. Turn off the heat and let the broth steep for 30 minutes. Strain the broth through a fine-mesh sieve. It can be refrigerated for several hours, but it is best used the same day.   MAKES 6 CUPS

Dashi

Put ½ ounce kombu (kelp) in a nonreactive saucepan, add 4 cups cold water, and let soak for at least 15 minutes. Put the pan on the stove over medium-high heat. When the water is just about to simmer, turn off the heat and add ½ cup *katsuobushi* (dried bonito flakes). Let steep for 10 minutes, then strain through a fine-mesh sieve. (The dashi can be prepared up to a day in advance.)   MAKES 4 CUPS

NOTE: Dashi can be used for simmering vegetables (page 319) or for making miso soup.

LINGERING AT THE TABLE

At my table, I'm inclined to have very simple desserts, if you can even call them desserts. A tiny dish of yogurt with a spoonful of honey or homemade jam or barely sweetened and cooked berries. Little bowls of dried fruits and candied ginger or citrus peel, some dark chocolate, a few biscotti. Maybe some ice cream.

Mostly, though, I want fresh fruit of every kind, each in its celebrated season. Strawberries, cherries, plums. Sliced peaches or nectarines. A fine bunch of grapes. A giant bowl of tangerines in winter. Blood oranges, cut into wedges. Juicy Asian pears. Ripe mangoes or pineapples. A platter of figs.

A little cheese instead of dessert (in the French manner) can be nice, especially if there's still wine in the bottle. A firm, sharp sheep's-milk cheese, or a creamy, sweet Gorgonzola, perhaps served with nuts in the shell and a nutcracker.

If I do make a dessert, the one most likely to appear is the open-faced apple tart on page 465, which I consider far superior to the fanciest cakes and pastries.

A dessert, no matter how simple, is always a welcome opportunity to linger longer.

Rustic Apple Tart

If there is one dessert that always pleases, it's a simple French apple tart. Sliced apples are fanned over an easily made flaky pastry dough, sprinkled with sugar, and baked. For a glaze, you can simmer the apple cores and peels in a sugar syrup, as directed here, or instead use good homemade jam, warmed and thinned with a bit of water (apricot and plum are especially complementary). Or a drizzle of warm honey.

Serve the tart with crème fraîche or vanilla ice cream, if you wish.

1 cup all-purpose flour, plus more for
*   dusting*
Pinch of salt
½ cup (1 stick) cold unsalted butter,
*   cut into ¼-inch pieces*

¼ cup ice water
2 pounds firm, tart apples
*   (4 to 6 medium), such as Cox or Gala*
1 cup sugar, plus more for sprinkling
1 cup water

Put the flour and salt in a bowl and add half the butter. With your fingers, work the butter into the flour until the mixture looks mealy. Add the ice water and the remaining butter and stir the dough for just a minute or two, until it comes together. It will be soft, a little sticky, and a little rough looking, flecked with bits of butter.

Turn out the dough onto a lightly floured work surface, sprinkle with a little flour, and pat into a rectangle about 1 inch thick. Wrap and refrigerate for at least an hour, or overnight.

Lightly dust the work surface with flour. Roll out the dough to a rectangle approximately 6 by 9 inches and about ⅛ inch thick. Trim the edges of the dough with a sharp knife and transfer the dough to a parchment-lined baking sheet. Set aside in the refrigerator, loosely covered.

Peel the apples and cut into quarters. Remove the cores and use to make a glaze: Put the cores in a saucepan with the sugar and water (add a handful of apple peelings for color if you wish), set over medium heat, and stir at first to dissolve the sugar, then simmer, stirring occasionally, until reduced to a thick syrup, 15 to 20 minutes. Strain the glaze and reserve. (You'll have more glaze than you need; just keep it in the fridge for the next tart.)

continued

Preheat the oven to 400 degrees. Thinly slice the apples, about $\frac{1}{8}$ inch thick. Arrange the apple slices over the pastry in rows, overlapping them like roof tiles, leaving a 1-inch border of dough all around. Fold the border over to enclose the apples. (At this point, the tart can be covered with plastic wrap and refrigerated for up to 8 hours. Bring to room temperature to bake.)

Sprinkle sugar generously (3 to 4 tablespoons) over the apples and bake until the apple slices are beautifully browned and the pastry is crisp and caramelized, about 45 minutes. Cool on a rack.

Just before serving, reheat the glaze. Slide the tart from the pan onto a cutting board. Paint the apples with the warmed glaze. Cut crosswise into rectangular slices or into wedges.   MAKES 6 TO 8 SERVINGS

ACKNOWLEDGMENTS

It is impossible to thank each one personally, but I wish to express my deepest gratitude to all who helped produce this cookbook— and to hardworking farmers and farm laborers everywhere, without whom we would perish.

To everyone at Artisan: Lia Ronnen, Michelle Ishay-Cohen, Renata Di Biase, Nancy Murray, Zachary Greenwald, Allison McGeehon, Judy Pray, and Elise Ramsbottom. And in the larger Workman Publishing firmament, to David Schiller, Elisabeth Scharlatt, Deborah McGovern, Judith Sutton, and most especially the extraordinary Ann Bramson.

To Evan Sung, for incredibly gorgeous photographs, and thanks to Kira Corbin.

To James Casey for intelligent, artful book design.

To agent and advocate Katherine Cowles.

To the cooking team: Oliver Monday, Michelle Fuerst, Maggie Trakas, Amalia Mariño, Mason Lindahl, Joel Hough, and Tina Dang.

To Jacob Greenberg, Elizabeth Klein, Zwann Grays, and Alison Roman, for editorial support.

To my colleagues at the *New York Times*.

To Susan and Bruce, Alice and Cie, Gilbert and Richard, Barbara and Stuart, Michael and Jill, Darina and Tim, Ignacio and Susannah, Fabrizia and Gianni, and many other dear friends, mentors, fellow cooks, and tablemates.

To RB, always.

INDEX

Page numbers in *italics* refer to photographs.

David Tanis has worked as a professional chef for over three decades, and is the author of several acclaimed cookbooks, including *A Platter of Figs and Other Recipes*, which was chosen as one of the fifty best cookbooks ever by the *Guardian/Observer* (London), and *Heart of the Artichoke*, which was nominated for a James Beard Award. He spent many years as a chef with Alice Waters at Chez Panisse in Berkeley, California; he ran the kitchen of the highly praised Café Escalera in Santa Fe, New Mexico; and he operated a successful private supper club in his seventeeth-century walk-up in Paris.

He is an advocate for simple home cooking, with a core belief that food needn't be fussy to be beautiful. An avid traveler, his first stop on any trip is at an outdoor market, finding inspiration in regional cuisines from hither and yon. He has written for a number of publications, including the *Wall Street Journal*, the *Guardian/Observer*, *Cooking Light*, *Bon Appétit*, *Fine Cooking*, and *Saveur*.

Tanis lives in Manhattan and has been writing the weekly City Kitchen column for the Food section of the *New York Times* for nearly seven years.

CONVERSION CHARTS

WEIGHTS

US/UK	Metric
1 oz	30 g
2 oz	55 g
3 oz	85 g
4 oz ($^1/_4$ lb)	115 g
5 oz	140 g
6 oz	170 g
7 oz	200 g
8 oz ($^1/_2$ lb)	225 g
9 oz	255 g
10 oz	285 g
11 oz	310 g
12 oz	340 g
13 oz	370 g
14 oz	395 g
15 oz	425 g
16 oz (1 lb)	455 g

VOLUME

American	Imperial	Metric
$^1/_4$ tsp		1.25 ml
$^1/_2$ tsp		2.5 ml
1 tsp		5 ml
$^1/_2$ Tbsp ($1^1/_2$ tsp)		7.5 ml
1 Tbsp (3 tsp)		15 ml
$^1/_4$ cup (4 Tbsp)	2 fl oz	60 ml
$^1/_3$ cup (5 Tbsp)	$2^1/_2$ fl oz	75 ml
$^1/_2$ cup (8 Tbsp)	4 fl oz	125 ml
$^2/_3$ cup (10 Tbsp)	5 fl oz	150 ml
$^3/_4$ cup (12 Tbsp)	6 fl oz	175 ml
1 cup (16 Tbsp)	8 fl oz	250 ml
$1^1/_4$ cups	10 fl oz	300 ml
$1^1/_2$ cups	12 fl oz	350 ml
2 cups (1 pint)	16 fl oz	500 ml
$2^1/_2$ cups	20 fl oz (1 pint)	625 ml
5 cups	40 fl oz (1 qt)	1.25 l

OVEN TEMPERATURES

	°F	°C	Gas Mark
very cool	250–275	130–140	$^1/_2$–1
cool	300	148	2
warm	325	163	3
moderate	350	177	4
moderately hot	375–400	190–204	5–6
hot	425	218	7
very hot	450–475	232–245	8–9